# Organizing the Lakota

## DATE DUE

| FEB 1 6 2000 | |
|---|---|
| | |
| | |
| | |
| | |
| | |
| | |
| | |
| | |
| | |
| | |
| | |
| | |
| | |
| | |
| | |
| | |
| | |
| | |
| | |
| BRODART | Cat. No. 23-221 |

# ORGANIZING THE LAKOTA

The Political Economy of the New Deal
on the Pine Ridge and Rosebud Reservations

Thomas Biolsi

THE UNIVERSITY OF ARIZONA PRESS

Tucson

NOTE ON PROTECTION OF HUMAN SUBJECTS
This book is written so that specific individuals on the
reservations are not identifiable from the text. This
procedure is intended to protect the anonymity of historical
actors on the local level. Only individuals of national note,
or senior federal personnel, are identified by name.

*Second printing 1998*
The University of Arizona Press
Copyright © 1992
The Arizona Board of Regents
All Rights Reserved

⊗ This book is printed on acid-free, archival-quality paper.
Manufactured in the United States of America

03  02  01  00  99  98    6  5  4  3  2

Library of Congress Cataloging-in-Publication Data
Biolsi, Thomas, 1952–
　　Organizing the Lakota : the political economy of the
New Deal on the Pine Ridge and Rosebud Reservations /
Thomas Biolsi.
　　　　p.　cm.
　　Includes bibliographical references and index.
　　ISBN 0-8165-1127-6 (cloth : alk. paper)
　　ISBN 0-8165-1885-8 (pbk. : alk. paper)
　　　1. Dakota Indians—Legal status, laws, etc.　2. United
States. Indian Reorganization Act.　3. Dakota Indians—
Politics and government.　4. Dakota Indians—
Government relations.　5. New Deal, 1933–1939.
6. Pine Ridge Indian Reservation (S.D.)—Politics and
government.　7. Rosebud Indian Reservation (S.D.)—
Politics and government.　I. Title.
E99.D1B56　1992
323.1'197'0783—dc20　　　　　　　　　　92-182
　　　　　　　　　　　　　　　　　　　　　　CIP
British Library Cataloguing-in-Publication Data
A catalogue record for this book is available from the British
Library.

The author's royalties from this book are assigned to the
Lakota Archives and Historical Research Center, Sinte
Gleska University, and to the Oglala Lakota Archives, Oglala
Lakota College.

To my father, Louis Biolsi

# CONTENTS

# ILLUSTRATIONS

# TABLES

# NOTE ON LAKOTA ORTHOGRAPHY

Lakota words in the text are rendered in a simplified form of one of several orthographies, a rendering which would be readable by a Lakota speaker. The reader should note that:

- *a*  is pronounced as f*a*ther
- *c*  is pronounced as *ch*
- *e*  is pronounced as th*ey*
- *ġ*  is pronounced as Spanish pa*g*ar
- *i*  is pronounced as s*ee*n
- *k'* is glottalized
- *n*  following a vowel is not pronounced separately but indicates that the vowel is nasalized
- *o*  is pronounced as *o*pen
- *p'* is glottalized
- *ś*  is pronounced *sh*
- *t'* is glottalized
- *u*  is pronounced as b*oo*t

On Lakota orthographies, see Buechel 1970:22; Powers 1975: 209–10; Walker 1980:286–87; Walker 1982:171–72.

# ACKNOWLEDGMENTS

Much of the material for this book was collected at archival repositories where I have depended upon the expertise and patience of librarians, archivists, and other professionals. At the National Archives in Kansas City, I worked with Mark Corriston, Diana Duff, Rita Klepac, Anne McFerrin, Alan Perry, and Reed Whitaker. At the National Archives in Washington, I was assisted by Richard Crawford, Don Jackanicz, Renee Jaussaud, Bob Kvasnicka, and Reginald Washington. Phil Bantin guided me through Catholic records at the Marquette University Library, as did Harry Thompson for Episcopal records at the Center for Western Studies. At the Richardson Archives I was assisted by Karen Zimmerman. Linda Ritter at Dakota Wesleyan University helped me locate documents in the Francis Case Papers. Laura Glum steered me through the manuscript collections of the South Dakota State Historical Society. Erv and Margaret Figert allowed me access to the files of the *Todd County Tribune* and the *Mellette County Pioneer*. Patsy Bjorling, Marcella Cash, Bob Gough, Chuck Hill, and Charlene Lapoint helped me with documents at the Lakota Archives and Historical Research Center. Rose Cordier assisted me in finding documents among the Rosebud Sioux Tribal records, and Ben Black Bear, Jr., provided access to Rosebud Tribal Land Enterprise records. At the Newberry Library I depended upon John Aubrey. The late Sam McCloskey and Maynard Wright of the Bureau of Indian Affairs in Mission provided a great deal of data, as did Agnes Tyon and Willamine White Eyes of the Bureau of Indian Affairs in Pine Ridge. Emil Her Many Horses helped me locate photographs in the Buechel Memorial/Lakota Museum.

While I was in the field in South Dakota, I had the assistance of a great many people. I am indebted to the following who consented to interviews, assisted in my project, or offered their hospitality and friendship: The Bad Hand family, Ben Black Bear, Jr., Florentine Blue Thunder, Mike Boltz, Simon Broken Leg, Ed Charging Elk, Leo Chasing in Timber, the late Elmer Compton, Tom Conroy, the late Leo Cordier, Cheryl Crazy Bull, Dwight Dam, Evelyn and Marvin Douville, Karen, Brian, and Meddore Douville, Margaret Douville, Victor Douville, the late Kate Fast Dog, Hanna Fixico, Bernard Flood, Sr., the late Nile Hollow Horn Bear, the late Henry Horse Looking, Sr., Mercy Iron Shell, Shorty Jordan, Calvin Jumping Bull, Rosemarie Kramer and family, the late John King, Louis Leader Charge, Shirley Leader Charge, Dave Leading Fighter, Sr., the late Alfred and Rose Left Hand Bull, Dennis and Rose Lessard, Alex Lunderman, Sr., Dorothy Lunderman, the late Sam McCloskey, the late Hattie Marcus, Nellie Menard, Ethel Merrival, Charlie and Titter Moe, Elva One Feather, Lloyd One Star, Angeline Rabbit, the late Stanley Red Bird, the late Willy Red Bird, the late Burgess Red Kettle, the late Ben Reifel, Fern Reynolds, Leo Running Horse, Neola Spotted Tail and family, Sylvan and Charity Spotted Tail, the late Nelson Stranger Horse, Ted Thin Elk, the late Charles Under Baggage, the late Cato Valandra, the late Tom Valandra, Julia Walking Eagle, Albert White Hat, Charlie White Pipe, and Josie and Joey Yellow. I also relied on the expertise of my father, Louis Biolsi, who helped me understand pre-Depression family farming.

This book also owes much to my academic colleagues. I am indebted to the members of my defense committee at Columbia University who helped me through the dissertation which was eventually to become this book: Stanley Freed, Ross Hassig, the late Bob Murphy, Bill Powers, and Nan Rothschild. I also want to express my gratitude to these other friends who read and commented on parts of the manuscript or otherwise offered advice: Martha Balshem, Barbara Brooks, Violet Brown, Sharon Carstens, Diane Ciekawy, Jim Clifton, Ray DeMallie, Loretta Fowler, Herb Hoover, Fred Hoxie, Miyako Inoue, Andrea Kambara, Cecil King, Paul Little, Nancy Lurie, Harvey Markowitz, Jay Miller, David Nugent, Sharon O'Brien, Don Parman, Frank Pommersheim, Joel Robbins, Nancy Shoemaker, John Sugden, Joan Vincent, Charlotte Lloyd Walkup, and Bob Weibe. I also want to express my thanks to Steve Cox at the University of Arizona Press and to Richard Allen, my editor, for careful and challenging readings of the manuscript.

The research and writing of this book was funded by several sources: two Columbia University President's Fellowships (1983–84, 1984–85), a Sigma Xi Society Grant-in-Aid of Research (1983), an American Philosophical Society Phillips Fund Grant (1984), a Whatcom Museum Foundation Grant (1984), a National Science Foundation Dissertation Improvement Grant (1984), a National Endowment for the Humanities Travel to Collections Grant (1988), a Rockefeller Foundation Fellowship (D'Arcy McNickle Center for the History of the American Indian, The Newberry Library, 1988–89), and a Portland State University Faculty Development Grant. Publication was subvented with a grant from the Portland State University Foundation.

# Introduction

In December 1933, a new commissioner of Indian affairs, John Collier, traveled to Rosebud Reservation in South Dakota to explain his plans for an Indian New Deal. His audience comprised Lakota people and local personnel of the federal Office of Indian Affairs (OIA). Collier spoke of reversing United States Indian policy, which had been left largely intact since the 1880s. Where the previous policy had been one of allotting tribal lands to individuals, Collier proposed reincorporating individually-held lands into a tribal estate. Where the previous policy had entailed supervision of reservation affairs by the OIA, Collier called for empowering the existing tribal council to take over administration of the reservation. Collier also called for tribal courts to replace OIA courts of Indian offenses, and he told the people that the present administration was looking forward to the day when local Indian people would choose the local OIA superintendent, if indeed there would even be one. "The present administration is not merely willing for you to govern yourselves," he told the people. "We are determined that you shall and must do it if we have the power to insist."[1]

Collier also condemned the previous federal prohibition or regulation of native religion, custom, and dance: "It was illegal, unconstitutional and wrong, and it is not going to be done anymore." Collier made it clear that he respected Indian ways, and he thought that both the old and the new were needed. Upon being presented with a beaded pipe bag, he said:

When I heard the old men singing when I came in this morning, it
gave me the best feeling I have had for three months. . . . And who is
there in the State of South Dakota—what white person—who can
make anything as beautiful and as fine as this? . . . Five hundred
years from now in the future, when there won't be any more railroad
trains, and probably there won't be any more automobiles or any
more skyscrapers, and when they will have forgotten about most of
the things happening in our time, five hundred years from now,
people all over the world will go and look at things like this and say
that they are beautiful and great, the work of a great people. This is
the old Indian life.[2]

Collier, in short, was proposing the political, economic, and cultural
*decolonization* of Indian peoples in the United States. Most of this
formidable agenda was given statutory expression in the Indian Reorganization Act (IRA) of 1934. The IRA, among other things, provided
for federally-recognized tribal constitutions and charters of incorporation. These instruments would establish tribal governments which
would, the hope was, usher in a new era of self-government in Indian
affairs. The process of drafting constitutions and charters, and of providing assistance and guidance for the new tribal governments, was
known in the OIA's lexicon as *organizing* tribes, and it was viewed by
its proponents as a liberal and humane—and by some of its opponents, both Indian and non-Indian, as a radical—revision of federal
Indian policy.[3]

Even if Collier had an almost mystical respect for Indian ways,
even if his Indian New Deal was humanely conceived in the supposed
interests of Indian people, and even if it promised decolonization and
Indian self-government, organizing the Lakota—the Western Sioux or
Teton Dakota—would not go smoothly, nor would the process go
unchallenged by the Lakota people of Pine Ridge and Rosebud reservations in South Dakota. From the beginning the OIA encountered
Lakota politicians who had their own ideas about what Indian self-
government should look like, ideas which departed widely from those
of the reformers in Washington who invented the Indian New Deal
and from those of OIA field personnel who were responsible for im-
plementing it. Some Lakota people who became known as new dealers enthusiastically—even zealously—embraced the notion of Indian
self-government. They believed that their newly-established tribal
councils, the Oglala Sioux Tribal Council on Pine Ridge Reservation

and the Rosebud Sioux Tribal Council on Rosebud Reservation, organized under the provisions of the IRA in 1936, should constitute the
governments of the reservations. They were not content with the rate
at which the OIA was prepared to transfer administration to Lakota
people, and many came to believe—not without good reason—that
organizing tribes was not being done in good faith by the OIA. They
continued to pressure the OIA to make good on its promise of Indian
self-government throughout the New Deal period.

Other Lakota who became known as old dealers perceived the
new IRA tribal councils as culturally-alien impositions which violated treaties and which were foisted on fullblood (traditional) Lakota
people by the OIA and mixedblood new dealers.[4] The old dealers
would not recognize the IRA tribal councils as governing bodies, and
they insisted that their organization known as the Treaty Council
was the legal and traditional Lakota body for making tribal decisions.
They argued that the Treaty Council had been ignored in tribal organization, and they sought a return to pre-New Deal reservation administration, which came to be called the old deal and which was
seen by the old dealers as consistent both with Lakota tradition and
with treaty law.

This book is a study of the politics of organizing the Lakota.
Its approach, as is indicated by the book's subtitle, is a political-
economic one. I mean by "the political economy of the New Deal" a
focus on what Eric Wolf has recently called structural power—power
that "organizes and orchestrates."[5] "Structural power shapes the social field of action so as to render some kinds of behavior possible,
while making others less possible or impossible."[6] This book will
focus on what was seen as politically possible and impossible from
the point of view of Lakota people during the New Deal, and on why
these conditions of political possibility and impossibility prevailed.
Of particular import will be the presence of the federal bureaucracy
and its remarkable technologies of surveillance and control. Also
critical will be Lakota resignation to this domination. This was not
a simple resignation; it was rather a complex one involving a good
deal of everyday resistance, yet it was a resignation nonetheless.
Why was life without the OIA not considered possible among Lakota
people? And why did Lakota resistance to domination on the reservations come to focus on their own tribal governments rather than on
the OIA?

Chapter 1 will describe the reservation system set up by the OIA after 1880 and which was in place when John Collier visited Pine Ridge and Rosebud in 1933. The technologies of power deployed by the OIA for the surveillance and control of individual and mass behavior will be examined—the law and order apparatus, administrative restrictions on the use of individual lands and funds, and the ration system. The resignation of the Lakota to this domination will also be examined. Chapter 2 will recount Lakota politics before 1934, paying particular attention to the indigenous Lakota reading of the Fort Laramie Treaty of 1868 in which "three-fourths majority rule" was adopted as the technique of tribal decision making on the reservations. Chapter 3 will narrate the events of 1933 and 1934 when John Collier and his colleagues in the OIA presented the idea of an Indian New Deal to the Lakota. Attention will be given to the understanding the Lakota had of the IRA when they went to the polls to vote for or against its application to Pine Ridge and Rosebud reservations. Chapter 4 will describe the drafting of the tribal constitutions in 1935 and will analyze the non-Indian model of Indian self-government inherent in the constitutions—a model which ignored the indigenous Lakota model of three-fourths majority rule. Chapter 5 will analyze the effects of the drought, Depression, and New Deal economic programs with respect to reservation politics. Chapter 6 will describe the disempowerment of the IRA tribal councils through the OIA's aggressive, preemptive technical assistance, formal supervision of council procedures, and retention of control over reservation personnel and critical economic resources. Finally, chapter 7 will analyze the resistance to the New Deal organized by the old dealers. This resistance involved systematic demands for the abolition, not of the OIA, but of the IRA tribal councils. The aim will be to explain the remarkable alignment of political loyalties in which the Lakota grassroots disowned their "own" tribal councils but not the OIA.

ORGANIZING THE LAKOTA

## CHAPTER I

# Domination, Resignation, and Dependence

In 1893, the OIA agent in charge of the Rosebud Agency reported: "This reservation is not adapted to agriculture, as has been practically demonstrated by both Indians and whites. Indians capable of working, however, are required to do some farming and not permitted to spend their entire time in idleness, which invariably breeds discontent and mischief." In 1895, his report was similar: "As has been practically demonstrated during each of the past twelve years of my residence here, this reservation is not adapted to agriculture, and, although Indians have made efforts each year, the results have been and are almost invariably the same, yielding no return for labor spent." Yet, "Indians have been required . . . to plow and cultivate each year. . . . " What mattered to the OIA in Washington was not that Indian agricultural labor pay off in particular cases but that Indians acquire the habit of industry, one of the main components of civilization. For present purposes, the point to note is the remarkable ability of the agencies to compel Indians to labor, even when that labor was irrational and nonproductive. What was the nature of this formidable power, and why were the Lakota resigned to it?[1]

During the period from about 1880 to the New Deal, the OIA instituted a mode of domination over the Lakota composed of a set of administrative technologies of power. These technologies included agency courts and police forces, trust restrictions on individual lands and funds, and the ration system. Together they formed an integrated system for the surveillance and control of both mass behavior, as in the case above, as well as the behavior of individuals and families down to the minute details of household composition and use of land

and cash. The purpose of this chapter is to examine the administrative technologies instituted by the OIA and to explain the resignation of the Lakota to them. I will argue that Lakota people submitted without open challenges to the administrative presence of the OIA because of their dependence upon the critical resources administered by the agencies in the artificial reservation economies.

## The Origin of the Reservations

The Oglala Lakota of Pine Ridge Reservation and the Sicangu (*Sicangu*) Lakota of Rosebud Reservation are two of seven subdivisions of a linguistic community variously called the Teton-Dakota, Teton Sioux, Western Sioux, and Lakota. A dialect of the "Sioux" language known as Lakota is spoken among all of the subdivisions. The seven Lakota subdivisions together comprise one of seven divisions of what was once called *Oceti Śakowin*, the Seven Fireplaces. Different dialects of the "Sioux" language, Dakota and Nakota, which are mutually intelligible with Lakota, are spoken among the other divisions of *Oceti Śakowin*. During the twentieth century, the constituent divisions that make up *Oceti Śakowin* have referred to their collective selves when speaking English as the Sioux Nation or the Great Sioux Nation. Most Lakota people now reside on reservations in the western half of South Dakota, although they have close ties—including marital ties—with the other divisions of the Sioux Nation.

Like most nomadic plains Indian groups, the Oglala and Sicangu—and the Lakota generally—were relatively recent arrivals on the short grass plains.[2] In the seventeenth century the Lakota were located in what is now Minnesota, where they practiced, as did the other six divisions of the Sioux Nation, a mixed economy involving horticulture, hunting and gathering, and fur trading. Pushed from the east by better armed Cree and Assiniboin competitors, and pulled from the west by the prospects of a rich, nomadic, buffalo-hunting economy enabled by horses, the Lakota permanently crossed the Missouri River onto the short grass plains in what is now South Dakota during the latter half of the eighteenth century.

Some Lakota bands entered into treaties with the United States as early as 1825, which provided for peace between the signatories, safe passage for traders and government agents, agreement that the Lakota would deal only with traders licensed by the United States, and recognition by the Lakota of the "supremacy" of the United States.[3] By the 1830s the Lakota had been more securely drawn into the world economy by trade; they were engaged in the production of buffalo robes to exchange with the American Fur Company—which operated steamboats on the Missouri River—for guns, powder and shot, and other manufactured goods.

Another compact with the United States followed in 1851 with the Fort Laramie Treaty which guaranteed peace between the United States and eight Indian "nations," including the Lakota, and delimited the territories of each party. It bound each Indian nation to choose a principal or head-chief—the Sicangu Brave Bear became the head chief of the Lakota—and it provided for annuities in the form of rations, domestic animals, and agricultural implements. It also established the right of the United States to build roads and forts in Indian country.[4]

The first major military engagements between the Lakota and the United States began in 1854 with the Grattan affair in which Brave Bear was killed. The Powder River or Red Cloud war, a contest over the Bozeman Trail through Lakota country in what is now Wyoming, was waged in 1866–68. United States forces were eventually withdrawn, forts in the area were abandoned, and hostilities ceased with the Fort Laramie Treaty of 1868.[5] This treaty established the Great Sioux Reservation, including all of present-day South Dakota west of the Missouri River, and reserved to the Lakota the right to hunt north of the North Platte River—in Nebraska and in the territories of Wyoming and Montana—and on the Republican River in Kansas and Nebraska. Major hostilities—including the Battle of the Little Big Horn—resumed in 1876 after Lakota who had been granted permission to hunt in lands reserved outside the Great Sioux Reservation were ordered to return to the OIA agencies. In the same year a United States commission compelled some Lakota to sign an agreement to cede the Black Hills out of the Great Sioux Reservation. The Black Hills Agreement[6] was a violation of the 1868 treaty, which required the approval of three-fourths of the adult males to execute any land cession; this violation was the basis of the well-known Black Hills claim against the United States. By 1877 the Oglala and Sicangu "hostiles" had been forced by military pressure and by the eradication of the buffalo to join their "friendly" cousins already at agencies on the Great Sioux Reservation.

The 1868 treaty provided for the establishment of OIA agencies in Oglala and Sicangu country, and Lakota friendlies resided at these agencies while their hostile comrades roamed, hunted, and engaged the United States Army. The treaty stipulated that the agencies would supply the Lakota with schools, instruction in farming, a physician, a blacksmith, a carpenter, an engineer, a miller, and seeds and agricultural implements. Perhaps the most attractive benefits of agency life were the rations provided for in the treaty for those who gave up nomadism, as well as protection from the army. The Whetstone agency was established on the Missouri River in 1871. Spotted Tail—recognized as the head chief of the Sicangu by the government—and his followers resided at this agency. The site of the agency for the Sicangu was moved several times until it was finally located on Rosebud Creek in 1878 on the Great Sioux Reservation, where its name was changed to Rosebud Agency and administration was turned over by the army, which had assumed command during hostilities, to the civilian OIA agent. A large house was built for Spotted Tail near the agency building.[7]

Red Cloud Agency, named for the man recognized as head chief of the Oglala by the government, was established near Fort Laramie on the North Platte River in Wyoming Territory in 1871. The agency was moved several times. Civilian command was restored at the Oglala's agency in 1877, and it was eventually located on White Clay Creek on the Great Sioux Reservation in Dakota Territory—its present location. Here its name was changed to Pine Ridge Agency, and a house was built for Red Cloud.[8]

The Great Sioux Reservation was partitioned in 1889 into six smaller reservations by the Great Sioux Agreement[9] (see chapter 2; see maps 1, 2, and 3). The Agreement established Cheyenne River, Crow Creek, Lower Brule, Pine Ridge, Rosebud, and Standing Rock reservations, and "returned" the eleven million acres not included in these six reservations to the public domain of the United States. Pine Ridge and Rosebud reservations were eventually diminished by the cession of "surplus" lands remaining after allotment. On Rosebud Reservation, "surplus" lands were opened to non-Indian homesteading in Gregory County in 1904,[10] in Tripp County in 1907,[11] and in Mellette County in 1910.[12] "Surplus" lands in Bennett County on Pine Ridge Reservation were opened to homesteading in 1910.[13]

## The Mode of Domination: Technologies of Power

With the hostiles militarily subdued and with civilian agents in charge of the agencies in Lakota country, the OIA began to create the reservation system by bureaucratically penetrating the populations. This involved deployment of a series of administrative technologies which together comprised an integrated system for the surveillance and control of the everyday lives of Lakota people.[14]

### The Law and Order Apparatus

One technology deployed by the OIA for controlling Indian behavior was the agency courts and police forces. In 1883 the Interior Department promulgated a code providing for a court of Indian offenses at each agency, to be presided over by three Indian judges appointed by the commissioner on the recommendation of the agent. The court had jurisdiction over misdemeanors and civil matters as these were defined under the laws of the state or territory in which the reservation was located. The court also had jurisdiction over what were termed Indian offenses. These included the Sun Dance, new plural marriages, the practices of medicine men, destruction of property, payment for cohabiting with a woman, intoxication, and trafficking in liquor. In actual practice, the agent often enforced the code without a court of Indian judges; he also had veto power over the decisions of judges. Punishments included detention in the agency guardhouse, fines in cash and/or hard labor, and withholding rations.[15]

The agent enforced the code with Indian policemen appointed and paid by the OIA, over which he served as commander. The Pine Ridge agent swore in fifty Oglala men in 1879 "to serve the Great Father [the president] and him only." Their first action was to prevent the departure of an armed Cheyenne party—some Cheyenne people resided on Pine Ridge—which intended to join Sitting Bull's band of hostiles in Canada. The leader of the Cheyenne party was shot and killed, and the agent reportedly told the Oglala, "Remember this . . . you have seen the power of the police; they represent the Great Father."[16]

The criminal cases actually handled through the law and order apparatus concerned, principally, not infractions by medicine men or Sun dancers, but the kinds of misdemeanors—particularly liquor vio-

MAP 1.    South Dakota Reservations.

lations—which one would find in any non-Indian community. There
was a heavy incidence, however, of cases involving illicit sexual relations and prohibited domestic arrangements (see tables 1.1 and 1.2).[17]
The OIA wanted to insure documentable paternity through legalized
marriage/divorce in order to facilitate the determination of heirs in
probating trust property (see below), and in order to prevent claims
for rations for children unsupported by a father. Toward this end, the
agencies systematically issued marriage licenses free of charge after
1900. Neither the agencies nor the courts of Indian offenses were authorized by law, however, to grant divorces.[18] The agencies punished
couples cohabiting without a license as well as legally married individuals who divorced by "Indian custom" and moved in with new
spouses while still legally married to the original spouse. These practices account for the numerous cases listed as adultery, bastardy, big-
amy, fornication, and illicit relationship. Sentences for such offenses
on Rosebud Reservation in 1930 ranged from thirty to sixty days
detention.[19]

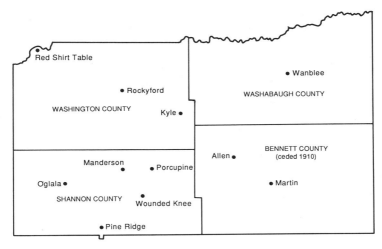

MAP 2.    Pine Ridge Reservation.

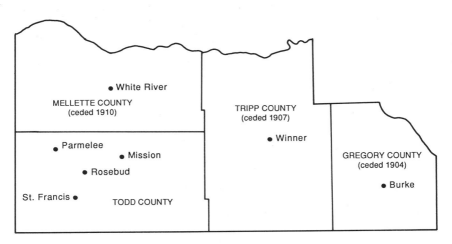

MAP 3.    Rosebud Reservation.

Table 1.1    Criminal and Civil Cases
in the Pine Ridge Agency Court

| Year and Case | N |
|---|---|
| **1905** | |
| Fornication | 31 |
| Adultery | 26 |
| Horse stealing | 15 |
| Drunkenness | 13 |
| Gambling | 12 |
| Wife beating | 10 |
| Disturbing the peace | 9 |
| Divorce and separation | 7 |
| Attempted assault | 6 |
| Fighting | 6 |
| Bastardy | 5 |
| Introduction of liquor | 4 |
| Disputes over stock ownership | 3 |
| Slander | 3 |
| Changing brands/fraudulent branding | 2 |
| Disobedience of orders | 2 |
| **1922*** | |
| Adultery | 30 |
| Bastardy | 10 |
| Assault and battery | 9 |
| Larceny | 7 |
| Gambling | 5 |
| Shooting with intent to kill | 3 |
| **1927** | |
| Adultery | 26 |
| Bastardy | 21 |
| Larceny | 16 |

* Liquor violations excluded.

SOURCES: RC, 1905, 337; Statistical Reports, 1922, 1927, 1934, Pine Ridge, Rolls 106, 107, SAR.

Table 1.1   *continued*

| Year and Case | N |
|---|---|
| **1927** *continued* | |
| Burglary | 4 |
| Liquor violations | 4 |
| Assault and battery | I |
| **1934** | |
| Intoxication | 106 |
| Adultery and rape | 66 |
| Assault and disorderly conduct | 21 |
| Cruelty and desertion | 13 |
| Forgery | 11 |
| Larceny | 11 |
| Possession of liquor | 2 |

## Trust Restrictions on Indian Land

The trusteeship of the federal government over individual Indian land was an elaborate administrative technology which facilitated surveillance and control of Lakota use of an important economic resource. Income from land sales and leases was critical in the subsistence of many Lakota people, but access to these sources was securely supervised by the OIA.

The Great Sioux Agreement of 1889 provided for the allotment in severalty of tribal lands on the reservations of western South Dakota. Allotments were to be held in trust for each allottee by the United States for a period of twenty-five years. Trust status meant that allotments could not be leased or sold without either the permission or the supervision of the Interior Department.[20]

There were two administrative agendas which informed the agencies' execution of this trust responsibility. One involved simply protecting Indians from their assumed incompetence. Except as specifically noted in individual cases, Indians were administratively classified by the OIA as *incompetent wards.* For individuals so designated, the OIA assumed the role of *trustee* over trust property and over

Table 1.2   Criminal and Civil Cases
in the Rosebud Agency Court

| Year and Case | N |
| --- | --- |
| **1921** | |
| General misconduct | 80 |
| Illicit relationship | 40 |
| Drunkenness | 6 |
| Theft of stock | 4 |
| Possession of liquor | 3 |
| Larceny | 2 |
| **1923** | |
| General misconduct | 40 |
| Illicit relationship | 15 |
| Drunkenness | 10 |
| Possession of liquor | 8 |
| Larceny | 4 |
| Bigamy | 2 |
| **1927*** | |
| Adultery | 32 |
| Trafficking in liquor | 11 |
| Fighting | 11 |
| Larceny | 6 |
| Perjury | 6 |
| Rape | 6 |
| Assault with a deadly weapon | 2 |
| Forgery | 1 |
| **1935** | |
| Drunkenness | 190 |
| Adultery | 46 |
| Assault | 24 |
| Larceny | 8 |
| Disturbing the peace | 6 |
| Parole violation | 3 |

* Some liquor violations excluded.

Sources: Statistical Reports, 1921, 1923, 1927, 1935, Rosebud, Rolls 118, 119, SAR.

"unearned" income from trust property or trust funds. The stated intent was to insure that Indians used resources wisely and received fair market value in their transactions, especially with non-Indians. The other agenda was to foster "self-support." "The chief duty of the agent," the *Regulations of the Indian Office* stated in 1904, "is to induce his Indians to labor in civilized pursuits." This meant that allotments were to be homesteads on which Indians became yeoman farmers, not sources of "unearned" income from frivolous leasing or sale.[21]

Leasing was attractive to Lakota families, however, because the return on land was ordinarily greater in either cash or product if the allottee leased the land to a non-Indian farmer or rancher than if he worked the land himself. This was because of, among other reasons, the capital deficiencies and checkerboarding of land holdings (the allotments of family members were not contiguous, and a single allotment was insufficient for commercial ranching) disadvantaging potential Indian operators. Leasing of allotments, nevertheless, was generally considered an evil by the OIA. The Pine Ridge superintendent (agents were called superintendents after 1908) reported in 1927: "In a great many instances, it would be more profitable so far as production is concerned for the Indian to lease his land to a white man, but the coming generation would not be getting the experience in farming which they so badly need." The commissioner warned the superintendents in a circular in 1911 that no allotment lease would be approved "unless it is impossible or impracticable for the lessor . . . to occupy and improve the land."[22]

Yet during the 1910s leasing became a major source of cash for Lakota families. Leasing was the largest source of income listed in the 1921 annual report of the Pine Ridge superintendent ($147,075). This situation came to pass both because leasing could provide budgetary relief for the OIA by offering a source of Indian subsistence other than rations or agency employment, and because most families simply could not make practical use of all their scattered tracts of land.[23]

For present purposes—outlining the mode of domination erected by the OIA—what is important to note is that access to the critical resource of lease income was fully controlled by the agencies. The agencies decided which allotments could be leased (even if those decisions were not rational in terms of returns on land), what the terms of a lease would be, and who would be awarded a lease. The only allotments which were approved for lease were those of the disabled or elderly, or of wives and minor children of able-bodied men, which were located at some distance from the family homesteads and therefore lay idle. The leasing procedure involved sealed bidding on tracts advertised for lease in local newspapers. The allottees were required to sign leases only with the highest bidder on each allotment; allottees were not allowed to sign leases with prospective lessees offering higher rents after the sealed bids were opened. The collection of lease money was originally handled by the agencies, and the funds went into Individual Indian Money (IIM) accounts, with expenditures by individuals regulated by the agencies.[24]

Land sales were another important source of income for Lakota people under agency control. The Rosebud superintendent reported in 1914 that $2 million had been realized in the previous six or seven years through land sales supervised by the OIA, and that most of the cash in the IIM accounts had come from that source. Supervised sales were intended to allow "incompetent" allottees with more land than they could use to sell some or all of it to meet certain categories of approved expenses, and the procedure was strictly regulated. Some sales were approved to allow elderly and indigent allottees to have subsistence funds. Sales were also approved to provide capital funds to allow able-bodied people to buy livestock, implements, and better land, to build homes, and generally to improve allotments. Land sales were also approved to allow allottees to meet medical expenses. The first step was for an allottee to file an application with the agency. Once the agency's recommendation for a sale was approved by the secretary of the interior, the allotment was appraised and advertised for sale with other allotments by the agency. Proceeds from supervised sales went into IIM accounts.[25]

Another dimension of the OIA's surveillance of and control over Lakota access to land as an economic resource is found in its administrative authority to remove trust restrictions. The Burke Act of 1906 enabled the OIA to declare a deserving individual allottee "competent" and to remove the trust status from his allotment, a process known as fee patenting. This allowed the allottee to lease, mortgage, or sell his allotment without supervision. Fee patenting was attractive to allottees because it enabled them to convert land into cash rapidly and to spend this cash without OIA supervision.[26]

One procedure for fee patenting involved voluntary application by the allottee. After notice was posted on the reservation of intended removal of the trust restrictions on the allotment, the agency forwarded to Washington a form supplying information from the applicant's file on his "competence." Final approval was at the discretion of the secretary of the interior, and fee patents were denied when individual competence was not considered sufficient. Fee patents were officially given not because of need for cash, but because of the assumed ability of the allottee to manage his own affairs. Yet there were almost daily applications for fee patents at the Rosebud Agency in 1914, the applicants attempting to justify their requests by appeals to their need for cash.[27]

What became known as forced fee patenting was another procedure for removing trust restrictions from allotments of "competent" Lakota. Toward the supposed end of terminating guardianship over such individuals and of directing attention to the affairs of the "incompetent," Commissioner Cato Sells ordered the fee patenting of all allottees of less than one-half degree of Indian blood in 1917. Degree of blood was one of the characteristics of individuals recorded by the OIA, and one of the more important components of the administrative and legal statuses of Indian people within the mode of domination being examined. There was an assumption—at least on the part of some OIA personnel, including Sells—that competence correlated with degree of blood. By 1934 the proportions of mixedbloods on Pine Ridge and Rosebud were forty-eight and fifty-four percent respectively, although Lakota people may have classified mixedbloods with high degrees of Indian blood as fullbloods.[28]

Fee patents were also issued on Pine Ridge in 1920 by an OIA competency commission. The commission investigated the educational, linguistic, and "industrial" backgrounds of 370 Oglala allottees of one-half or more Indian blood. Some apparently voluntarily applied, others did not. The commission declared the competency of about 100.[29]

## Individual Indian Money (IIM) Accounts

Another administrative technology deployed by the agencies in the twentieth century to monitor and control Indian use of an economic resource—cash—was IIM accounts. What the OIA called "unearned" income was not usually allowed to go directly to individuals but was doled out by the agencies in conformity with OIA regulations from individual trust accounts. Income passing through IIM accounts could include lease rentals from allotments, proceeds from the supervised sales of allotments or inherited interests in allotments, per capita payments from (usually the interest on) tribal trust funds, pro rata shares of the principal of tribal trust funds, and the substantial annuities, known as Sioux benefits, that allottees received under the provisions of the Great Sioux Agreement to get them started on their allotments.[30]

As in the case of trust restrictions on land, there were two administrative agendas behind IIM procedures. One involved insuring that cash was spent providently—on genuine needs and with fair value received. It was believed at all levels of the OIA that Indians did not understand or care to understand financial transactions, and that they might spend formidable sums on frivolities or alcohol. The other agenda was fostering self-support, and it was also believed at all levels of the OIA—probably correctly—that an Indian with access to "unearned" cash or rations would neglect agricultural work on his allotment or other gainful employment. Therefore, funds in IIM accounts were not generally disbursed for subsistence. The OIA, thereby, presumably hoped to convert "incompetent" wards into either yeoman farmers or wage workers.[31]

Cash was, in general, regularly disbursed only to the aged or disabled, who received monthly subsistence payments if their account balances were sufficient. Able-bodied men were not generally disbursed cash, but could apply for purchase orders to buy such things as clothing, seeds, livestock, land, and implements, and to obtain material to build homes, barns, fences, corrals, and wells. Equipment or livestock bought with a purchase order was defined as trust property and could not be liquidated without the permission of the OIA. Funds were also disbursed for special medical and educational expenses.[32]

An individual who wanted access to his IIM funds via a purchase order visited the OIA farmer (also called the farm agent or boss farmer), a subagency official stationed at the local farm station in the reservation district. The farmer was charged, among other things, with intimately knowing the business and personal affairs and "progress" of each family in his district, and he affixed his recommendation to a form which was mailed to the agency. There, the chief clerk entered additional information upon the form concerning the applicant's age, marital status, income, and "advancement." The superintendent then passed on each case, dispatching a purchase order to those applicants whose requests were approved. After a merchant supplied the item, it was inspected by the farmer, and the merchant was paid by the agency.[33]

The IIM system facilitated the bureaucratic penetration of the everyday lives of Lakota people, as is clear from the written appeals from Lakota wards that survive in the records. One Rosebud man wrote to the superintendent in 1930 regarding proceeds he was expecting from a supervised land sale: "My wife will [give birth] soon. I want to ask for advance purchase order for baby clothes for $50 and other necessary things to prepare for this." Another man wrote, pleading, "[the] farmer gave me a purchase order for $40. Now, I got a big family I have to support. This is hard time for take care of my family account of I got no money. Please very respectfully ask you help me for a purchase order for groceries. And I remain respectfully, _____."[34]

## The Ration System

Because the Lakota were dependent upon rations, the manner of their issue was an administrative technology which allowed direct and immediate control of Indian behavior. Rations had originally been provided for the Lakota via the Fort Laramie Treaty of 1868. The subsequent Black Hills Agreement stipulated in article five that in consideration of the Sioux Nation's cession of the Black Hills to the United States, the government agreed to provide the following daily ration for each individual: one and one-half pounds of beef (or one-half pound of bacon), one-half pound of flour, and one-half pound of corn. For every one hundred rations, the government was to issue four pounds of coffee, eight pounds of sugar, and three pounds of beans. These rations were to be "continued until the Indians are able to support themselves." The agreement also provided, however, that when Indians became located on lands suitable for cultivation, rations would be issued only to those who labored. The Lakota were keenly aware of article five of what they called the Black Hills Treaty, and they considered rations to be not a form of temporary assistance they would receive until they learned to farm but just compensation for the Black Hills.[35]

The agencies, however, had the key to the commissary, and one can almost detect a note of glee in the descriptions by OIA officials of the ease with which both individual and mass Indian behavior could be managed with rations. The Pine Ridge agent reported in 1882 that he had found withholding rations a useful tool for controlling the Oglala. He simply withheld rations for unauthorized activities (such as butchering stock issued for breeding purposes): "'Poor Lo,' not unlike his white brother, is peculiarly sensitive in the gastric region."[36]

Withholding rations was, along with the OIA police and courts, an important method of sanction used by the agencies against misconduct by individuals. A 1917 case from Rosebud illustrates how this power could be exercised. A man had arranged with the local farmer to live on his son's allotment, which was two and one-half miles from a day school his children attended. "The understanding was," according to the superintendent, "that if he would move there and behave himself, that the farmer would give him rations at such times as he needed them, but that if he did not stay there that the rations would not be forthcoming." The man, who had only one horse, decided, however, to move with his family and camp on land closer to the day school in order to make it easier for his two children to attend school. It was the policy of the OIA to discourage "roaming"—it was no doubt believed to have been an uncivilized proclivity ingrained by the nomadic buffalo days—and to instill a discipline for self-support on one's allotment. When the family moved, the rations were cut by the farmer. The superintendent sustained the action, and when the man complained in a letter to the commissioner, the superintendent responded: "Moses is physically and mentally able to work and support his family but is too lazy and worthless to do so. I suggest that the office write him a good straight letter and tell him that until he goes back to his home and attempts to do something for himself and his family that no assistance will be given."[37]

The commissioner's office sustained the actions of its field personnel in a letter to the man, obviously based on data from his individual case file as supplied by the superintendent:

> This matter has been investigated, and it appears that you are thirty
> six years of age, in good health, and fairly well educated. That up to
> the summer of 1915 you lived in eastern Mellette County, where
> there was considerable drinking and idling, in both of which you participated. That in the summer of 1915, the farmer arranged with you
> to move to the allotment of one of your children two and one-half

miles from the Butte Creek farmer station and near a day school, with the understanding that if you remained there, behave yourself, and work hard, you would be given rations at such times as you needed them, but if you did not stay there the rations would be discontinued.

It is difficult to imagine a more impressive example of precise and efficient surveillance and control of individual behavior outside of a "total institution" such as a school, prison, or asylum.[38]

Rations could also be used for large-scale social engineering. Rations were issued weekly on Rosebud in 1884 in order to prevent Indians from leaving the reservation on horse-stealing raids or for other purposes. As an OIA inspector reported, the agency relied in this case on "the bond between the commissary department and the Indian conscience, which is supposed to lie very near the region of the stomach." When in the early twentieth century the OIA sought to compel Indian men to work for the agencies on a per diem basis so as to train them in labor discipline (see below), ration cuts were the key to compliance. Charles Dragenett, supervisor of Indian employment for the OIA, described the method of enforcing per diem labor to the assembled conferees of the Lake Mohonk Conference of Friends of the Indians and Other Dependent Peoples in 1907: "The Indians have a natural disinclination to work hard. They are not lazy, but, like many whites, they do not work for pure love of it. It is generally prompted by necessity. In fact, about the best way to promote it is to cut off the rations."[39]

## Resignation and Dependence

The mode of domination erected on the reservations included not only the integrated administrative technologies of surveillance and control described above. It also included the cultural representation of this power by the OIA. This representation explained and legitimated—at least for the administrators[40]—the presence of the OIA and its technologies on the reservations. There developed after 1880 an elaborate ideology of wardship and guardianship, involving the now familiar theory of the incompetence of Indians, of the necessity to civilize (almost a technical term in the OIA's administrative lexicon) them, and to administer their affairs—individual, family, and tribal—until they had traveled sufficiently far along the road to civilization to be competent to manage their own affairs. This representation of power on the reservations was reinforced in the language and official criteria involved in every administrative interaction between the wards and their guardians.

But there is little reason to assume that this representation of power was accepted by the Lakota; the mode of domination described above did not go unchallenged. The most well-known, open challenge was, of course, the Ghost Dance movement on Lakota reservations in 1890, when some Lakota people destroyed their homes and fences, armed themselves, committed depredations, and put on bullet-proof shirts in preparation for the imminent millennium.[41] This was not the only case of open civil disobedience. The Pine Ridge agent reported in 1902 that when he explained the plan to drop able-bodied men from the ration rolls and to compel them to work for $1.25 per diem, "they became ugly and showed a great deal of resentment, made all sorts of threats, declared emphatically that they would not submit to the change. The old chiefs and headmen called councils in the several districts and advised the younger element to resist the proposed change. Some went so far as to advise the young men to get their guns and ponies ready for trouble."[42]

But the Oglala *did* submit to per diem labor, and such calls to mass disobedience and even violent resistance were unusual.[43] Most resistance to the administrative technologies did not involve the threat of force or *call into question the presence of the OIA* or directly challenge *the existence of the administrative technologies themselves.* Most resistance took the form of dissimulation, appeals for administrative reconsideration of specific cases, appeals for reform or liberalization of procedures, or requests for investigations.

The resignation of the Lakota regarding the *presence* of the United States government in the particular form of the OIA is reflected in the deference shown by the Lakota in public and face-to-face interactions with the colonial agents (this must, of course, be recognized as only a "partial transcript"):[44] The Lakota referred to their superintendent as *ateyapi* (their father), "father," or even "papa," and to the president of the United States as *t'unkśilapi* (their grandfather) or "the great father." This kinship idiom was, of course, consistent with the representation of power as a relation between wards and guardians.[45]

How can we account for the resignation of Lakota people to technologies which imposed the administrator's gaze and control over sexuality, family life, household budgets, and use of supposedly individually owned land? How can we account for the fact that what Lakota resistance there was to OIA domination took the form, not of insurgent action or demands for removal of the OIA or its administrative technologies but of dissimulation and conformist/reformist demands which would leave the administrative technologies intact? Part of the answer is that these tactics were the most realistic and effective "weapons of the weak"[46] in the day-to-day situations faced by the Lakota on the reservations.

Dissimulation, for example, could be an effective way around administrative structures, a tactic for circumventing the intentions of the OIA. In 1881 the Pine Ridge agent reported that he had achieved a savings by issuing the Oglala less than the full ration stipulated in the Black Hills Agreement, yet they did not complain. They did not have to. Rations were allocated to districts on the basis of census counts, and the Oglala had been able to convince the agency that their number was on the order of seventy percent more than it actually was. This was accomplished by families which had already moved through the line past the census enumerator getting back in line and giving other names, or lending their babies to families waiting in line to be counted. The enumerators may have been mixedblood Oglala who also served as interpreters and who may have winked at, if they did not actively invent, this subterfuge. An accurate census was finally achieved in 1886 only under guard.[47]

The same padding of the census rolls took place on Rosebud. This may explain a most interesting census taken on Rosebud in 1885 in which a series of English translations of dubious Lakota names were recorded: "Bad Cunt," "Shit Head," "Dirty Prick," "Cunt," and "Shit," for example. It is not difficult to imagine that these entries represent people who got back in line after already being enumerated and who gave—not without a certain contemptuous wit—fictitious names the second time through.[48]

There were also definite *channels* which were open, even to Indian wards, and this also helps explain why Lakota resistance did not openly challenge the presence of the administrators. The OIA was a modern, rational bureaucracy in the technical sense—it was staffed with civil service personnel who operated and were evaluated (both within the OIA and without) according to publicly disclosable, universalistic, professionalized standards. There was, thus, a structural limit on the level of abuse of the wards which the system would tolerate.[49]

The Lakota understood clearly that the agencies were expected to manage blindly and humanely Indian affairs in the interests of Indians (as, of course, those interests were defined by the OIA), and that favoritism, corruption, and other malfeasance would not survive administrative scrutiny or other oversight. They knew that farmers and clerks answered to the superintendent, that the superintendent reported to higher OIA officials in Washington, and that the OIA was supervised to some extent by the secretary of the interior, the president, and Congress, and was also answerable to the courts and even to powerful Indian welfare organizations such as the Indian Rights Association. Even unfounded allegations of malfeasance from Indian people, if directed to the right place, could bring on scrutiny. Any complaint to the commissioner or to a congressman would produce at least a letter of inquiry. The Lakota also knew that OIA inspectors (called "cats" and "big cats")[50] frequented the reservations, and they sometimes got these inspectors to listen seriously to and even investigate their complaints. In 1929 Lakota complainants on Pine Ridge and Rosebud gave testimony about OIA mismanagement and malfeasance to three traveling United States senators holding hearings of the investigating subcommittee of the Senate Indian Committee. It is not difficult to imagine the effect among the Lakota of seeing the superintendents and other agency personnel pointedly questioned in an open hearing by the senators regarding the charges of the complainants.[51]

True, complaints and appeals from the wards seldom resulted in actual reversed decisions or procedural liberalization, but the existence of channels offered some protections. What is more, their use brought real trouble down on the heads of the bureaucrats who monitored and controlled the everyday lives of the Lakota. Using the channels was clearly an "everyday form of resistance."[52]

On the other hand, resistance which went beyond mere dissimulation and lawful and peaceful channels could clearly have dire consequences. Fort Robinson and Fort Niobrara were within easy striking distance of Pine Ridge and Rosebud reservations, respectively, and during the Ghost Dance panic, the United States Army dispatched more combat troops to the Lakota agencies than were assembled at any other time between the Civil War and the Spanish-American War. The 1890 Wounded Knee massacre of perhaps as many as 300 Lakota people on Pine Ridge Reservation, and the mass burial of more than 150 bodies, indelibly inscribed in the practical memories of the Lakota people the preparedness of the United States to use swift, brutal, and indiscriminate force to maintain order on the reservations. The Lakota were not allowed to forget the threat of mass terror. After the Wounded Knee massacre, Indian troops from Fort Niobrara (including men from Rosebud) were taken on reconnaissance marches on Rosebud; the pacifying effect of this display of troops on the reservation after the massacre can be imagined. Lakota people were well aware of the superintendents' telegraph link to troops stationed at Fort Robinson and Fort Niobrara. Regular combat troops were not withdrawn from Fort Niobrara until 1906, or from Fort Robinson until 1919.[53]

## The Artificial Economies and Dependence

The resignation of the Lakota is not ultimately explained, however, by the effectiveness of dissimulation or "going through channels," or even by the threat of organized, mass terror, although these factors cannot be ignored. The reluctance of the Lakota to challenge systematically or radically the presence of the OIA and its administrative apparatuses is ultimately rooted in the *dependence* of the Lakota upon the resources administered by the OIA.

After the destruction of the pre-reservation mode of production, it became necessary to provide for Indian subsistence in new ways. The official intent on the part of the OIA was to make Indians self-supporting through agricultural enterprise on their own allotments. The OIA assumed that the Lakota would be dependent upon rations and other resources provided by the OIA as the process of civilization was taking place, but the assumption was also that Lakota families would eventually take their place alongside white families as independent farm families. Some progress was made toward this end. The Lakota raised subsistence gardens on their allotments. They also became petty commodity producers, selling agricultural products on the market. Beef cattle, stock crops, wild hay, and vegetables were among the commodities produced on Lakota allotments. The Rosebud superintendent reported in 1931 that the average plot cultivated by families was 25 to 35 acres, with some farming 160 acres or more. In addition to petty commodity production, Lakota people performed seasonal labor for lessees and for Nebraska potato farmers. Wage work was also available from railroads and other businesses.[54]

The importance of these "industrial" pursuits, as the OIA called them, in the subsistence of the Lakota varied with seasonal, climatic, and economic conditions, but all in all they were not sufficient to support the reservation populations. Western South Dakota, as everyone knew, could not sustain commercial dry farming for long: rainfall was unpredictable and often insufficient (even subsistence gardening was unreliable in this climate), soils were poor, and local markets or nearby shipping points were not always available. What is more, the Lakota could not compete with the better-capitalized white commercial farmers. Ranching was better adapted to the weather and geology of western South Dakota, but here the Lakota were again hampered by insufficient capital, and (ironically) by insufficient land, in comparison to non-Indians. And wage labor was not a realistic alternative, since there was simply not enough local employment to allow most families to make ends meet. The subsistence of the Lakota would, therefore, necessarily have to be guaranteed by another source. That source was the OIA, which delivered a range of resources upon which the Lakota became dependent during the period under consideration. The same bureaucracy which deployed the administrative technologies for surveillance and control of the Lakota also delivered resources which were necessary for Lakota survival.

In the case of rations, the technology of surveillance and control was also the technology of resource delivery; the linkage between domination and dependence was direct here, and domination may have been less visible to all concerned because of this linkage. The high point of dependence on rations was during the period of 1880 to 1900, when all families were issued rations on Pine Ridge and Rosebud. Although the Lakota were receiving in 1900 only about seven-tenths of the value of the ration provided for in the Black Hills Agreement (they received the full ration only immediately after the Wounded Knee massacre), they still received the equivalent of about one pound of beef and five and three-quarter ounces of flour per capita, per diem.[55]

During the twentieth century, the OIA made concerted attempts to compel the Lakota to be self-supporting through per diem labor for

Table 1.3    Monthly Ration for One Person,
Pine Ridge Reservation, 1906

| 40 lbs. | beef * |
|---------|--------|
| 2 oz. | baking powder |
| ½ lb. | coffee |
| 3 lbs. | corn |
| 12 lbs. | flour |
| 2 oz. | salt |
| 1 oz. | soap |
| 10 oz. | sugar |
| 2 lbs. | bacon |

* Gross weight: "on the hoof"

SOURCE: RC, 1906, 353.

the agencies and/or agricultural enterprise. Nevertheless, 5,700 of the 6,700 residents on Pine Ridge in 1906 were on the ration roll at some point during the year. The monthly ration for an individual on Pine Ridge in 1906 is presented in table 1.3. The surviving records indicate that the ration rolls were diminished during the 1920s, although ration recipients continued to comprise significant proportions of the reservation populations. The ration rolls climbed again with the onset of the drought and depression of the 1930s (see tables 1.4 and 1.5).[56]

Another major source of subsistence pumped into the reservations by the OIA was agency employment. Freighting work was the most important form of agency employment available on Pine Ridge and Rosebud in the nineteenth century. There were other jobs available for a fortunate few Lakota people from the earliest days of the reservations. The agency police forces have already been mentioned. The 1890 roster of the Rosebud Agency included twenty-four regular Indian employees (additional and assistant farmers, laborers, a watchman, an interpreter, an assistant issue clerk) and twelve irregular Indian employees (herders, a cook, and an assistant carpenter), in addition to three officers and forty privates on the agency police force. Annual pay ranged from $30 for the cook and assistant carpenter to $720 for an additional farmer. Agency employment was the third

Table 1.4    Reservation Population and Ration
Recipients, Pine Ridge Reservation, 1920–33

| Year | Population | Ration Recipients |
|------|-----------|-------------------|
| 1920 | 7,225 | 841 |
| 1921 | 7,267 | 1,757 |
| 1922 | 7,362 | 1,571 |
| 1923 | 7,455 | 1,546 |
| 1925 | 7,625 | 1,700 |
| 1929 | 7,911 | 745 |
| 1930 | 7,994 | 795 |
| 1931 | 8,103 | 666 |
| 1933 | 8,294 | 1,452 |

SOURCE: Statistical Reports, 1923, 1925, 1929, 1930, 1931, 1933,
Pine Ridge, Rolls 106, 107, SAR.

Table 1.5    Reservation Population and Ration
Recipients, Rosebud Reservation, 1920–33

| Year | Population | Ration Recipients |
|------|-----------|-------------------|
| 1920 | 5,430 | 1,710 |
| 1921 | 5,466 | 1,063 |
| 1922 | 5,516 | 1,248 |
| 1923 | 5,572 | 1,004 |
| 1925 | 5,700 | 519 |
| 1927 | 5,839 | 817 |
| 1928 | 5,975 | 785 |
| 1929 | 6,039 | 444 |
| 1930 | 6,077 | 359 |
| 1931 | 6,109 | 405 |
| 1932 | 6,215 | 615 |
| 1933 | 6,280 | 1,486 |

SOURCE: Statistical Reports, 1920–23, 1925, 1927–33, Rosebud,
Rolls 118, 119, SAR.

most important source of cash income on Rosebud in 1895 ($15,886), after beef cattle sales ($48,101)[57] and freighting ($17,003).[58]

The most significant form of agency employment in the first decade of the twentieth century was per diem labor. In January 1901 the commissioner issued an order to the agencies that able-bodied men be dropped from the ration rolls and offered work by the agencies at the rate of $1.25 per diem. The rationale was to instill labor discipline in Indian men and to prevent them from becoming ration loafers. The Rosebud agent reported in 1904 that nearly all able-bodied men had been engaged in per diem labor for six months. The federal expenditures on per diem labor on Rosebud in 1907 are presented in table 1.6. This was clearly a source of labor for developing and maintaining reservation infrastructure, but the main purpose was to wean Indian men off rations and to teach them to work for their keep. Thus, it is not surprising that the two largest expenditures on Rosebud in 1907 were for labor by allottees on their own allotments, for their own benefit. Per diem labor was never again as important as it was in the first decade of the twentieth century, but some irregular Indian labor continued to be hired by the agencies—along with a handful of regu-

Table 1.6   Expenditures on Per Diem Labor, Rosebud Reservation, 1907

| Type of Labor | Amount |
| --- | --- |
| Improving allotments | $25,737.54 |
| Making hay on allotments | 20,000.00 |
| Building and repairing dams and reservoirs | 13,000.00 |
| Constructing fireguards | 10,000.00 |
| Receiving and distributing cattle | 6,312.50 |
| Building and repairing roads and bridges | 5,965.50 |
| Rounding up, branding, and dipping cattle | 4,000.00 |
| Riding and repairing government fence | 4,000.00 |
| Total | $89,015.54 |

SOURCE: Report, 4 September 1907, File 75225-1907-150, Rosebud, CCF.

lar agency employees—until New Deal relief work became available in 1933.[59]

The agencies also administered per capita payments from tribal trust funds. In consideration of the cessions made by the Lakota through the 1889 agreement, and through the acts opening "surplus" lands within the two reservations, Congress provided for certain per capita payments to be made to tribal enrollees. The OIA had discretion over the distribution of some of these payments, as provided for in the legislation and even when not expressly provided for in the legislation. In 1910, for example, the Rosebud Agency cabled the commissioner: "Earnestly recommend authority be granted for thirty dollar per capita payment from Gregory County funds. Large number of Indians in destitute condition and unless payment is made soon, there will be great amount of suffering and many deaths this winter." Per capita payments under the 1889 act were the third largest source of cash disbursed to the Oglala by the Pine Ridge Agency in 1905 ($30,767), surpassed only by per diem labor ($73,213) and the purchase of beef cattle ($34,686). Per capita payments were a crucial source of cash for many families during the 1910s especially, when both rations and per diem labor had been drastically cut.[60]

In addition to the above resources, the OIA also supplied some credit to Lakota people for agricultural operations, both subsistence and commercial. Since the trust status of allotments prevented allottees from securing loans from private banks with land, the OIA was the *only* source of credit open to allottees who had not been fee patented. Under what was called the reimbursable plan funded by a federal budget item termed "Industry among Indians," the agencies provided individuals with seed, livestock, and even implements on credit. Lakota people on Rosebud were also eligible to borrow from a $30,000 revolving fund established for them out of funds credited to the tribe under the provisions of the 1889 Act. Thus, even where the Lakota did produce part, or occasionally all, of their subsistence from labor on their allotments, they were still dependent upon the OIA.[61]

One more point about Lakota dependence upon resources administered by the OIA needs to be made. The OIA not only managed the local allocation of resources on the reservations. It also *made the flow of some of these resources from Washington possible* because it was in a position to lobby Congress and the secretary of the interior for the necessary funding. There was obviously some overlap in the interests of the Lakota and those of OIA personnel regarding the federal appropriations for Indian affairs. The funding from Congress which sustained—and expanded—the bureaucracy inhabited by OIA personnel simultaneously provided resources for the Lakota. No matter how much the OIA skimmed off funds appropriated for Indians, it secured the continued flow of those funds. In this one sense, the OIA was the Lakota's best advocate, because no other agent or organization would as faithfully or could as successfully lobby for Indian appropriations. The Lakota, of course, were aware of this.

None of this is to suggest that the resource flows administered by the OIA were *sufficient*. As James Mooney pointed out in his study of the Ghost Dance, "The highest official authorities concur in the statement . . . that the Indians were driven to outbreak by starvation." "There is no question," the Pine Ridge superintendent wrote in 1925, "but that the Pine Ridge Sioux have suffered considerably during the winter and spring on account of insufficiency of food." This situation no doubt contributed to the high mortality rate ascertained by the Meriam commission for South Dakota reservations in 1925. The rate was 23.5 deaths per 1,000 population. This compares unfavorably with the figures of 9.1 and 7.9 deaths per 1,000 for the states of Nebraska and North Dakota respectively. The point in the above description of resources provided by the OIA is not that the Lakota were not poor, but that no matter how insufficient the subsistence base, such subsistence base as there was owed its existence to the OIA.[62]

The political economy of Lakota reservations, then, was essentially a situation in which a people recently extruded from their pre-reservation, "contact-traditional"[63] niche had become dependent upon "foreign" administrators—the colonizers—for the reproduction of their physical bodies, their families and communities, and the social and cultural matrix of those families and communities. Given this dependence, is it any wonder that the presence of the OIA agencies and the imposition, maintenance, and expansion of the administrative technologies of surveillance and control described above went unchallenged (or, at least without challenges which called into question the *presence* of the agencies or directly attacked the *existence* of surveillance and control)? The Lakota endured the bureaucratic penetration of their everyday lives by the OIA because the OIA made their everyday lives possible.[64]

This does not mean that the Lakota were given a "good deal" by the government; they paid a dear price for the resource flows—their lands. The effects—sometimes intended, sometimes not—of what Frederick Hoxie has called the OIA's "colonial land policy" was what Janet McDonnell calls "dispossession"—delivery of Indian lands into the hands of non-Indian farmers and ranchers through sale and lease, often at bargain rates. The Lakota ceded 11,000,000 acres via the Great Sioux Agreement in 1889 (see chapter 2). Additional lands were lost through the opening of "surplus" lands to settlement on Pine Ridge and Rosebud, and there is strong evidence that the "surplus" lands in Gregory County on Rosebud were sold to homesteaders at prices below market value.[65]

Fee patenting was another mechanism by which non-Indians— banks, real estate companies, and farmers and ranchers—obtained Indian lands at bargain rates. From the point of view of an allottee, the value of a fee patent was that land he could not make productive use of could be mortgaged or sold for cash—cash which did not go into an IIM account and which could be spent without supervision. According to the Pine Ridge superintendent, seventy-five percent of the fee-patented allottees mortgaged their land. Mortgages were signed for one-half to one-quarter of the value of the land, for a period of two years. Many allottees mortgaged their holdings to more than one party, and most defaulted on their payments and lost their lands through foreclosure. Twenty-five percent sold their land outright.[66]

It has also been pointed out that the capital and land disadvantages suffered by potential Indian operators—disadvantages partly produced by OIA policy and federal Indian law—created a situation in which it was more profitable for an allottee to rent land to non-Indian operators than to work it himself. By 1918 almost all of Pine Ridge Reservation was leased to white ranchers—75,000 to 100,000 head of non-Indian stock on nearly 1,000,000 acres of Indian land— and the leasing department at the agency was in arrears. Almost 1,000 new allotment leases were contracted on Rosebud during fiscal year 1915—30,000 non-Indian cattle on approximately 200,000 acres of Indian land.[67]

But this domination of Lakota people with respect to their land does not alter the fact that the artificial reservation economies by which the Lakota lived were underwritten by the OIA (and ultimately, of course, Congress). One of the ironies of federal Indian policy before the New Deal is that, the civilization—which is to say, *assimilation*—discourse notwithstanding, the reservations in fact served as "homelands" (in Hoxie's terminology) or "sustained enclaves" (in George Pierre Castile's) allowing the maintenance of modified traditional ways of life that would have fast been liquidated if Lakota people had been directly exposed to the market forces of the agrarian economy. It must have quickly become inconsistent with Lakota *common sense* understandings—because it would be inconsistent with their obvious and immediate interests—to contemplate seriously reservation life without the oia.[68]

## Treaty Rights

The concept of resignation as it is used here is meant to draw attention to the fact that, except for notable exceptions, the Lakota *did not systematically challenge the presence of the oia bureaucracy* either in political discourse—at least in "frontstage" discourse—or in political action. This does not mean that the Lakota participated completely in their own domination, that they freely consented to the surveillance and control imposed on them by the oia, that the oia had "legitimacy" among them, or that they accepted the oia's representation of power. "Resignation to what seems inevitable," James Scott tells us, "is not the same as according it legitimacy, although it may serve just as efficiently to produce daily compliance."[69] Lakota people were, at best, deeply *ambivalent* about the oia. The Lakota *acquiesced* regarding the presence of the oia, but they developed an alternative representation of their relations with the United States government, the treaty rights ideology. Resources and political arrangements on the reservation were not matters to be left by wards to the wise discretion of fatherly bureaucrats, in the terms of this ideology, but matters clearly provided for in law (*woop'e*)—in the treaties and agreements by which the Lakota had ceded land to the United States.

One element of this ideology concerned the way in which tribal decision making was to take place under treaty provisions—"three-fourths majority rule" (see chapter 2). This could have critical implications for the legitimacy of oia power, as one Oglala complained to the investigating subcommittee of the Senate Indian Committee, visiting Pine Ridge in 1929: "The 1868 treaty says it is to be three-fourths majority to run everything," but, "The agent here is pushing us down all the time."[70]

The other element of this ideology concerned the origin of rations and other resources and services provided by the OIA. The Lakota knew well the terms of the Black Hills Agreement regarding rations. Scudder Mekeel found that during the early 1930s, Oglala people between the ages of thirty and the late fifties—the group from which the major political actors were drawn—saw rations as a right: "Their stomachs started on government rations and their minds were turned to a parasitic life [sic!] which was regarded as their inalienable right by treaty." Both Erik Erikson and Everett Hagen, who visited Pine Ridge, commented on what they called the "compensation neurosis" of the Lakota—they expected compensation for the ceded lands. The Pine Ridge superintendent explained to the investigating subcommittee of the Senate Indian committee in 1940: "To the older Indians the treaty of 1868 was simply a guaranty of rations forever. . . . Ideally, these older Indians would have an Indian Service set-up which would consist of schools, medical service, extension service, and the other divisions as at present, plus rations for everybody."[71]

To the Lakota, of course, rations were not "free" and their consumption by the people was not "parasitic" or part of a "neurotic compulsion" for compensation. The rations had been paid for long ago by the millions of acres ceded to the United States. In return the government had promised to feed the Lakota until they were able to feed themselves, and given economic and agricultural conditions prevailing on the reservations, how were they to feed themselves? As an Oglala man told the Senate investigating subcommittee in 1939, "Today, practically all the Indians on our reservation are unable to support themselves but the Government is not supplying them with the agreed rations."[72] We can reasonably surmise that an appeal to treaty rights was one of the rallying cries when the Oglala chiefs sought to organize resistance to per diem labor, and force was even threatened, in 1901. In general, however, the Lakota did not put this ideology to use in challenging the presence of the OIA and its technologies of surveillance and control. Indeed, the execution of treaty rights *required the presence of government agents of some kind to deliver resources*, although, of course, this delivery did not require relations of wardship/guardianship. The treaty rights ideology would emerge in the 1930s in resistance not to the presence of the agencies but to the presence of tribal councils composed of some Lakota people who claimed to speak for all Lakota people.

The mode of domination described in this chapter entailed the bureaucratic penetration of a colonized people by the technologies of the state, technologies that facilitated the efficient surveillance and control of populations. This bureaucratic penetration of Indian lives went so far as to include the recording of the menstrual cycles of girls in the federal boarding schools by OIA matrons—so that administrators would know of pregnancies and could take appropriate action.[73] The struggle described here—the perennial struggle in reservation political economy—was over the presence of the state apparatus; it was over what Anthony Giddens calls "administrative power" and Michel Foucault calls "disciplinary power" and the "bio-politics of the population."[74] That the struggle on the part of the Lakota was contained within strict limits, that they were resigned to the penetration of the state even while carefully resisting its power over them on a day-to-day level, was the political effect of their dependence upon resources delivered by the same state apparatus that dominated them.

## CHAPTER 2

# Tribal Politics before the New Deal

Social systems, as Sally Falk Moore tells us, "like souped-up automobiles are constructions made out of new and used parts." When John Collier first visited Pine Ridge and Rosebud reservations in December 1933 to explain his plans for an Indian New Deal, he met, among others, men from the Oglala Tribal Council and the Rosebud Sioux Council. It would be difficult to imagine better examples of what Moore calls the "*bricolage* of the present," of the historical blending of the old and the new, than these two tribal councils.[1]

On the one hand, they operated under constitutions the OIA had some hand in drafting, which provided for representative democracy, and meetings were conducted according to parliamentary procedure. On the other hand, chiefs had a prominent role in these councils, and traditional dancing and feasts accompanied council meetings. What is more, the central political principle under which these bodies operated, "three-fourths-majority rule," was based on an indigenous Lakota reading of treaty law and the tribal constitutions. It was originally a legal provision inserted in the Fort Laramie Treaty of 1868 by the Interior Department. This principle was used by the United States in 1889 to undermine the authority of Lakota chiefs in order to obtain a land cession from the Lakota. The principle was soon embraced by the Lakota and their chiefs, however, as the proper, the legal, and— eventually—the *traditional* method of tribal decision making. The purpose of this chapter is to outline the history of Lakota tribal politics before John Collier's visit in late 1933.

## Chiefs

While what we know of nineteenth-century Lakota sociopolitical organization is very sketchy, that organization is best seen as seasonally and opportunistically variable along a continuum running from small units with little formal political structure to large units with more formal organization. Neither corporate groups nor fixed boundaries were characteristic of Lakota political organization, and units of all sizes were fluid. The smallest unit was the band, based in part on kinship and assembled around a chief. This was an achieved status, although there is some indication that it was partially hereditary. The Oglala consultants of Clark Wissler and James Walker made it clear that a would-be chief and his followers could form a new band by simply establishing a new encampment. If Francis Parkman's 1846 description of an Oglala chief is representative, no authority to issue commands accrued to the chief of a band: "Each village has a chief, who is honored and obeyed only so far as his personal qualities may command respect and fear. . . . [T]he usages of his people have provided no means for enforcing his authority."[2]

At the opposite end of the continuum were large, temporary associations composed of more than one band, such as the summer Sun Dance encampments. Wissler's and Walker's Oglala consultants differed a great deal on the specifics of political organization in these groups, probably because both historical change and geographic variation made typification difficult, but there were several levels of chiefly authority.[3]

An association of older men, the chiefs society (*naca ominicia*) or big bellies, comprised, according to Wissler, "the majority of the efficient older men of forty years or more," at least among the Red Cloud division of the Oglala. It selected from without seven *wicaśa it'ancan* (men chiefs) to serve for life, candidacy being partially hereditary. The *wicaśa it'ancan* in turn chose four "owners of the tribe" or "shirt wearers," who were the "supreme councilors and executives" responsible for providing good hunting and selecting good campsites. The chiefs society, *wicaśa it'ancan*, and shirt wearers together selected four *wakicun* to serve for one year. The *wakicun* in turn appointed two soldier chiefs (*akicita it'ancan*), who appointed two others, and the four soldier chiefs together selected eight to

ten men or a military society to act as a camp police force. Wissler
wrote that

> all the civil and economic affairs of the camp are in the hands of the
> wakicun. On all these matters, they are free to instruct and can en-
> force their orders through the akicita. They decide when to break
> camp, where to go and again select the new site. Hunting must be
> carried on when and as they direct. They also see that every person
> receives a fair share of the meat and is provided with enough robes
> to make the winter endurable. They settle disputes, judge and com-
> pound crimes, and make rules to ensure proper decorum in camp.

People who disagreed with the authorities, however, could apparently
leave the larger camps just as people could leave the bands. At all
levels of organization, Lakota people could vote with their feet.[4]

This timeless ethnographic description of Lakota political organization is of little use, however, without a consideration of historical context. The power of chiefs was first enhanced by contact
with United States officials, and then drastically diminished on the
reservations.

Centripetal forces began to appear in Lakota politics after 1850;
these originated in the United States government's need to deal with
Indian tribes as legal and political entities over which it had not yet
instituted the administrative technologies of surveillance and control
described in chapter 1. The government's tactic was to identify and
support individuals who could negotiate and execute agreements for
the Lakota—conduct foreign affairs, in effect—and who could also
govern the internal affairs of the "Sioux Nation." The United States
systematically recognized chiefs who would, at least as far as it was
concerned, speak for the Lakota. The Fort Laramie Treaty of 1851, for
example, established a head chief for each "nation" which was a sig-
natory. A head chief was selected for the Lakota only after much insistence by them that there could be no one chief. In 1856 General
William Harney negotiated a treaty with the Lakota—which was
never ratified by the Senate—in which each division named chiefs,
subordinate chiefs, and soldiers to enforce the chiefs' orders. Eventually, Spotted Tail came to be the head chief recognized by the government among the Sicangu, and Red Cloud among the Oglala, and
the government built houses for them at the agencies. These chiefs,

as well as lesser chiefs and headmen, negotiated and signed the Fort Laramie Treaty of 1868 and a series of cession and other agreements. They were also given certificates by the OIA recognizing their positions, much like commissions.[5]

Chiefs were not only legally recognized by and drafted to negotiate with the government, but were also relied upon by the agencies to help maintain order on the new reservations. It is certainly true that the Lakota chiefs recognized by the United States government may not have been seen by the Lakota as having the authority to govern, particularly outside their own bands. But their influence was apparently significant as is indicated by the Rosebud agent's comment on the death of Spotted Tail in 1881: "The loss of this chief is irreparable. There is not one on the reservation who can fill his place. The value of his services to the government in the past cannot be too highly estimated, and he was ever on the side of law and order, and to him is greatly due the credit of its maintenance on this reservation."[6]

Chiefs were given special treatment by the agencies as officially-recognized middlemen. Federal law stated that annuities—clothing and yard goods provided for in the 1868 treaty—could be "distributed to the tribe by the chiefs in such manner as the chiefs may deem best."[7] The agent at Spotted Tail Agency, who served in 1869 and 1870, wrote that Spotted Tail was given extra rations because of the hospitality he had to extend as head chief. Rations at that time were also provided in bulk to some favored chiefs for distribution to their followers. These chiefs skimmed some of the rations for their own use and were thus "able to give grand feasts" and surpass rival chiefs who were not so favored by the agency.[8]

This intermediary role of the chiefs—distributing annuities and rations—in the early stages of the artificial economies of the reservations clearly enhanced their power. It even gave them some autonomy from the agencies. The Pine Ridge agent complained in 1882 that turning annuities over to the chiefs for distribution had the effect of "the bolstering up and supporting of the chiefs." He explained:

> If an individual Indian tries to aid civilization and progress by cutting
> loose from the tribe, and adopt the white man's ways, he will meet
> his reception when he attends the annual distribution of annuities
> under his chief: He will be told by the chief . . . 'I am the chief; the
> Great Father told me when I was in Washington he has sent to *me* all

these goods. You have worked against the good old Indian ways, you have worked against your chief, you have taken the part of the white man, you can have none of these things; they are for Indians.'

The agent wrote that in 1879 annuities at Pine Ridge were issued in bulk to seven chiefs, and all who had joined the agency police force or otherwise worked for the agency were deprived of their share of the annuities.[9]

By the late 1870s, however, government policy regarding chiefs was beginning to change. Chiefs came to be seen as a hindrance to the new policy of civilizing the Indians. It was also clear that chiefs could interfere with relations between the agencies and the emerging jural individuals being constructed by the administrative technologies of surveillance and control described in the last chapter. In 1879 the new agent at Pine Ridge explained in his annual report that previously the only way to feed and control the Indians had been "through and by the assistance of the chiefs" because they "held undisputed and absolute sway, and that we should as a government deal with them *as savages*, through their chiefs, was natural." But if it was government policy to civilize the Indians, and not simply to feed them from cradle to grave, "these chiefs in the control of their tribes must soon outlive their usefulness." The Indians must "individualize themselves, and not remain mere machines to be ordered into rebellion against the government at the mere whim or desire of their chiefs." While he no doubt exaggerated the power of chiefs, chiefs did constitute a threat to the authority of the agencies.[10]

One method of dealing with this threat was simply to *depose* chiefs. Since the power of a chief on the reservation depended upon government recognition to some extent, the government was in a position to undermine chiefs by withdrawing recognition. In 1880 Red Cloud wrote to the president and Congress complaining that the Pine Ridge agent had tried to "throw me away," and that the agent had tried "to trample me in the dust and make a dog of me." In 1881 the Rosebud agent requested permission to depose a particular chief, and a group of chiefs at his agency wrote to the president, obviously with his encouragement, asking for the deposing of a chief who had lied to whites.[11]

Another method of undermining chiefs was to abolish their prerogatives in distributing annuities or rations. The Pine Ridge agent reported in 1882: "A short time before the issue in 1880, I notified the Indians that the annuities were not the property of the chiefs alone, but were sent for all the Indians, as were the rations, and that the Indians might draw their annuities by families, bands, large or small, or through the chiefs." While there had been seven divisions of the annuities in 1879—issued to seven chiefs who distributed them to their followers—in 1881 there were twenty-five to thirty divisions, and in 1882 the annuities were split into sixty-three divisions. "This method is practically and rapidly breaking up the old tribal system and the power of the chiefs," the agent wrote in 1882. "It is to be hoped," he wrote in 1880, "that the time is not far distant when there will be as many bands as there are families; in other words, every head of family his own chief."[12]

Organizing agency police forces was another means of undermining chiefs, because it gave the agents a source of power independent of them, and the chiefs resisted the agents' control of the police at first. The Lakota men who joined the police forces clearly saw them as continuous with the *akicita*, and described their preparedness to die in the line of duty for the government in the way a member of a pre-reservation Lakota military society would have described his readiness to risk his life in combat with an enemy. The captain of the Pine Ridge agency police force said during a visit to Washington in 1888: "We have a good deal of trouble among the people to get them to do what the Government wishes them to do. I am in the service of the Government. No matter what comes before me I am willing to go ahead and do whatever the Government desires me to do." Another policeman said: "I have forced myself into being powerful for the Government and have worked very hard. Of course, when I have this uniform on my life is nothing, if I have anything to do that the Government orders me to do. Anything I am told to do, I walk right into it." Such men, of course, would have taken their orders from the *wakicun* and other chiefs before they were coopted by the agents.[13]

## Three-Fourths Majority Rule

One of the most significant blows to chiefly authority came with government negotiations for the Great Sioux Agreement in 1889, which the Lakota sometimes called the Crook Treaty after one of the commissioners, General George Crook. The government proposed the cession of eleven million acres from the Great Sioux Reservation established by the Fort Laramie Treaty of 1868—which originally included all of what is now South Dakota west of the Missouri River—and the establishment of six smaller reservations. In consideration of the cession, a trust fund of $3 million would be established. The agreement would also provide for the allotment of remaining reservation lands in severalty and the issue of livestock, agricultural tools and implements, and cash to individual allottees, which became known later as Sioux benefits. Since the proposition included a land cession, it had to be executed by three-fourths of the adult males of the Lakota, in conformity with article twelve of the 1868 treaty. This was crucial in the view of the Interior Department. Although the Black Hills Agreement had been ratified by Congress in 1877 with only ten percent of the adult males signing, Congress had refused to ratify an earlier version of the 1889 cession agreement because of the failure of the commissioners to obtain the consent of three-fourths of the adult males. The concern on the part of Congress to abide by the 1868 treaty was no doubt motivated by fear of a Lakota claim against the government.[14]

With concern to follow to the letter article twelve of the 1868 treaty, the Crook commission traveled in 1889 to all the Lakota agencies to explain the cession and allotment proposition, to answer questions, and to obtain signatures on an agreement from the adult males. They encountered difficulty, however, and reported: "The commissioners at every agency found that their greatest obstacle was to reach the individual Indians. In spite of the Indian department policy to break up the control of chiefs and to deal only with individuals, it was found that in all matters of general interest the influence of the chiefs was almost as great as ever."[15]

The Lakota were aware of the proposal, had information on an earlier version of it in the Lakota language provided by the Indian Defense Association in Philadelphia, and had selected speakers to make their wishes known to the commission. But the commission used the three-fourths majority provision to drive a wedge into this attempt to maintain a united front at both Rosebud and Pine Ridge.[16]

At Rosebud General Crook chose to emphasize not the land cession but the provisions for allotment in severalty. He explained to the Lakota that patents for individual allotments—the privatizing of tribal property—was the only way the Indians could protect their land from Congress. Congress would take tribal land with or without tribal consent in the future, but it could never take patented land against the wishes of the allottee. His appeal was made directly to individual men with families: "Those of you with families should make some provision for them when you die. . . . And if you don't take my advice, and you have nothing for your families, can your chiefs give them anything? Will they have any land to give them? Those persons who have any love for their families at all must think well over this matter. Now, each one will have the privilege of voting just as you desire."[17]

Some of the chiefs on Rosebud wanted the agreement to be negotiated by a body of twelve leading men representing all of the Lakota agencies. They believed that universal male voting on the proposition without hard bargaining by a few selected leaders would harm Lakota interests in the agreement. But other Lakota, probably responding to the government's appeal to the interests of individual families, believed differently: "Every man is supposed to have his own opinion in regard to this business. It is not left with a body of men to decide upon in this matter."[18] This political sentiment—not inconsistent with the picture of Lakota politics painted by Francis Parkman in 1846—was reinforced by the government's intention to enforce the (emergent) "right" of individuals to decide as individuals on the matter. One of the local white traders spoke in council: "The opportunity will be offered each and every one of you to sign this bill, if you so desire. And you must not fear you will be persecuted for signing the bill, for the United States Government will sustain you."[19]

By such means the commissioners obtained the signatures of 1,455 of the 1,476 adult males on Rosebud.[20]

On Pine Ridge the commissioners encountered much stronger opposition to the agreement. There were those in favor of the agreement, one man stating that he supported the bill even though he had been "under these head-men and chiefs and listened to them."[21] But the chiefs had been advised by Dr. T. A. Bland of the Indian Defense Association to refuse to accept the agreement. The commissioners were able to obtain the signatures of only 684 of the 1,366 adult males on Pine Ridge. The agreement was deemed approved by three-fourths of the adult males of the Sioux Nation, however, since the commissioners obtained the signatures of 4,463 out of 5,678 adult males at all the agencies combined, and the agreement became law.[22]

The 1889 negotiations were the first time that the franchise for males was employed as a decision-making mechanism among the Lakota. Although the three-fourths majority provision had been inserted as article twelve in the 1868 treaty, it had not been an indigenous concept. Similar provisions are found in at least six treaties with other tribes in the 1867–68 period. The intent of Congress in the provision was to protect small groups within the Sioux Nation: "As different tribes and bands were . . . located on different portions of this large reservation [the Great Sioux] held in common by them all, in order to guard the rights of each in the whole and protect each one from a combination of the others to part with any portion of the territory to the injury of any other band or tribe," it was provided that all future land sales would require approval of three-fourths of the males eighteen years of age and over. In 1889, however, the three-fourths majority provision was used to undermine the influence of chiefs in cession negotiations, and it is likely that the provisions for allotment were inserted into the cession agreement by the Interior Department as a tactic to persuade individual men to accept the cession against the wishes of the chiefs who had some experience at dealing with government commissioners.[23]

When combined with the general administrative policy of bypassing chiefs and individualizing wardship, the effect of what the Lakota came to call three-fourths majority rule on chiefly authority can well be imagined. In 1891 the Rosebud agent reported that the "real cause" of the Ghost Dance uprising on his reservation was to be found in the "nonprogressive" chiefs who had opposed the 1889 agreement, which had been accepted by the majority: "This element, who heretofore considered themselves as the authority of the tribe, could not be reconciled to the fact that the younger element now assumed equal authority."[24] How much things had changed is indicated by the remarks of a young man at a Rosebud council with the government in 1897: "Of course, when the Great Father made that law for me about the young men 18 years of age I was so crowded by the chiefs that nobody could see me, but now you see me. Now I do not ask anybody's advice nor take anybody's word; I think for myself according to that law General Crook made for us." He concluded, "All the young men 18 years old want to vote without anybody's wishes and you take that vote home to Congress."[25]

The administrative fostering of the power of chiefs had, thus, given way to a policy of *individualizing* Indian tribes and allowing chiefs to fade into oblivion. This policy was directly related to the growing bureaucratic presence of the OIA on the reservations.

The position of chief, however, was not eradicated. The original bands had settled separately in the river valleys on both reservations with their chiefs, and communities derived in part from these bands, often with recognized chiefs, were still present in the 1930s. Band chieftainship was apparently passed from father to son. Scudder Mekeel found the chiefs society extant on Pine Ridge Reservation in 1930 and 1931, with each of the thirty bands on the reservation having a chief, and fourteen chiefs in White Clay District alone. He also found at that late date that an individual still might serve as *akicita*—probably glossed as soldier or sergeant-at-arms in English—under a chief. A "Chief Day Celebration" was held in the spring at the Grass Mt. dance hall on Rosebud Reservation in the 1930s, and in 1935 seven living chiefs were honored at that celebration.[26]

Rather than disappearing in the new environment, the chiefs accommodated by espousing the principle of three-fourths majority rule and acting as spokesmen. From the transcript of the 1889 negotiations it is apparent that some bands voted on the agreement en bloc and conveyed their sentiments to the commission through their headmen or chiefs. At the series of councils with the government between 1901 and 1911 for the cession of "surplus" reservation lands, Lakota speakers, some of whom were chiefs, sometimes prefaced their remarks by explaining that they were chosen by the people in a band or district to make their wishes known. There were requests that proceedings be halted so that the matters could be discussed with the people. Sometimes papers were handed by the spokesmen to the government negotiator with the desires of groups set out. It is clear that men who would be chiefs were careful to pay attention to the desires of the people they would represent.[27]

Three-fourths majority rule, originally inserted in the 1868 treaty to protect the Lakota and employed in 1889 to break down resistance to land cession, thus became—or, at least a Lakota interpretation of it became—the accepted means of making agreements with the United States. It became a critical element in the treaty rights ideology which was mentioned in chapter 1. Along with the claim examined in chapter 1 that rations and other benefits from the government were *compensation*, the principle of three-fourths majority rule also defined for the Lakota relations with the United States. Or at least it defined how those relations should justly and legally be conducted *according to the Lakota*, because the government was soon to abrogate the three-fourths majority principle in its dealings with the Lakota.

The Interior Department first considered in 1897 negotiating with the Lakota to obtain their voluntary modification of article twelve of the 1868 treaty in order to make future land cessions less difficult procedurally. OIA Inspector James McLaughlin, who was asked by the Interior Department to seek such an agreement, reported that the Lakota were not disposed to discuss such a proposition since they regarded article twelve "as their greatest protection and safeguard in any future negotiations affecting their common interests." It was clearly a protection both against the government and against a minority of chiefs or others who might presume to speak for and make decisions for the Lakota people without their knowledge or approval (even though it could be used *against* the Lakota, as it had been in 1889).[28]

The United States Supreme Court settled the matter of tribal approval of land cessions, however, in 1903 with *Lone Wolf v. Hitchcock*. The court held that Congress had plenary power in Indian affairs, which is to say, authority to abrogate Indian treaties without consulting the Indian signatories, and, as guardian of its Indian wards, it could enact legislation affecting Indians, including land cessions, without their consent.

The import of *Lone Wolf* was first explained to the Lakota by McLaughlin on Rosebud in 1903, while he was negotiating for the opening of Gregory County. The main spokesman for the Rosebud people, a prominent chief, responded: "We are Indians yet, and we remember the laws that have been made for us. The Great Father has made a law that there must be three-fourths of the people consenting before any action shall be taken by Congress. If they shall consider that law, they should not open that Gregory County without our consent. If they do I shall feel like a prisoner in my own country."[29]

McLaughlin first explained the plenary power doctrine on Pine Ridge at a council for tribal land cessions in 1909. One Oglala responded to his explanation: "a three fourths majority have always ruled and that is the way we desire all of our business transacted as we have done before and furthermore we have never been informed before that Congress had the right to open up surplus lands without the consent of the Indians."[30] The president of the Oglala Council told McLaughlin: "You refer to this southern Indian, Lone Wolf by name, whatever kind of animal he is, or who he is, we are not of the same class." The denial of the force of article twelve by the *Lone Wolf* decision only served to heighten the significance of three-fourths majority rule for the Lakota because it became a treaty provision which was in their view *broken* by the government.[31]

The principle of three-fourths majority rule was not only a model for relations with the United States government. It also served as a model for tribal decision making (of course, *tribal* decisions never had to be made before the establishment of the reservations). The model, in its simplest reading among the Lakota, provided that all tribal decisions be made by all adult males enrolled in the tribe. This, of course, was easier said that done because of logistics. Round-trip travel from some parts of Rosebud Reservation to the agency required seven to ten days by team and wagon in 1920. Furthermore, the agencies wanted to discourage allottees from traveling and neglecting their crops and stock.[32]

What were called general councils, mass meetings, or three-fourths majority councils (*okaśpe yamni*) attended by a significant proportion of the adult males were held on both reservations at the time of Fourth of July celebrations and during the annual reservation agricultural fairs. The OIA also called general councils for special matters, as with the surplus land negotiations mentioned above. Such councils, however, could not meet often enough to conduct all the tribal business that came to need attention throughout the year.[33]

A workable solution was for local general councils to meet regularly in each farm district and to dispatch a number of representatives to a central meeting to make popular wishes known. Members of any central council in this model were more on the order of delegates than elected officials or public administrators. The model was one of grassroots democracy with the delegation of limited authority to representatives who did not presume to *govern* or to use their initiative or better judgment without the consent of the men who choose them, and who certainly did not presume to impose unpopular decisions on tribal members. The proper role for a representative, be he a chief or not, was to act merely as a "word carrier."[34]

This model for tribal decision making developed historically out of the OIA's own introduction of three-fourths majority rule in 1889, and the agents had some role in the elaboration of the model because they had some hand in drafting tribal constitutions, as will be seen below. The model also resonated with the new social status of the formally free, jural individual that was instituted by the administrative technologies of surveillance and control which individualized affairs among the Lakota, as seen in chapter 1. In addition, this model was not inconsistent with, although it was very different from, the individual freedom inherent in nineteenth century Lakota political organization—a fact that may have allowed the model to be persuasively presented as the *traditional* Lakota way of making tribal decisions, as it was by the old dealers in the 1930s.

## Tribal Councils on Rosebud

In 1911 the Rosebud superintendent decided that a general council was too impractical—"simply a 'mob'"—and he organized a Business Committee with representatives selected by local general councils in each farm district, plus two representatives selected at large, totaling twenty. Selections of representatives to the Business Committee by the district councils were probably made by a show of hands or a rising vote, not by secret ballot. The superintendent could and did "summarily dismiss" any man elected whom he considered to be of "undesirable timber."[35]

In 1916 a new superintendent reorganized the Business Committee, which he complained had been only "partially elective"[36] and had been much too concerned with fostering traditional dances.[37] A constitution was drawn up, apparently by the agency, for the Rosebud Tribal Council which provided for the election of one member from each day school community and band camp on the reservation for a two-year term. All male allottees of at least twenty-five years of age were eligible for membership, and male allottees over twenty-one were entitled to vote in the elections, but it is not clear from the constitution whether election was by a show of hands or a rising vote, or by secret ballot. The district councils—each district included several day school communities and band camps—were authorized to meet just before and just after each Rosebud Tribal Council meeting for the purposes of conveying petitions to the council and of being apprised of council actions. This, of course, was consistent with the model of three-fourths majority rule. The purpose of the Rosebud Tribal Council was "to represent the Rosebud tribe of Sioux Indians in all matters which by law or custom have heretofore devolved upon the common council of the tribe or the Rosebud Business Committee. It shall be the purpose of this council to maintain harmonious cooperation with the Secretary of the Interior, the Commissioner of Indian Affairs, and the Superintendent of the Rosebud Agency." The members would receive per diem allowances to help defray their travel expenses.[38]

Not all Lakota, however, saw the Rosebud Tribal Council as sufficiently representative of their interests. In fact, as soon as the new council had been organized in 1916, an elderly man who signed his name with the title chief requested permission from the commissioner to hold a three-fourths majority council. The superintendent had advised the commissioner in 1915 that this man was among the "ultraconservative" and "dancing element" of the reservation, one of the "typical old time dance leaders and would-be Indian chieftains." Now he reiterated that evaluation and advised the commissioner against granting permission since there was already an elective council on the reservation. Permission was denied by the commissioner. The same chief and others again requested permission for a council in 1917. This time they had encouragement from Charles Eastman, the noted Dakota Indian physician and former OIA employee, who had wired the men that he was coming out from Washington with an attorney and that they should call a meeting to discuss the Black Hills claim. The superintendent again warned the commissioner not to allow what the Lakota called a three-fourths majority council. Such a meeting could not be as representative as the Rosebud Tribal Council, he said, because younger men would not be likely to rise in an open meeting to oppose the opinions of older men, and, therefore, "old, ignorant or reactionary" men would control the meeting. Again, the commissioner denied the men permission for the meeting.[39]

It appears that the new council superseded older men who had previously been prominent in tribal decision making. The superintendent said of the constitution:

I feel that this instrument marks one of the most important mile-
stones in the forward progress of the tribe. . . . One of the principal
things resulting from it is to very largely do away with the influence
of the old self-styled chiefs who are very retrogressive in their influence. So long as they can secure recognition as speaking for and representing the tribe they can maintain a following. It is this following
that enhances their power and influence for retrogression. If their following is destroyed their influence goes with it. While this instrument is not hostile to the old people, it will very largely take away
their following, and through that, their influence for holding back
the younger element of the tribe.

The new constitution may have diminished the influence of chiefs
and older men by making smaller camps and day-school communities
rather than the district councils, where the chiefs probably dominated, the units of representation; and by altering the method of election from a show of hands or rising vote to a secret ballot, although
this is not clear from the record.[40]

But it was not just a matter of the new council superseding the
chiefs. To the extent that elected councilmen acted beyond the express desires of the people as represented in district councils, the new
arrangement would also have been seen as a violation of three-fourths
majority rule, the model for tribal decision making. This indeed seems
to have happened. The superintendent reported:

As a result of this organization the old time neighborhood dances are
being very largely done away with and pretty nearly one half of the
local dance halls in the reservation will be destroyed during the summer. This is not done through any arbitrary act on the part of myself
or the government but through the influence of this tribal council,
and several communities heretofore maintaining local dance halls
are being brought together in fewer numbers.

Dance halls were built by communities for meetings and for Lakota
social dances such as the *Omaha* Dance. The council probably pursued this restriction at the insistence of the superintendent, but it is
clear that these actions were not in conformity with the desires of the
people whose dance halls were destroyed or whose dances were limited. This was a far cry, indeed, from three-fourths majority rule.[41]

There continued to be requests for councils outside of the official
Rosebud Tribal Council. (Some of these attempts to hold councils
were instigated by attorneys seeking to obtain a contract to handle

the Black Hills Claim.) In 1919 the superintendent instructed the farmers to advise the Indians that any camp holding an unauthorized meeting or dance would be "dealt with in annuity payment."[42]

There remained, however, general dissatisfaction with the Rosebud Tribal Council, and in 1920 the agency consented to a referendum in which a "large majority" voted to replace the Rosebud Tribal Council with the general council. What the leaders of the opposition wanted, however, was not a literal return to the general council—that would have been impractical—but new elections in the districts for delegates to a tribal council. The superintendent interpreted this as merely a political tactic to turn the rascals out: "I now find that it would be entirely satisfactory to nearly all Indians of the reservation to announce a date for election of members to represent the tribe as a whole and call them tribal councilmen instead of business councilmen." The opposition's intent, however, was not merely to replace the incumbents, although that is a likely enough factor, but to reorganize the operations of the council so that it did not have autonomy from the district councils and could not impose decisions unpopular with the tribal members. In short, they wanted a council of representatives consistent with the model of three-fourths majority rule. Three-fourths majority rule meant that the councilmen would represent and act on the desires of the people as they were expressed in district council meetings, and that they would not impose decisions on the people.[43]

A new constitution was drafted in 1920 by, or under the supervision of, the agency. This constitution remained in effect, with minor amendments, until it was replaced by the IRA constitution in 1935. It provided for district councils which would have representation on a central tribal council through two classes of tribal councilmen— advisors and delegates—to insure that both older chiefs and younger people were fairly represented. A 1933 form of the constitution of the Rosebud Sioux Council provided for a Board of Advisors of twenty "subchiefs or members with good characters," allocated to the districts on a population basis and elected by the district councils (probably by a show of hands or rising vote) to two-year terms. The constitution also provided for twenty-seven delegates allocated to the districts on a population basis and elected by the district councils to one-year terms. Each district delegation was also authorized to bring one camp soldier (*akicita*) to each meeting, with rights equal to those of a delegate. The advisors, delegates, and camp soldiers met jointly. The constitution did not specify whether or not women could vote or serve on the council, but no women served on the council. According to contemporary consultants, women did not vote at district council meetings.[44]

The council operated in only loose conformity with the constitution. Minor amendments that were made over the years were, according to the superintendent in a 1934 questionnaire, "kept somewhat in the traditions of the council rather than on paper." Certification of duly elected councilmen was often informal, unclear, or problematic and contested; the superintendent reported in the questionnaire that the "Indians are a little hazy on just what constitutes their council." Apparently men who were not duly elected attended council sessions and may have voted. At one meeting in 1930 there were more than one hundred present.[45]

Yet, the Rosebud Sioux Council organized in 1920 survived until the New Deal period without serious challenges to its operations by nonmembers, probably because the advisor-and-delegate system helped insure wide representation and because the council acted (arguably) in conformity with the Lakota model of three-fourths majority rule: it did not *regularly* (although it did occasionally) take actions beyond the express desires of the people or, at least, the men. Regular meetings of the Rosebud Sioux Council were held quarterly at a different local meeting or dance hall. Members brought their families by team and wagon and camped around the meeting hall, and dances and feasts were held when the council was not in session. Proceedings began with a prayer and conformed broadly with parliamentary procedure, although this was a vernacular version, and the superintendents complained of unbusinesslike procedures as well as the unwieldy size of the council. Proceedings were conducted in both Lakota and English, and minutes were taken by the secretary in English.[46]

The council was recognized by the agency and the OIA office in Washington as representing the Lakota, but its authority was limited to expressing tribal opinion and acting on a few tribal matters, such as executing leases of tribal land. Most business consisted of acting on resolutions submitted by the local councils and was, essentially, a matter of expressing the opinions of the people rather than governing or adopting resolutions that were in any way binding on anyone. The topics ranged widely: a resolution that the federal and state courts and the superintendent be legally empowered to deal effectively with reservation "moral conditions" (1923); a resolution supporting erection of a federal monument to Rosebud men who fought in World War I (1922); a resolution to circulate a petition to be sent to the state board of pardons pertaining to a Rosebud man in prison (1922); resolutions that allotment leasing by bidding and that the purchase order system be abolished (1929); a resolution calling for the abolition of the OIA positions of extension agent, home demonstration agent, forest ranger, day school inspector, school principal, field nurses, general mechanic, chief engineer, and special law enforcement officer, among others (1933); a resolution to authorize only one traditional dance hall in each district (1928). Resolutions were sent to the superintendent who commented on them in writing to the council secretary. The council also entertained correspondence and addresses from the superintendent and sent delegations to the OIA office in Washington and to meetings of the Black Hills Council, the inter-reservation assembly of delegates from tribes with an interest in the Sioux Nation Black Hills claim.[47]

It is important to recognize that the Lakota people on Rosebud Reservation referred to this council as *okaśpe yamni*, three-fourths majority council. The constitution of the Rosebud Sioux Council stipulated that "the membership of this organization shall constitute every individual member of the Rosebud Sioux Tribe of record." Clearly, not all tribal members were members of the council; only a relative handful of men were elected to it. Yet because the district councils—open to everyone (again, at least all men)—were part of the "organization," and because the legitimate role of the Rosebud Sioux Council was only to take up business delegated to it by the district councils, the fiction was that all members were represented in decisions by the Rosebud Sioux Council.[48]

Of course, this *was* a fiction. There would always be a wide range of minority opinions "in the districts" which might not be favorably acted upon, and which might not even receive a serious hearing, at tribal council meetings. In fact, the council clearly attempted to contain opposition and to insist that all public opinions be channeled through it, an understandable enough agenda in dealing with the federal government. The 1924 draft of the constitution provided "that no protests or complaints by individual members or parties of men against the action of the 'Rosebud General Council' shall be submitted to the Honorable Commissioner of Indian Affairs . . . unless such action is submitted by the said Council as a 'minority report'."[49]

But even if the council sought to impose decisions on minorities, the extent to which this was possible was strictly limited by the OIA. Although the successive superintendents—and there was a high turnover rate—recognized the authority of tribal councils to different degrees, in general the councils were not allowed to *govern*. Thus, the Rosebud Sioux Council did not appear to violate the three-fourths majority principle, and the archives are devoid of evidence of grassroots challenges to this body.

## Tribal Councils on Pine Ridge

The Pine Ridge agent had organized an "Agency Board of Councilmen" in 1885 to replace what in his opinion were the "superannuated chiefs," but this body apparently did not survive the administration of the subsequent agent. A more permanent body, the Oglala Council, was organized circa 1891. It was composed of delegations from the various district councils. In the early twentieth century, it had a membership of approximately 300, including elected officers, and it met monthly. The meetings commenced with a prayer and were conducted with an indigenous variant of parliamentary procedure. Chiefs and headmen were prominent among the speakers, and the tension between older and younger men remained despite the supposed operation of three-fourths majority rule. The agent reported in 1907 that "this Oglala Council in its makeup is composed of the older and non-progressive Indians. They shut out the younger element and absolutely control the proceedings." By 1909 the Oglala Council was apparently being represented by twelve standing delegates, two from each of the district councils, who were authorized to present business to the OIA. The superintendent wrote of the Oglala Council in 1909: "The principal business of their councils was to discuss old treaties, figure out how much money the Government owed them on account of the Black Hills Treaty and other treaties, find fault with the government generally and especially with laws and rules made for government of the reservation, and make things as unpleasant as possible for the agent and other employees."[50]

By 1911, however, he was more sanguine about the council in a report to the commissioner: "Very little trouble is experienced with this council, as they have learned to put their complaints or suggestions in writing—to be acted upon by this office and your office. From time to time a committee waits upon the superintendent to support the written complaint or suggestion and all discussions have been very amicable." In 1914 he reported that the council, although composed mostly of fullbloods, was divided into a "progressive and a non-progressive" wing, but that it was "ready to reason and be reasoned with." The superintendent called upon the Oglala Council to execute leases on tribal land and to act on applications for enrollment and allotment.[51]

By 1916 the Oglala Council had a constitution, apparently drafted by members without supervision by the agency. The constitution provided for ten councillors elected—probably by a show of hands or a rising vote—by each of the district councils, and it stipulated that only duly elected councillors were authorized to vote at Oglala Council meetings. A regular meeting required the presence of representatives from three-fourths of the districts, a provision—perhaps mistranslated into English—obviously in keeping with the democratic spirit of three-fourths majority rule. But the constitution, like that on Rosebud, also provided a mechanism for the suppression of minority opinion: "Any party or parties transacting any business [with the OIA] without the knowledge or consent of the President of the council will be fined $15.00." The constitution also sought to protect the positions of chiefs, and it provided that the "making of new chiefs and the and making of new bands will be managed by the chiefs at their camps at home, and not to be handled within the Council." The constitution was approved by the superintendent.[52]

By 1918, however, there were several factions claiming to be the leaders of the Oglala Council or the local chapter of the inter-reservation Black Hills Council on the reservation. In order to establish a body with which the OIA could deal officially, the new superintendent called an election of three delegates from each district to serve for two-year terms, with balloting by men aged twenty-one and over. It is likely that balloting significantly altered the composition of the council. Understandably, the Oglala construed the intention of the agency at the time the election was called to be the replacement of the Oglala Council.[53]

The new council was authorized to meet only at the pleasure of the superintendent and to operate under his supervision. He would not approve a constitution the councilmen drafted at their first meeting because he insisted, among other reasons, that the district councils provided for in the instrument were unnecessary. His general reason for not approving the constitution was most likely that he did not want the council to have jural authority to exist as a recognized body beyond his administrative discretion. Indeed, this council did not meet regularly and quickly became defunct.[54]

Because the elective council foundered, the tribal affairs of the Oglala during the early 1920s were officially—as far as the agency was concerned—in the hands of a standing committee of seven delegates elected in 1921 by the district councils to the inter-reservation Black Hills Council. Some Oglala, however, were not content with this arrangement, and there were requests throughout the period for the approval of constitutions for tribal councils and for the assembly of general councils, with Congressman William Williamson (R., S.D.) and Ralph Case, attorney for the Sioux Nation, even interceding with the commissioner on behalf of Oglala correspondents. The superintendent and the OIA office in Washington resisted all these initiatives.[55]

Yet the Oglala Council, or at least a group of men who called themselves by that name, continued during the mid-1920s. The meetings were probably composed of delegations from the district councils, which also continued to meet.[56] The superintendent described the Oglala Council in 1926 as composed of men "who are anxious to receive more gratuity money; men who are not willing to work for a living, but who carry the impression, and attempt to set themselves up as leaders in a movement that the Government still owes them a living."[57] They were, in the superintendent's opinion, "the Bolshevik element" on the reservation—the reference being to general agitation, not literally to communist activity—and the council was "a mighty poor piece of machinery."[58]

Because both the agency—under a new superintendent—and some of the Oglala had become dissatisfied with the situation, an officially-recognized elective council was again organized in 1928 under a constitution drafted by some Oglala and redrafted by the OIA office in Washington. The new council, which became known as the Oglala Business Council or the Council of Twenty-One, was composed of three delegates elected for two-year terms in each of the seven districts by ballot in elections supervised by the district councils. The constitution did not specify if "voting members" in the districts included women. Any chief, sergeant-at-arms (*akicita*), or other tribal member might "have a voice in the discussion of questions purely for the purpose of advice for a peaceful, intelligent discussion and transaction of business," but only elected delegates and officers were entitled to make motions and to vote. The understanding at the time was that the Business Council was to function for one full term, and if it was not found satisfactory, it would be replaced with the old Oglala Council or with a new body. The councilmen apparently intended to operate according to the model of three-fourths majority rule, and at their first meeting they passed a motion to retain the district councils as branches of the Business Council and where council business would originate. In this respect, the council operated much like the Rosebud Sioux Council of the same period. There was even a resolution proposed—in Lakota—by one of the delegations that the new council be called the "Three Fourths Majority Council." That is to say, at least some of the councilmen believed that their job was to act as word carriers for the district councils.[59]

Yet the models of parliamentary democracy and three-fourths majority rule were not so easily reconciled on Pine Ridge. There was wide recognition that these were two conflicting models of decision making, and in January 1931, at the close of the first term, the Business Council entertained the question as to whether or not it should be maintained as the representative body of the Oglala Lakota. The councilmen discussed two forms of government: the representative form favored by younger people and under which they operated, and the "Council of Chiefs," which is to say, three-fourths majority rule in which the chiefs were prominent—the old Oglala Council favored by the older people. Fifteen councilmen cast their votes in favor of the Business Council, four in favor of the old Oglala Council. Having thus settled the matter as far as they were concerned, they set the date for the next Business Council election.[60]

The Business Council, however, was about to face a serious crisis of authority. In February 1931 a general council composed of "representatives, chiefs, councilors, and of members of the tribe" met and voted to disband the Business Council, which was "declared ceased and void," and to reinstate the old Oglala Council as the tribal council of the reservation. They requested that the superintendent rescind official recognition of the Business Council. They also put into circulation a petition which would "establish properly the true authority of the tribe," the Oglala Council, which they said had existed for more than thirty-five years. The petition, they said, would indicate the will of the three-fourths majority of the tribal members at least twenty-one years of age (importantly, women's names were among the signatures on this petition).[61] The petition eventually received 575 signatures, hardly three-fourths of the adult members, but a substantial indication of dissatisfaction with the Business Council nonetheless.[62]

The participants in the general council complained that the last Business Council election had been conducted "improperly, illegally, and unfairly."[63] The specific complaint was apparently that the Business Council members had, in the words of an OIA official, "scouted around and secured votes before the duly appointed day for the election, by making various threats and promises."[64] There may also have been more clear cases of what a non-Indian observer would call "crookedness,"[65] but a distinction between violations of fair play on the one hand and common electioneering on the other was not made by the complainants, and older men who were not able to compete with younger educated men probably thought electioneering was improper, illegal, and unfair.

The complainants also insisted that the election had been generally ignored by tribal members "because of the new form of the Council which is contrary to the methods of the former Council which had given the people more freedom in speech and expression and the methods that the tribe was more accustomed to."[66] This point referred to the fact that only elected members could vote at Business Council meetings. It also no doubt referred to the autonomy of the Business Council. As an OIA agent put it, council members "do not take up with the tribe in general anything they want to put before the Department, or the Superintendent, and then they do not return to their districts, and explain at an open meeting, or in any other way, what they have been doing." What is more, the president of the Business Council had, the complainants insisted, threatened to have jailed any person who expressed opposition to the council. All of this constituted a gross violation of the model of three-fourths majority rule. The proceedings of the general council were confirmed by the signatures of twenty-four men who called themselves chiefs, no doubt members of the chiefs society that Mekeel reported extant at the time, as well as by thirteen men who called themselves sergeants-at-arms (*akicita*) of chiefs.[67]

Those who wanted the Business Council disbanded also introduced the degree of blood issue. A fifty-seven-year-old fullblood man who had some reservation day school education—and who would later become an old dealer—wrote to both Congressman Williamson and to the commissioner that the Business Council had been organized by fee-patented mixedbloods living in the off-reservation town of Martin (in the ceded county of Bennett). Citing article twelve of the 1868 treaty, he informed them that "the threefourth majority (which consists of full bloods) demands your power to strengthen their request." He understood that Williamson and the commissioner approved of the reinstatement of the Business Council, and he asked if they had consulted with the chiefs, and also, "Have the half breeds the same right as the fullbloods own?"[68]

In fact, only four of the twenty-one members of the Business Council were mixedbloods, but these included the secretary and treasurer, both of whom were also fee-patented (the president was a trust-patented fullblood). Most of the opposition was composed of trust-patented fullbloods, although there were also some fee-patented and/or mixedblood men among them. The appeal to degree of blood was an attempt to discredit the members of the Business Council as not fully Indian people who had no right to speak or act for real, i.e. fullblood, Lakota people. They had gotten themselves elected by slyly using corrupt and/or non-Indian tactics, and now they were operating the council in a way which violated three-fourths majority rule.

The members of the Business Council, naturally, had their own view of the conflict. They did not see the opposition as a group of grassroots Oglala demanding more fair representation. The treasurer, a thirty-five-year-old, fee-patented mixedblood with some education, wrote to the commissioner regarding the council:

> For the first time in the history of the tribe it gave to every member of age the privilege to vote without intimidation for the most capable members of their Tribe to represent them in Tribal affairs. . . . The younger generation, on whom the government is spending millions of dollars annually to educate, now have a chance to be elected to the Business Council. . . . The old Oglala Tribual [sic] Council consist [sic] of men who must be a descendant of some Chief, regard-

less of their utter incompetence. They are illiterate, many of them depending on the government for rations. The meetings called by the old Oglala Tribal Council are usually conducted in a haphazard way and culminate in a dance and feast, with no beneficial results to the Tribe as a whole and to the disgust and embarrassment of the civilized members of the Tribe.[69]

The treasurer also wrote to Williamson and asked him to convey to the commissioner his endorsement of the Business Council, pointing out that if "incompetent, illiterate Indians" came to power and displaced the Business Council, which was "composed of the most competent and intelligent younger Indians," it would be a "grave injustice." "It would be," he insisted, "like electing incompetent men to represent the people in Congress." The treasurer had connections with the Republican organization in the state and had a hand in the large reservation vote received by Williamson and Senator Peter Norbeck (R., S.D.) in the previous primary election. His letter must have carried weight with Williamson, because the congressman wrote to the commissioner, supporting the Business Council.[70]

The secretary of the Business Council, a thirty-eight-year-old mixedblood, apparently educated, wrote to the commissioner, pointing out that his organization was composed mostly of literate returned students (from boarding school). His criticism of the "ignorance and weakness of these royal rulers of the Indians"—the chiefs who sought to reorganize the Oglala Council—was clear: "To revive such an organization at this time would be like trying to put a 1910 model automobile on the market today. One is just as out of date as the other, and they cannot cope or compete with modern day conditions." He consigned the motives of the chiefs to petty jealousy and personal pride, and he pointed out that their belief that their ancestors were empowered by the government in the treaties—and that this is what authorized them to rule—was simply false. "We, the younger generation, contend that today we are enjoying equal advantages with the most despotic old chiefs since 1924, because the franchise act of that year [the Indian Citizenship Act] put all the Indians on the same footing and gave them all the same privileges." He also argued the essential worthlessness of the treaties since the government had not negotiated them in good faith, but merely to end hostilities. They, therefore, could not be relied upon as a guarantee of any kind, "and it is going to require real wide awake fellows, and it is going to take younger and more enlightened Indians. All that the old fellows like to do is feast and sleep." "The [old-time] councils were replete with traditional ceremonies which called for plenty of eating and sleeping but no heavy brain action."[71]

In the end, the conflict between the Business Council and the Oglala Council was decided by a general council called by the agency and attended by ten delegates from each of eight districts. The vote on the question of abolishing the Business Council was seventy-eight in favor and two opposed. On the question of reorganizing the Oglala Council, the vote was eighty in favor and none opposed. At another general council in December, delegates adopted a constitution and elected officers for the Oglala Treaty Council (the term "Treaty" was soon dropped from the title and replaced with the term "Tribal"). The officers, importantly, included both fullbloods and mixedbloods. The constitution provided that each district council would appoint (by a rising vote) five members to serve only for the duration of an Oglala Treaty Council meeting. The officers, to be elected in general council arranged by the "Tribunal of Chiefs," would serve for two-year terms. Officers would be sworn in by a chief. The election of chiefs and sergeants-at-arms was, as in an earlier constitution, left to tribal custom, "and it shall in no way be arranged by the Tribal Council." Only council members could vote on an issue, but the council could transact business with the government concerning tribal property only "after securing the consent of not less than three-fourths of all adult members of said Tribe or Band of Sioux Indians." The principle of three-fourths majority rule had triumphed over the principle of elective government on Pine Ridge Reservation on the eve of the New Deal.[72]

When John Collier visited Rosebud and Pine Ridge reservations in December 1933, it was with members of the Rosebud Sioux Council and the Oglala Tribal Council, among others, that he met. Collier told the councilmen that he meant to systematize the authority of the councils. He tried to explain to the Lakota that his Indian New Deal would help them build up what tribal organization they already had. As will be seen, however, tribal organization, or reorganization, under the IRA brought about a radical rupture with the form of tribal decision making described here and with relations with the OIA. Secret ballots replaced open voting, on Rosebud "communities" replaced districts, women were extended the franchise, elected *tribal officials who made law and otherwise presumed to govern* replaced three-fourths majority rule, and men (and two women) who became known as new dealers replaced men who became known as old dealers. We turn in the next two chapters to the OIA's efforts in organizing the Lakota under the IRA.

## CHAPTER 3

# The New Deal Comes to Lakota Country

In March 1934 the OIA assembled representatives from eighteen northern plains tribes in Rapid City, South Dakota, to explain the Indian New Deal. The potential of the new policy to bring about dramatic change was immediately perceived in South Dakota. On Friday, March 2, when the Rapid City congress opened, the *Sioux Falls Argus Leader* ran a front page article describing the meeting in quaint, patronizing terms: "Where once they and their ancestors hunted buffalo and pitched their tepees, an area now in the midst of civilization, close to 300 Indians of many tribes gathered here today for a council with the great white father, John Collier." Two days later, after Collier and other officials had described their plans to foster Indian use of Indian resources and to turn reservation administration over to Indian governments, the same newspaper ran a front page headline proclaiming: "Indians of 18 Tribes Hear About Radical Scheme For New Relations with Whites."[1]

Unprecedented changes were, of course, taking place all over in the mid-1930s. In 1932 the national economic crisis swept a reform administration into power in Washington. If a new economic policy was to save capitalist private enterprise, a new image of the social responsibility of government for citizens' welfare was to save the state from mass civil disobedience. As part of this new agenda, John Collier was appointed commissioner of Indian affairs by Interior Secretary Harold Ickes. Collier had been a prominent and effective critic of the OIA in his role as director of the Indian Defense Association in the 1920s. He was appointed by Ickes—who was himself a proponent of reform of federal Indian policy and had been considered by some as a candidate for the commissionership—in order to bring about change in the OIA and in the administration of Indian affairs. The extensive changes which Collier would propose—both statutory and administrative—became known as the Indian New Deal. The purpose of this chapter is to narrate the presentation of the Indian New Deal to, and its reception among, the Lakota in 1933 and 1934.

## The Indian New Deal is Conceived

Upon his appointment as commissioner, Collier began his reforms boldly. By the summer of 1933, he had already issued instructions that the agencies were to consider the wishes of the tribal councils in their planning for road work and for Indian Emergency Conservation Work (the Indian division of the Civilian Conservation Corps; see chapter 5) projects on the reservations. Also in the summer of 1933, Collier issued an executive order ending all allotment in severalty.[2]

During the fall Collier and others in the OIA, and Nathan Margold and Felix Cohen in the Interior Department Solicitor's Office, worked on an omnibus bill which would incorporate the additional reforms deemed necessary. The legislative proposal prepared by the Solicitor's Office in 1933 included the issuance of a charter to each tribe or community by the secretary of the interior enumerating specific tribal powers. These were to be based on "careful study and negotiation," and the original charters were to be in effect for a one- or two-year trial period. The charters could entail restraints on tribal powers, if necessary, to assure the preservation of tribal resources and to protect against "factional discrimination, the arrogance of petty officials and the domination of property interests." Such restraints were to be put in place judiciously after an analysis of the resources, standards of living, class divisions, and political structure of each tribe. The proposal also provided for supervision of the transfer of OIA administrative functions to the tribe by an agency other than the OIA, such as an independent board, if considered necessary to overcome bureaucratic resistance within the OIA. Obviously, the intention was to avoid boilerplate charters and to produce machinery fine tuned to local reservation social and political conditions and capable of assuming substantive administrative responsibilities transferred from the OIA agencies.[3]

In December 1933 Collier traveled to Lakota country to explain his new program. On Rosebud, as was seen in the introduction, he spoke of his plans to systematize the power of the tribal council, to establish tribal courts, to put land back into tribal ownership, to halt illegal government interference in the free exercise of Indian religion, custom, and dances, and generally to diminish the arbitrary power of the OIA over Indians. He also, it will be recalled, indicated to the people his almost mystical regard for Lakota culture.

On Pine Ridge Collier delivered an address at a banquet attended by 350 agency employees and Indian leaders. He outlined a three-part plan. The first part involved ending allotment, halting the leasing of lands to non-Indians, and eliminating the checkerboarding of fee-patented land with allotted land. The second part would entail the preservation of Indian heritage. Collier explained the position he shared with Interior Secretary Harold Ickes and Agriculture Secretary Henry Wallace on this matter:

> We believe that the government should eliminate the old policy
> on the Indian's heritage. We believe that your Indian heritage is just
> as practicable and good, and just as much needed by America as is
> the Anglo-Saxon heritage or the German heritage or the Scotch or
> Irish or Norwegian heritage. . . . Hundreds of different tribes of Indi-
> ans built up the old Indian traditions through ages of toil and prayer
> and struggle with nature and with man, and that which was worked
> out in those olden days was an achievement of the human spirit just
> as bravely as that which was worked out in England, Italy, or by the
> Jewish race. . . .

The third part of the program would entail a transfer of administration from the OIA to the tribes via legislation. During the meeting, the Oglala performed a ceremony in which a pipe was passed to Collier. The pipe is the Lakota sacred symbol of social unity and the connectedness of all things in the universe. There was a "death like stillness" in the room, according to the superintendent, when Collier accepted the pipe as a token that he would always be a friend and speak the truth.[4]

In January 1934 Collier promulgated three major policy changes directly affecting Indian people, agency personnel, and missionaries in South Dakota. One was his circular on Indian religious and cultural freedom, which stated: "No interference with Indian religious life or ceremonial expression will hereafter be tolerated." In South

Dakota this had particular reference to the formidable opposition to the Native American Church (also known as the peyote religion) by the agencies, missionaries, and some Lakota.[5]

Another policy change was to circumscribe the operations of denominational boarding schools in South Dakota. Toward this end, Collier promulgated an order which facilitated the transfer of Lakota children from denominational (and government) boarding schools to government day schools. The boarding schools would handle only "institutional" cases (orphans or children from "demoralized" or impoverished homes identified in a survey conducted in 1934) or students living excessive distances from day schools. The OIA was in a position to enforce this plan because of funding for denominational boarding schools. Originally tuition in the schools was paid out of tribal, not federal, funds, which allowed Indian parents to send their children to boarding schools at their discretion free of charge. By the time of the New Deal, however, the tribal funds had been depleted, and the only source of funding for the boarding schools was federal gratuity funds—monies appropriated by Congress for expenditure by the government for Indian affairs. This funding arrangement allowed the OIA to dictate enrollment. Collier also issued an order signed by the secretary of the interior which prohibited compulsory religious worship or instruction in schools supported with either gratuity funds or tribal funds.[6]

Collier also got his new policy on Indian self-government under way with a circular. It provided an outline for discussion at tribal council meetings, including: (a) the deleterious effects of the allotment system; (b) the correction of these problems through self-government and community life; (c) the possible structure of self-governing machinery; (d) the functions of Indian community government; (e) corporate landownership; (f) Indian control over tribal funds; (g) Indian control over agency personnel; and (h) law and order jurisdiction. Perhaps the most portentous (or ominous, depending on point of view) passage in the circular stated:

> Powers of government now exercised over Indians by employees of the Indian Bureau should be gradually transferred to the chartered Indian community, as its members progress in the ability to administer the functions of government. Meanwhile every effort will be made to train and employ Indians qualified for the service. While federal employees continue to exercise governmental powers over Indians, they

should be responsible to the chartered Indian community, should be required to report their plans and achievements to the regular government of the Indian community, and should be subject to transfer from the reservation at the request of the Indian community where they are unable to work effectively with the community.[7]

Collier's visits to the reservations in December and his policy directives in January made quite a stir in South Dakota. The Pine Ridge superintendent reported that the Oglala were "rather dazed" by Collier's December visit,[8] which had been the topic of "unusual interest and heated debate." The fee-patented mixedbloods who had lost their land were in favor of the land plan, according to the superintendent, but those holding trust land were "naturally" opposed. The fullbloods were concerned that the mixedbloods would get control of fullblood trust land through Collier's scheme. Some Oglala parents were also "worked up," the superior of the Jesuit Holy Rosary Mission on Pine Ridge wrote in March 1934, about the OIA's new policy to determine which children would attend boarding school and generally to curtail boarding school education. One Oglala chief called for the removal of the OIA personnel who were making the selections regarding which children would be enrolled at Holy Rosary at government expense.[9]

The Rosebud superintendent wrote to Collier regarding the self-government circular: "I have never seen a situation among the Sioux such as your circular has created." He warned that the greatest difficulty would be the animosity between mixedbloods and fullbloods, which could be easily exacerbated by such a program. "The fullbloods seem to feel that you are selling out to the mixed-bloods because, as a rule, the full-bloods have kept their land and the mixed-bloods have not. The mixed-bloods seem to feel that you are offering a political expediency to gain fame. Both groups are conjecturing as to what effect it will have on my position with the tribe and what effect it will have on the established group of employees here." The superintendent also predicted that no non-Indian in South Dakota would support the Indian New Deal.[10]

In February 1934 the Rosebud Council met to discuss the Indian self-government circular. The meeting began with the chairman, a bilingual mixedblood with some college training, pointing out that the program offered the independence and freedoms that the non-Indians had fought for in the American Revolution. The superintendent explained the tenets of the circular, and the councilmen asked questions regarding the Black Hills claim, what would happen to individual allotments, what would happen to fee-patented land, and other topics. One councilman noted that civilization had required two thousand years to develop and that Collier should not expect Indians to become civilized and govern themselves in a mere fifty years. The Oglala council also met in February to discuss the new program. Collier wired the superintendent to assure the council that land would not be taken from those who had it to give to the landless, and that the equities of landowners would be fully protected when allotments were turned in to the tribal corporation. It is evident from tribal council minutes that there was little understanding among the Lakota as to what Collier's program really would mean in practical terms.[11]

If the Lakota were confused about the program, the agency employees and missionaries were surely apprehensive. Collier had directly threatened the missionaries with his religious freedom order, legalizing the Native American Church and other native religious practices, and with his restrictions on missionary activity. The missionaries particularly resented the OIA's insistence that it would decide on student placement in schools; they—like the Lakota—believed that this was the right of the Indian parents. One Jesuit missionary believed Collier's plan tasted of "Communism": "The child is no longer the child of the parent but the child of the Government." The Jesuits told the Lakota that the new OIA policy regarding missions was equivalent to "what Russia did to religion," according to a Lakota correspondent.[12] The agency personnel were obviously concerned about what self-government meant for agency operations and for their very jobs. The superintendents were "simply shocked" over the Indian self-government circular, according to a Jesuit missionary.[13]

While tentative opinions and alignments on the Indian New Deal were being formed—amid much confusion—in South Dakota, the legislation was drafted by the OIA and Solicitor's Office staffs and introduced by Senator Burton K. Wheeler (D., Mont.) and Congressman Edgar Howard (D., Neb.). The Wheeler-Howard bill was a very ambitious piece of legislation with four titles.[14]

Title I provided for Indian self-government and declared the policy of Congress to be the transfer of administration of Indian affairs to the tribes. A charter would be issued to each tribe for ratification by a three-fourths vote, specifying the powers of the tribal government and providing for the gradual elimination of federal supervision. The possible tribal powers of self-government were enumerated in the bill. In addition to these enumerated powers which could be extended in a charter, the bill would automatically extend certain powers over the OIA to the organized Indian community. The OIA would be required to make regular reports to community authorities on reservation administration and would "advise and consult" with these authorities, who were to be given free access to agency files. The community would have the power fill vacancies in the local OIA staff, subject to the commissioner's approval, and the community would have the power to compel the transfer of OIA personnel, subject to guidelines established by the commissioner. OIA budgets would be presented to the community for recommendation, and community funds in the federal Treasury (tribal funds) would only be expendable by community authority. The commissioner of Indian affairs was to inventory local administrative functions and draw up a program for transfer of these functions to the tribes, and the community would be able to initiate transfer by requesting it through a three-fourths vote. Clearly, the intent of the legislation was to make the local agency staffs at least partly answerable to Indian people and to their officials.

Title II concerned Indian education. It declared the promotion of the study of Indian civilization to be the policy of Congress. It also provided for training Indian people to fill administrative positions in the OIA and Indian community governments, and it set up a loan and grant program for Indian education.

Title III dealt with Indian lands and provided for the return of individual allotments to corporate ownership by the chartered community in return for pro-rated individual shares in the community estate. This would be accomplished voluntarily, through the mandatory descent of allotments to the community upon the death of the allottee, and otherwise through compulsion by the secretary of the interior. Title III also provided for the appropriation of $2 million for the purchase of additional land for organized communities.

Title IV provided for a Court of Indian Affairs to be composed of seven circuit judges, appointed by the president. The Court would have jurisdiction over a range of criminal and civil cases involving non-Indians who were either living on reservations or doing business

with chartered Indian communities. It would also handle disputes between Indians and their community governments as well as appeals
from lower Indian courts in the chartered communities. Locally-
elected judges and community-based codes would replace the courts
of Indian offenses administered by the OIA in the new communities.

## Selling the New Deal to the Lakota

In March Collier and a contingent of senior OIA and Solicitor's Office
personnel took to the road for a series of Indian congresses around the
country. The aims were to explain the bill to Indian people, to get
Indian suggestions, and to secure Indian endorsement with which to
persuade the congressional Indian committees, where the reformers
knew they would encounter opposition. The Rapid City congress was
held on March 2 through 5, 1934 and was attended by delegates from
eighteen northern plains tribes, including Rosebud and Pine Ridge.
The Washington contingent included Collier, Ward Shepard (OIA land
policy specialist), James Stewart (chief of the OIA Land Division), Walter Woehlke (OIA field representative), William Zimmerman (assistant commissioner), and Melvin Siegel and Felix Cohen (assistant
solicitors in the Interior Department). The explanations by the Washington men were simultaneously translated into the languages of
those tribes present. All the delegates from Lakota-, Nakota-, and
Dakota-speaking reservations—who constituted a majority of the
delegates present—used a single interpreter.[15]

The proceedings began with Collier asking the delegates to maintain open minds and to concentrate not on the specific provisions of
the bill—they would in any event be altered by Congress—but on the
broad intentions of the bill. These were preserving and extending the
tribal land bases, and helping tribes to organize, since in "the white
world, the unorganized people are powerless."[16] Collier explained
that an organized Indian community "could, if it desired, take over
many of the things that are now being done by the Indian Bureau and
the money being spent on those things would be transferred to the
organized body of Indians and they would spend the money and they
would hire their own employees." To this there was "mild applause"
among the delegates.[17] Collier assured the delegates that their individual property rights in allotments would be protected in this bill,
that the courts would not allow any "crazy plan" which would inter-

fere with "due process" as it pertains to private property. The delegates also applauded this assurance.[18]

On the second day of the congress, Collier began with a discussion of the effects of heirship fractionation and checkerboarding of
Indian lands under the OIA allotment policy. One allotment on Sisseton Reservation had sixty heirs, said Collier, with the interests varying from the value of a postage stamp to one dollar. And every year
the interests became smaller as more heirs died intestate and their
heirs—as determined by state law—in turn received shares in the es-
tates. Under such conditions, the OIA was forced to sell or rent the
land and divide the minute proceeds among the multiple heirs. The
situation was made worse by checkerboarding in which fee-patented
or heirship land that had been sold to non-Indians was intermingled
with Indian trust land in a pattern which made Indian use of their
land unprofitable. James Stewart distributed detailed, multicolored
maps to the delegates to illustrate the Sisseton situation. The effect
of the allotment system was that Indian people were not making productive use of their own land. In addition, the bookkeeping job of
administering trust allotments was enormous ($2 million per year),
explained Collier, and the mushrooming administrative load would
lead a future administration to "simply force fee patents on all of
you."[19]

Collier saw the solution to the Indian land problems in two parts.
First, the Wheeler-Howard bill would set up a $2 million annual fund
for the purchase of additional tribal lands and a $10 million revolving
loan fund to facilitate Indian use of Indian land through economic
development. At one point during the congress, Collier explained that
the loans would not bear interest for individuals and that the repayment period could be arranged for as long as thirty years. Tribes could
also expect outright gifts of submarginal land purchased by the government from farmers bankrupted by the drought and depression.
Collier insisted, however, that more land would not solve the Indian
land problem unless the land tenure system was modified. What the
bill proposed was a system of tribal community tenure, "which will
not take away anything from any individual Indian, but which will
only increase what any individual Indian has got, while giving something to the Indian who has got nothing."[20] The reformers believed
that conveying allotments and inherited estate shares to a tribal corporation—in return for corporate shares—would allow Indian lands

to be more productively used by the owners. For example, an individual with inherited tracts spread across the reservation could convey his land interests to the corporation for shares and convert those shares into lifetime access to a consolidated piece of land in the community estate. The plan also involved providing land for fee-patented individuals who had lost their land, but Collier assured the delegates that new land would be acquired for this purpose and that individual trust allotments would not be made available to the landless. The Indian delegates were particularly concerned about the provision in the bill giving the secretary of the interior the power to compel transfer of individual allotments to the chartered community. Collier explained that he expected the transfers to be voluntary once allottees realized the advantages of corporate holding, and that the provision had been included in case a single individual irrationally held out and blocked the corporate consolidation of land. He yielded to the wishes of the delegates, however, which were consistent with the views of the congressional Indian committees, and announced that he would recommend the elimination from the bill of secretarial power to compel transfer of allotments. To this announcement there was "great applause."[21]

Title I, self-government, was discussed by Collier, Ward Shepard, Walter Woehlke, and Henry Roe Cloud, a Nebraska Winnebago and head of the Haskel Institute. It was pointed out that an Indian community of any size might organize under Title I; a large reservation might break itself down into two, three, or four governments—an important point for reservations like Rosebud and Pine Ridge with serious factional divisions as well as dispersed, kinship-based settlements. Shepard explained the plan to transfer gradually administrative functions and control over tribal and agency funds from the OIA to the communities. The government would provide an education system to train tribal members to assume these responsibilities. He added that the bill did not impose any particular form of self-government on the communities. Rather, it would allow Indians to form governments consistent with their diverse histories and traditions. And even before the formal transfer of functions, Shepard explained, the Indian community would have the right to appoint Indians to vacancies in the OIA staff, provided they had the requisite qualifications.[22] Collier added, backhandedly, "Now there might be here not a single tribe that wasn't completely satisfied with all of the Indian Bureau employees on the Reservation. Maybe that is the condition. But if there is a tribe in North Carolina or Oklahoma or California, that would like to take a vote on whether it wants to keep its Superintendent, you would not object to them having that privilege, would you?"[23]

Walter Woehlke explained that he had discussed the bill with the Northern Cheyenne delegation and that they had approved of the land and credit provisions but were afraid of self-government. Woehlke attempted to assuage the concerns of the delegates by explaining that self-government would come into operation only as the community sought it. The bill merely set a "table" of self-government with various self-government "dishes" from which the community could choose. The federal government would advise caution since the Indians had not had a dish of self-government for 100 years, so "don't eat too fast," Woehlke told them. The Indians would not have to eat anything they did not want to and could start off with "soup" and gradually work up to the "roast beef."[24]

On the third day of the congress, representatives from the eighteen delegations expressed their opinions on the bill or otherwise responded to the government explanations. The chairman of the Rosebud Sioux Council spoke for the Rosebud delegation. He explained that they were "not at liberty to make any decision one way or another here," and that their role was "to listen, thresh out the whole thing and bring the meat home and leave the bones up here." The Pine Ridge representative also commented that the delegates were not to take action on the bill but were to bring the information home to the people.[25]

This would be difficult because of the complexity of the issues. The Rosebud chairman said that the delegation had been studying Collier's proposals, but "the more we study the less we know." "We are in a deep sea for the last few days."[26] Personally, he thought the education and land titles would prove useful, but regarding self-government and the court of Indian affairs: "I hate even to look at them. I don't know whether we can look at it at all or not self-government at this time because we are very lacking in material— good material—men as leaders." He doubted that there was anyone on the reservation who could "take hold of" or "make a success of" self-government: "In every critical crisis point in history there has always been the rise of the man of the hour and now for the last three or four months we have tried to find some man that will rise up to be the man of the hour and we cannot find him." (Importantly, he saw this lack of leadership as the legacy of the "systems, Bureaucracy, absolutism holding the Indians down," which is to say, the OIA.)[27]

On the last day of the Congress, Collier warned that there

> will be increasing efforts to frighten you Indians and to stampede you. Throughout the local communities around the Indian Reservations there are interests that do not want the Indian property protected and you all know that. (Applause.) Your interests are, of necessity, in opposition to many local interests around you. You want to keep your lands, and of course there are other people who want to get your lands. That is inevitable. You want your lands to be exempt from taxation, and of course there are people who want to put taxes on them. You want to have the capital to put stock on your own lands and yourself enjoy the profits of the cattle business, and of course there are white cattle men and lessees and banks that don't want you to do it.[28]

Baptist, Congregational, Episcopal, Jesuit, and Presbyterian missionaries also attended the Rapid City congress, concerned probably more about Collier's religious freedom and Indian education policies than about the Wheeler-Howard bill. The missionaries met with Collier, and he even had dinner with the Roman Catholic bishop of Rapid City, but the missionaries found Collier "too radical" to give them reassurance about their future on the reservations.[29] They met in a private session at the congress, unanimously opposed the bill, and intended to write to the president, but then decided that the latter action might antagonize Collier. They did adopt a statement which was circulated in religious circles in which they opposed those features of the bill that perpetuated segregation and tax exemption (trust status for land) and that enhanced the authority of the secretary of the interior over Indians.[30] The missionaries were clearly scandalized by Collier, and in June the Bureau of Catholic Indian Missions in Washington circulated a questionnaire to the field soliciting data on "defections to paganism" that were "traceable to Collier's announcements on Indian culture."[31]

In April Henry Roe Cloud traveled to Pine Ridge and held eleven meetings to explain the bill further. According to one of my South

Dakota consultants, an Oglala man challenged Roe Cloud at a public meeting with a humorous metaphor, a common Lakota oratorical technique. The man noted that stockyards have a trained cow which cattle follow to the slaughterhouse. At the last moment, a gate is opened and the trained animal is diverted, while the herd continues in to be slaughtered. The man asked Roe Cloud if he was not a little like that animal. Nevertheless, the superintendent reported that Roe Cloud was greeted "as a brother" by the Lakota and changed the sentiment toward the bill "quite materially."[32]

There was a range of opinions among the Oglala about the Wheeler-Howard Bill in the spring of 1934. An Episcopal missionary on Pine Ridge—who was himself from Standing Rock Reservation—reported on reactions to the New Deal in the Corn Creek area at the time. He detected four opinions. Some admitted ignorance of the bill but had decided "Let'er come." Others wanted continued trust status for land but thought self-government was "too involved now when we want action for our people in distress." A smaller group believed that laws would not help Indians much and that what they needed was OIA employees "who will love the Indians more than they love their pay check." Another group rejected the New Deal and believed that "Indians ought to cut loose, no matter how badly and landless and whipped and beaten they find themselves. Those who survive will have been made and on their own hook and nobody will keep them down then."[33]

A nonbinding referendum on the bill was held on Pine Ridge in April. The results were 1,542 votes in favor of the bill and 953 opposed.[34]

The Rosebud Sioux Council held a meeting upon the return of the delegates from Rapid City. The council concluded that the Rosebud people must move slowly in order to understand the bill completely. The chairman reported that he had translated the bill into Dakota for publication by the OIA, but he had experienced some difficulty since there were no Dakota words for many of the legal concepts. The delegates to the Rapid City congress also attended district council meetings to explain the bill—as best they could.[35]

In April Henry Roe Cloud made a speaking tour of Rosebud. At a meeting in Parmelee he called the Wheeler-Howard bill a "big boat" to help Indians who could not "swim" get "across the river" to self-sufficiency, allowing them plenty of time to "learn to swim." He also emphasized the "power of organization," pointing to how much more several beavers could do as compared to one. But he assured the Lakota that self-government could be taken at their own speed, and that they could wait five, ten, or fifteen years to take over administrative functions. Administrative responsibilities could be assumed from the government severally, and funding would be transferred from the OIA budget to the community as functions were transferred. He also pointed out that the bill would provide for a $10 million credit fund which would set a man up with a horse, saddle, chaps, and cattle, with thirty years to repay with no interest: "What bank will start you in the cattle business?"[36]

One Rosebud man, who would later be active in the opposition Treaty Council, felt that Roe Cloud's campaign was an attempt to pressure Lakota into acceptance of the bill, and he thought that the Black Hills claim should be settled and the bill considered for another one or two years before a decision was reached. Roe Cloud answered that those who wanted to take advantage of the chartered communities should be allowed to do so. Any individual not convinced could "stay out" as long as he wanted to. Roe Cloud attempted to assuage the fears of the landowning fullbloods that landless Indians would get control of their land through the chartered community by assuring them that a separate community would be set up for the landless.[37]

There were strong forces arrayed in opposition to the bill on Rosebud. Collier's clear position on the use of Indian range land by Indians directly threatened many non-Indian ranchers. It also threatened many allottees who realized that their return per acre was higher if they rented their lands to non-Indian operators rather than operating on it themselves (see chapter 1). The West River Stock Growers' Association, composed of non-Indian lessees of and holders of grazing permits on Indian land, was opposed and may have influenced the Indian landowners. The president of the Rosebud Permittees Association—also composed of non-Indian grazing permittees on Indian land—thought that "this new idea of Mr. Collier's," the idea of getting Indians into the agricultural business on their own land, would not be as fruitful as generating employment for Indians through such programs as the Civilian Conservation Corps. Governor Tom Berry (D.), a large cattle operator on Indian land, advised some Indian people in White River just before the poll that he would vote against the bill.

There were also Episcopal missionaries counseling Rosebud people against the bill, and a fee-patented mixedblood who was a lay worker in the Catholic church actively campaigned against the bill—in all likelihood, influenced by the clergy—and even transported voters to the polls. A prominent, local non-Indian who ran a store patronized by Rosebud people protested to Senator Peter Norbeck (R., S.D.) that the bill was a "detriment to the Indian, and a menace to the white people living on Indian reservations or in adjacent territory."[38]

The former superintendent on Rosebud was also opposed to the bill. He was presently the state assistant director of taxation and saw the bill as a "right-about-face" from the previous—and in his opinion more humane—policy. Also, of course, he, more than anyone else on Rosebud, understood the serious state revenue problem attending the economic crisis. In 1935 nineteen percent of the land in the state was tax delinquent. The Berry administration had sustained deep cuts in the state budget, yet the legislature was still forced to enact an income tax bill in 1933 to raise funds. The Wheeler-Howard bill would keep millions of acres of Indian trust land permanently off the state tax rolls. The former superintendent had intimate contacts with people on Rosebud, had organized the Todd County Democratic Club with Indian members, and made weekly visits to Parmelee where he owned a garage. We can assume that he did his best to influence his Lakota Democrats.[39]

Notwithstanding these forces against the bill on the reservation, the Rosebud nonbinding poll on the Wheeler-Howard bill went 975 in favor and 399 opposed.[40]

At the time of the Roe Cloud campaigns, the Wheeler-Howard bill was being modified in Washington as a result of the Rapid City and other Indian congresses, pressure from Indian welfare groups, and the opinions of the members of the congressional Indian committees. Among other amendments, the provision giving the secretary of the interior the power to compel transfer of allotments to the chartered community was removed. This was requested by the Lakota delegates to the Rapid City congress and by the Oglala Tribal Council. The new, amended version also provided that the act would not in any way affect tribal claims and that no appropriation under the act would be calculated as an offset against any future recovery in a tribal claim against the government. This too had been requested by the Oglala

Tribal Council. The new bill also allowed allotments to continue to descend in accordance with wills and state probate laws rather than to revert automatically to the tribal corporation. The powers of tribes were also severely curtailed in the final draft. Most of the possible powers enumerated in the original draft were removed, as were almost all of the provisions for making the OIA agencies answerable to the tribes. The provisions for a court of Indian affairs were also deleted.[41]

The House and Senate Indian committees reported out their drafts of the amended bill in late May. Several additional amendments were added on the Senate floor both to exclude Oklahoma Indians from the act and to protect non-Indian mineral and water interests. The Indian Reorganization Act was enacted into law on 18 June. It ended allotment, extended the trust period indefinitely, and authorized the secretary of the interior to acquire additional lands for tribes with an annual $2 million fund. It established a $10 million revolving loan fund for economic development, as well as an education loan fund. It also provided for Indian preference hiring in filling OIA positions. It provided for organizing tribes under constitutions subject to tribal ratification by majority vote. In addition to unspecified powers vested in tribes "by existing law," the IRA stipulated that the constitutions could vest tribes with certain other powers including employment of legal counsel, control over tribal lands, and negotiation with federal, state, and local governments. The IRA also authorized the secretary of the interior to issue a charter of incorporation to an organized tribe, allowing it to conduct business as a legal corporation. The IRA would not be applicable on any reservation where a majority of adult members voted against it in a referendum.

In the summer of 1934, campaigns financed and organized by the OIA began on both reservations to explain the IRA in preparation for the binding referendums. On Pine Ridge a district farm agent, who was a bilingual, college educated, mixedblood member of the Rosebud Sioux Tribe, began giving "chalk talks." Traveling from district to district, he summarized the provisions of the IRA, translated them into Lakota, and illustrated them on a portable chalk board. He was considered so effective by the OIA that he was later sent to other South Dakota reservations to explain the IRA. On Rosebud the mixedblood chairman of the tribal council (who had testified in favor of the

IRA at Senate hearings and who was in the employ of the federal government at this time) went on a campaign tour. He was also bilingual and had some college education. In each district, a meeting would be held of one or two days duration, with families coming in to camp at the district farm agent's station. The IRA was explained, discussed, and debated. The main selling point of the IRA at the Rosebud meetings, according to one of my consultants, was the education, land, and credit provisions, particularly as they would benefit future generations.

By September the campaigns were beginning to gear up. Joe Jennings, the supervisor of Indian education in South Dakota, explained the IRA to the Rosebud Tribal Council. The Pine Ridge superintendent used OIA day school teachers and what Jennings called "influential Indians" to campaign for the IRA. These included thirty men chosen from the reservation districts, as well as eight Oglala who were in the employ of the agency. The superintendent reported on 28 September that he was "constantly hammering." A translation of the IRA into Lakota was circulated on the reservation. Ralph Case, an attorney for the Sioux Nation handling the Black Hills claim, circulated a flyer on Pine Ridge advising the Oglala to "Take Your Attorneys' Advice" and "make an X in the square that votes 'YES'" for the IRA. The flyer insisted that the IRA had many advantages and few disadvantages, that it protected tribal claims, and that it was "the sunrise of a new day for your people." Case also mailed a report endorsing the IRA—at the request of the OIA—to 400 Indian leaders among the parties to the Black Hills claim.[42]

The OIA attempted to maintain strict control of the referendums to insure fairness. Neither the Indian people in the educational campaigns—except for those who were already federal employees—nor the members of the election boards at the polling places were paid. The Indian members of the election boards were instructed to prohibit campaigning at the polling places. The ballots were printed in English and Lakota and each polling place was allowed two interpreters. In addition, the superintendents were instructed by the OIA to guard the ballots carefully. A consultant recalled that the ballot boxes on Pine Ridge were sealed and locked by the farm agents and brought in to the agency where they were further secured by the superintendent.[43]

The IRA was approved on Pine Ridge by a vote of 1,169 to 1,095 (a total of 55.5 percent of the 4,075 eligible voters going to the polls). The Rosebud people voted 843 to 424 to accept the IRA (a total of 40 percent of the 3,126 eligible voters going to the polls). Thus, about 29 percent of the electorate accepted the IRA for Pine Ridge, and 27 percent approved the IRA for Rosebud.[44]

## What Did the Referendums Mean?

### Misunderstanding

The positive votes in the referendums were not based on the *informed* opinions of the Lakota (nor were the negative votes, for that matter). To begin with, there was the matter of the complexity of the IRA and the difficulty even a native English speaker familiar with legalese would have understanding it, let alone someone who attempted to understand it through a translation of its provisions into Lakota. A Yankton Indian delegate at the Rapid City congress commented that "the things that are contained in that Bill would baffle the brains of a Huxley or a Darwin."[45]

Furthermore, as it turned out, both the Rapid City congress and the Roe Cloud campaigns provided a good deal of information inconsistent with the final draft of the IRA and its actual implementation by the OIA during the ensuing years. It was, for example, not possible for the Lakota to accept the act but postpone assuming self-government as they had been repeatedly told they could. Only one community could be organized on a reservation, not two, three, or four as had been explained in Rapid City. Nor would there be a separate community for landless mixedbloods, of which Roe Cloud had spoken. Once a tribe organized under the IRA, all tribal members were affected; one could not "stay out," as Roe Cloud had put it. What is more, almost all the provisions for making the agencies answerable to the tribes were removed from the IRA. The explanation of the credit program in the spring of 1934 was also inconsistent with actual implementation, since the thirty-year, interest-free loan terms never materialized.

There is good reason to believe that the positive votes on the IRA were not a mandate for tribal organization under the IRA—for Lakota self-government. True, as will be seen in subsequent chapters, some Lakota—the new dealers—came to believe strongly in Indian self-government and took seriously the promises made to them in 1933 and 1934 of transferring reservation administration. But most Lakota people were probably more intent on making the bureaucracy answerable—or at least responsive—than in actually taking over reservation administration from the OIA. To these people, the prospect of removing superintendents and boss farmers and perhaps even filling the positions with Indians, and getting access to agency and farmer's office files, may have been attractive. (Of course, these powers never came to pass because they were deleted from the final draft of the IRA.) But running the reservation was another matter, particularly in the midst of a depression and drought. There was concern, it will be recalled, that there was no Lakota "man of the hour." The Pine Ridge superintendent may have been exaggerating slightly, but he was probably representing the convictions of many Lakota when he told Collier in April 1934 that there was "nobody on the Reservation that believe[d] that the self-governing feature has any merit to it."[46]

Most Lakota probably voted in favor of the IRA because of the *material benefits* they anticipated. According to anthropologist Scudder Mekeel, who was actively engaged in organizing the Lakota in 1935 (see chapter 4), some Lakota people believed that liberal credit funds would be given as a reward for voting favorably for the IRA, with no responsibilities attached. *The Word Carrier*, a Congregational organ published by the Santee Normal Training School in Nebraska, reported in the fall of 1934 that the average voter had "not forgotten the great emphasis that was placed on the financial benefits, which probably created expectations that are not likely to be realized." And there was also the promise of more land, something which must have been very attractive to fee-patented families which were landless or owned only small, scattered tracts of heirship land. This benefit too did not materialize in the way hopeful families probably expected in 1934.[47]

The wondrous things that at least some Lakota (erroneously) believed—or hoped—would happen under the IRA is indicated by the testimony of an Oglala old dealer who explained at a Senate hearing in 1938 why people had voted affirmatively:

> By telling the Pine Ridge Indians that John Collier will give the Black
> Hills claim back to the great Sioux Nation, and they will soon be
> millionaires, and the Wheeler-Howard Act will chase all the Ameri-
> can white people off the reservation. The fullblooded Indians will
> have the first preference to borrow money and buy livestock with,
> and chase all the white employees from the Indian Service and man-
> age their own affairs. John Collier will have the power in the United
> States to see that the Indians will live on buffalo and all that. For
> that reason Mr. Indian vote for the Wheeler-Howard Act.

This witness believed that John Collier's intent was "to fool the
people." I heard similar complaints of misunderstanding and exaggerated campaigning from Lakota consultants on Rosebud (some of these
claims may actually apply to the charter or constitution campaigns
and not to those prior to the IRA referendums). Campaigning under-
taken by the "influential Indians" and "educational leaders" who
were not paid by the OIA may have involved exaggeration of benefits
under the IRA.[48]

In all probability, however, the OIA employees who campaigned
in the summer and fall of 1934 provided technically accurate (except
for the specific—and significant—points noted above), albeit confus-
ing, information about the provisions to the Lakota. OIA employees
were, in fact, warned against disseminating "information not in harmony with the official interpretation of this legislation as contained
in memoranda issued by the Indian Office."[49] But this, of course, not
only had the effect of preventing wild exaggeration of benefits. It also
prevented any critical comment on the IRA by the people most likely
to be able to envision its effects. An Oglala employee of the agency
road department was threatened with dismissal for his criticism of
the bill in the fall of 1934. Opponents of the IRA did not receive funding from the OIA for dissemination of their ideas, and, therefore, many
Indian people perceived paying agency Indian spokesmen to explain
the benefits of the IRA to be graft.[50]

### Who Voted How?

It was commonly believed among the Lakota (and is to this day) and
among OIA personnel that alignment on the IRA followed the fault
line of degree of blood and allotment status. The Pine Ridge superintendent had reported early in 1934, it will be recalled, that while
the fee-patented mixedbloods favored Collier's plan, the fullbloods

were afraid that the mixedbloods would get control of their land and were "naturally" opposed. This statement was either inaccurate, or the situation changed by April, since the vote in the village of Oglala, White Clay District—which Scudder Mekeel called "the most backward and full-blood on the reservation"—was 81 in favor and 38 opposed. In the October binding referendum, the vote in Oglala went against the IRA, 57 to 49, but the vote was still close enough at this predominantly fullblood polling place to make one suspect the proposition that alignment was based primarily on degree of blood.[51]

The surviving records pertaining to Pine Ridge do not indicate clearly which particular Oglala people supported the IRA in 1934. A statement by two prominent, trust-patented, fullblood leaders in 1934, however, suggests that they supported the IRA, even if they distrusted some mixedbloods:

> The full-blood Indians on our reservation are willing to cooperate with the methods that Mr. Collier has presented, but it seems like that the most of these mixed-blood Indians pretend to be smarter than the Commissioner or Councilmen; . . . we found out that they were only seeking for personal benefit, and not for the benefit of the Tribe as a whole, and this is the reason why we, the full-blood Indians remain silent during the while these mixed-blood Indians are criticizing the new method of self-government which is being under consideration for us full-blood Indians.

Among those actively opposed to the IRA were two fee-patented mixedbloods and one trust-patented fullblood. The fullblood was responsible for large majorities against the IRA at three polling places in the October referendum. According to the superintendent, this man was embittered because he had been dismissed from employment by the OIA for intoxication.[52]

The records indicate that four Lakota on Rosebud had actively campaigned for the IRA in 1934, one in the employ of the OIA. Three of these, including the latter, were fee-patented mixedbloods; the fourth was a fee-patented fullblood. An elderly fullblood also wrote a letter to the editor of the *Sioux Falls Argus Leader* in the spring, lauding Collier's ideas: "We are on the eve of a 'new deal' and we like to see it." Of the four people mentioned in the records as actively working against the IRA on Rosebud, three were mixedbloods, and all were fee-patented.[53]

The results of the April 1934 nonbinding referendum on Rosebud also demonstrate clearly that degree of blood was not the basis of alignment on the New Deal, at least at that time. At St. Francis the vote was 111 (78 percent) in favor of the bill and 31 (22 percent) opposed. At least 76 fullbloods participated in the referendum in St. Francis, meaning that even if we assume that all the opposed votes were cast by fullbloods, a majority of the fullbloods voted in favor of the IRA. If the St. Francis vote is representative, most fullblood Lakota people who voted, voted in favor of the IRA in April 1934.[54]

It is possible that fullblood people came to oppose the IRA by the time of the binding referendums in October. On both reservations the absolute number of votes in favor declined and the absolute number opposed increased in October in comparison to April (although the proportions in St. Francis did not change significantly: 126 positive and 49 negative votes). We have no way of knowing, however, if the increased opposed votes were cast by fullbloods.[55]

In the fall of 1935, the chairman of the soon to be officially defunct Rosebud Sioux Council wrote to the South Dakota congressional delegation that many fullbloods had not appeared at the polls in 1934 because they did not understand what was at issue. At the 1938 Senate Indian Committee hearings, an Oglala opponent of the IRA explained: "Because they think they do not want it, so they do not go there to vote." It is possible that Lakota people believed that the IRA would not apply to them as individuals if they did not go to the polls. They had been told in Rapid City and by Roe Cloud on the reservations that those who wanted to form an organized community could do so, while those who wanted to stay out could do that. According to Joe Jennings, however, the Lakota on Lower Brule and Crow Creek reservations realized "that a 'stay-at-home' vote [was] equivalent to a yes vote" because a majority had to vote against the IRA to prevent its application to the reservation. Except for the assertions made by old dealers at the time in order to undermine the legitimacy of the IRA and tribal governments, there is no reason to assume that fullblood people on Pine Ridge and Rosebud did not also know that they had to go to the polls to prevent the New Deal from coming to their reservations.[56]

A related claim is that the fullbloods organized a boycott of the IRA referendum. According to Robert Burnette, a chairman of the

Rosebud Sioux Tribal Council during the 1960s: "As the date of the referendum neared, the fullblood faction made a terrible mistake. Thinking in Indian rather than white terms, they urged their partisans to show their feelings by boycotting the election and staying away from the polls. On reservation after reservation, the tribes voted to accept the Indian Reorganization Act by a slim margin." It is, however, difficult to sustain the argument that fullblood leaders who were politically astute enough to organize a boycott were so ignorant as to make a "terrible mistake" about how elections work. Lakota people had been voting in general elections since 1924, and some of the principal old dealers had for years been in correspondence with the South Dakota congressional delegation, asking for political favors. They must have had a good working knowledge of how non-Indian elections work. In fact, the chairman of the pre-IRA Rosebud Sioux Council, who would shortly become one of the most prominent old dealers, was involved in the Republican campaigns on Rosebud before 1934. Graham Taylor has suggested that a boycott may have been perceived as a strategy by fullbloods since at least thirty percent of the eligible voters had to go to the polls to make the referendum binding. This provision, however, was an amendment to the IRA enacted in 1935, after the binding referendums on Pine Ridge and Rosebud.[57]

Thus, the evidence from both reservations indicates that most of the active public supporters of the New Deal were fee-patented mixedbloods, but people of this status also actively opposed the New Deal, and many trust-patented fullblood people voted for the New Deal. In short, both trust-patented fullbloods and fee-patented mixedbloods were found among both the supporters and the opponents of the New Deal in 1934.

The Indian New Deal in general and the IRA in particular were clearly not Indian ideas. The IRA was conceived and drafted by technical specialists in Washington who did their best to design a plan that would grant self-government to Indian people and would protect tribal resources. The reformers also sought to explain their complex plan to Indian people so that the latter could make informed decisions on the value of the plan. As has been seen here, however, Lakota people did not understand the IRA when they went to the polls in 1934 to vote on it. It was probably their (erroneous) belief that generous material benefits would accrue to them which accounted for the positive votes on the IRA on Pine Ridge and Rosebud.

Accepting the IRA was only the first step of tribal organization, however. It would now be necessary for the OIA to draft tribal constitutions and secure their ratification by popular vote among the Lakota, events to which we now turn.

## CHAPTER 4

# Establishing Tribal Government

The stated policy of the senior OIA and Interior Department Solicitor's Office staff in Washington was that the constitutions which established tribal self-government should reflect not only Indian wishes but, specifically, tribal cultures and social organizations. The Indian New Deal was to be not only government *by* Indian people, but self-government *as* Indian people wanted self-government organized—if indeed they wanted it at all. In replying in 1940 to charges at a Senate hearing that the Oglala constitution had been "foisted" on the Lakota, Collier wrote that the process of organizing under the constitution represented a "cooperative endeavor on the part of the Indians and the Department to work out a mutually satisfactory document." Collier wrote in his memoirs in 1963 that "each tribe . . . drew up a constitution fitted to its needs, and according to its cultural patterns and traditions." The role of the OIA and the Solicitor's Office in the establishment of tribal government was only to provide technical assistance, according to senior staff in Washington. OIA chief counsel Theodore Haas, surveying ten years of tribal government under the IRA in 1947, commented: "The Department offers its assistance in the preparation of such documents [tribal constitutions], but only to the extent that such assistance is required. Scrupulous care is exercised to see that the document as drafted represents the wishes of the Indians."[1]

These representations of the drafting of the tribal constitutions form the U.S. Interior Department's origin myth of tribal government. They are very euphemistic and more than a little distorting. Tribal governing machinery based on the constitutions was designed by the OIA, not by Lakota people, who had little input into these instruments. As Vine Deloria, Jr., and Clifford Lytle put it, "Self-government is not an Indian idea." Its origin was "in the minds of non-Indians who have reduced the traditional ways to dust, or believe they have, and now wish to give, as a gift, a limited measure of local control and responsibility."[2]

This chapter will narrate the events by which the constitutions were drafted, explained to, and ratified by the Lakota people. It will then examine the non-Indian model of Indian self-government—invented in Washington, and to a lesser extent by the Rosebud super-intendent—on which the constitutions were based.

## The Rosebud Constitution

The Rosebud Sioux Council took the wording of section sixteen of the IRA literally and thought it was up to the tribe to "organize for its common welfare" and to "adopt an appropriate constitution and by-laws," and in December 1934 it appointed a small committee to draft a provisional constitution. The council members evidently felt they were about to take a historic step because "a short prayer was of-fered . . . for benefit of the By-Laws Committee." The superinten-dent realized, however, that the government was not going to allow any tribe to organize and adopt a constitution on its own, and he wrote to Collier on 10 January requesting information on drafting a constitution which would be "acceptable to the Office" in terms of tribal powers and supervision of tribal operations by the OIA.[3]

By June 1935 an OIA field agent, who was himself a Shoshone, had been dispatched to Rosebud to supervise the drafting of the constitu-tion. This field agent, along with others, had received training in Washington on drafting the constitutions. Drawing on an outline is-sued by the OIA, the agent and an enlarged Rosebud committee that included representatives from all the districts completed a tentative draft, which the committee members then explained to the people in their districts. An OIA observer reported that he was impressed with the "harmony" of the meetings, and the "cooperation" the field agent received from the committee. The constitution was translated into Lakota by the Oglala agency clerk.[4]

In July additional work on the constitution was concluded by the committee working with Joe Jennings (at the time supervisor of Indian education in South Dakota, but soon to be on the staff of the OIA Organization Division), an enrolled Rosebud mixedblood who was the OIA field agent for Lakota country, and a Laguna Indian OIA field agent. The superintendent submitted the completed draft to Fred Daiker of the OIA and Felix Cohen, assistant solicitor in the Interior Department in Washington. The superintendent was evidently surprised at the extent of the tribal powers written into the constitution. He noted that the Rosebud people feared giving too much power to a tribal council and concluded: "I do not know how this constitution will be received by the Rosebud people."[5]

After they had reviewed the document, Cohen and Daiker arrived from Washington and worked with the constitution committee for about one week. On 2 August 1935 the Rosebud Sioux Council discussed the amended document. Although there was a favorable attitude on the part of the councilmen toward most of the provisions, they would not call for a referendum on ratification because of concern over what was called the community plan. This was a provision for the allocation of representation to smaller communities rather than the larger districts, as was presently the case for the Rosebud Sioux Council. The community plan had been included in the constitution on the advice and pressure of the superintendent, and the secretary of the tribal council told the field agent for Lakota country that the community plan was "wrong," that the "old members of the council do not want to give up their type of council." The constitution was to be translated again and distributed for discussion.[6]

Division over the constitution was apparent at a meeting of the Rosebud Sioux Council in September. The chairman, a seventy-five-year-old, trust-patented fullblood who did not speak English, "made a lengthy speech against the Wheeler-Howard Act as unworkable, against the wishes of those who still retain their allotments, and contrary to certain old treaties which are still in effect." He also criticized the community plan as "outrageous" and "causing much friction amongst councilmen," and pointed out the lack of fair play in the OIA field agent, a Rosebud Lakota himself, receiving pay to campaign for the constitution. The chairman obstructed discussion of the matter, and the council finally voted to refer the matter to the people at large before it took any action on calling a referendum.[7]

The Rosebud Council met again in October with the vice chairman presiding, the chairman having voluntarily relinquished the chair. The deliberations, which the superintendent described as a "battle royal," centered on the community plan, with ardent arguments on both sides. The alignment did not follow lines of degree of blood or status of allotment. Fullbloods and mixedbloods, and fee-patented and trust-patented people spoke on both sides of the issue. The vice chairman of the council called the community plan "the only workable form by which the whole reservation can be represented equally in the new tribal council." The Lakota OIA field agent was present and also spoke in favor of the community plan, as did Scudder Mekeel, who had conducted fieldwork on Pine Ridge for his Yale Ph.D. in anthropology and who had just been hired by Collier as an applied anthropologist. In addition, the superintendent's Oglala agency clerk was working behind the scenes with the board of advisors of the council. One of the opponents of the community plan argued "that majority of the people do not understand new bylaws. Therefore such bylaws should not be forced down the throats of the people." Nevertheless the council voted seventeen to ten to accept the new constitution for tribal referendum.[8]

After the constitution was accepted by the council, the OIA campaign began. The superintendent was instructed by Assistant Commissioner William Zimmerman to mimeograph the document in English and see to its explanation among the rank and file: "You, in cooperation with the Indian Council, are expected to so organize your personnel and Indian leaders that the constitution will be fully and clearly explained to all of the Indian voters of your reservation. This is distinctly your responsibility and should be given precedence over any other work." Zimmerman also instructed the superintendent to post copies of the formal order for the referendum from the secretary of the interior, since it was believed that this would "add to the importance of the occasion, and indicate to the Indians the personal interest of the Secretary." The campaign included explanations in the various communities by the field agent, another OIA official, and the farm agents. Collier also visited Rosebud in November prior to the referendum to campaign for acceptance, but no record of his remarks survives.[9]

There were several criticisms of the constitution among the Lakota in the fall of 1935. One concerned the community plan. Lakota people on Rosebud may have objected to the community plan because it would have replaced the district councils which were already in place and which had a long history on the reservation (see chapter 2); the people may have been "district minded" (see below). What is more, some councilmen rejected the community plan because they feared they would not be elected in the communities in which they resided. At the time, the Rosebud Sioux Council was composed of two kinds of representatives: advisors and delegates. Both were allocated to districts on a population basis and were elected by the district councils, probably by a show of hands or a rising vote (see chapter 2). A change in the voting precincts, as would be brought about by the community plan, in combination with the secret ballot and the enfranchisement of women, could result in an entirely new set of incumbents. What is more, the board of advisors supposedly included chiefs and sons of chiefs who claimed hereditary office. The new basis of representation made no provision for such offices.

A second criticism concerned the speed and aggressiveness with which the OIA was moving, and the resulting procedural irregularities. The chairman of the council and another fullblood opponent of the constitution protested to Collier the action of the 11 October meeting during which the constitution had been accepted for referendum. They claimed, among other things, that a quorum had not been present. The chairman explained (with obvious assistance, perhaps from a missionary or merchant, since he did not write English): "I am not against the Bill, but I am opposed to the Constitution and By-Laws, which were really drafted by Government employees and is [sic] now being rammed down our throats by the help of employees and twenty-five members of the tribe."[10]

Another criticism concerned the failure of Lakota people to understand the constitution. The people on Rosebud who could not read English well could only have had a poor understanding of it. The Lakota translations of the provisions orally and in writing were not effective, and complaints about misunderstanding were made to Senator Peter Norbeck (R., S.D.) and Congressman Theodore Werner (D., S.D.). The chairman of the Rosebud Sioux Council requested (again, with obvious assistance) that they secure a postponement of the referendum. The constitution, he wrote, appeared to be a "radical departure from the present set up" which would have a "permanent character," and, therefore, should not be decided upon hastily. It was unfair of the government to expect uneducated Indians to understand the issues in so short a period, especially when the information on the constitution had been presented by politically- or financially-interested parties. "There are many old full-blooded Indians who are uneducated, . . . and . . . many of these . . . full-bloods did not appear at the polls because they did not know what is was all about." Senator Norbeck shared the view of the Rosebud tribal chairman that there was not a clear understanding of the constitution, and he requested a postponement of the referendum by Collier, but it was not granted.[11]

A fourth criticism of the constitution was rooted in the common fear among fullblood people that the landless mixedbloods would get control of tribal government and use it to enrich themselves at the expense of fullblood people, who were less familiar with non-Indian ways. The chairman of the Rosebud Sioux Council sent a petition to Interior Secretary Ickes with forty-two signatures, mostly people living in the St. Francis area (copies of the petition were also sent to Norbeck and Werner). The petitioners identified themselves as "all fullblooded Sioux Indians" who still owned their allotments under trust patents. They had preserved their allotments, resided on them, and made a living from them in conformity with the treaties and allotment laws. A "great majority of the younger generation of mixed-blood Indians who have been allotted lands in trust have voluntarily alienated the said lands by conveyance," however, "in utter disregard of spirit and intent of allotment acts." They had never intended to live on their allotments, and the proceeds from sale were "in a great majority of cases dissipated with no thought of provisions for the future." The "present movement under said Reorganization Act is a belated act on the part of said particular class of Indians to benefit by the conservation of land and property on the part of these particular applicants and others." Those who signed the petition probably did not understand the English wording well, but they were frightened by the constitution's provisions for corporate tribal land holding, for conveyance of allotments to the tribe, and for assignment of tribal land to landless families; they probably signed the petition because they were told it opposed the constitution.[12]

The petitioners also protested that they and many other fullbloods were "not versed or skilled in political manipulation and organization," while the "mixedblood element on this and other reservations by reason of their employment by the government and in other ways have become more adept and skilled in these respects than these petitioners." They deemed majority vote an "inequitable and unconscionable method of bringing into effect or enforcing the terms of said Reorganization Act" since fullbloods were in a minority. Congressman Werner wrote to Ickes about the trouble at Rosebud, but the secretary assured him that landless Indians would not get control of individual allotments, and that the community plan of council representation would insure fullblood participation in tribal government.[13]

These criticisms notwithstanding, the constitution was ratified on 23 November 1935 by a vote of 992 to 643. Almost four hundred more voters participated in the constitution referendum than had in the IRA referendum in 1934. The favorable votes cast were reduced from sixty-seven percent in 1934 to sixty-one percent in 1935. The increase in the number of favorable votes was only 149, while the increase in number of opposed votes was 220, suggesting that there was increasing sentiment against tribal organization on Rosebud by November 1935, but that the Rosebud people were quite divided on the matter and that there was not a movement toward a consensus either way.[14]

In December 1935 the old Rosebud Sioux Council held its last meeting, or at least its last meeting as the tribal body officially recognized by the OIA on the reservation. The chairman gave a lengthy speech in which he called the community plan "unworkable" and argued that the constitution committee had acted without authority from the council in including certain provisions. He pointed out that the old council had been working in the tribe's interests, conducting research into treaty rights and claims against the government, and he called for the preservation of the "heritage of old council for the old men, which should be continued to be respected and adhered to in the future, and other authorities as granted by certain treaties shall not be undermined." The business of the tribal council should be to "investigate old treaties for such claims as may be beneficial, instead of directing too much effort toward the 'New Deal', which is . . . 'bunk'." Several other men spoke on both sides of the New Deal question, the "old dealers"—the first mention of the term in the archives—arguing that "the majority yes vote by the Rosebud referendum is an impardonable insult." The meeting adjourned without it being at all clear if the old council would continue, and if so, what its relationship would be to the New Deal council.[15]

## The Oglala Constitution

Work on the Oglala constitution began in January 1935. One committee of eight mature returned students (and one non-Indian, a Bennett County judge) and another composed of eight men from the Oglala Tribal Council worked on separate drafts and then met in a joint session. The superintendent had invited the returned students to work on the constitution. The proposed draft was submitted by the joint committee at a meeting of the Oglala Tribal Council, which, after a discussion, voted to distribute copies of a Lakota translation.[16]

The preamble listed among the purposes of the document the following: to protect the legal rights of the Oglala; to assume the responsibilities of government on the reservation to the full extent of the law; "to acquaint ourselves with our own affairs and other Tribal matters that are now entirely in the hands of Whitemen"; "to guard against the encroachments of designing exploiters and their followers"; to secure educational and credit opportunities; and "to regain that very distinct, self-sustaining fearless character which we once possessed." The constitution provided that the tribal council would have all powers vested in it by existing law, including the IRA, as well as several additional powers. These included the powers to adopt resolutions; to regulate the use and disposition of tribal property; to cultivate art, crafts, and culture; to administer charity; to protect the health, security and general welfare of the community; to appoint guardians; to administer tribal funds entrusted to the tribe by the government; to create a tribal council fund; and to cooperate with the agency. These powers were taken almost verbatim from the list of possible community powers in the original draft of the Wheeler-Howard bill.[17]

As was the Rosebud constitution committee, the Oglala were under the mistaken impression that they were to draft their own constitution, and the document was produced before the OIA distributed its circular on the tribal constitutions and before a procedure for constitution drafting had been worked out in Washington. As did his counterpart on Rosebud, the Pine Ridge superintendent realized that the Lakota would not be allowed to design their own tribal government: "I thought it best to allow them to continue thinking of and discussing the matter, and this would keep them interested," he wrote to Collier. "There is no doubt that the Constitution and By-Laws they

are sending you will have to be gone over carefully by the legal department and there may be other changes which will be necessary."
Assistant Commissioner Zimmerman warned the council that work
on the constitution must proceed slowly and carefully: "It might be
best if the Council would indicate to this Office what is wanted in
the constitution and let the solicitor do the work of putting the provisions together in the right order and right words."[18]

The Oglala's draft constitution was not considered seriously by
the OIA because it was not consistent with the official OIA outline for
tribal constitutions, and in June the superintendent and the Lakota
and Laguna OIA field agents discussed plans for drafting an acceptable
constitution with the Oglala Tribal Council. The council nominated
a committee of two representatives from each district to work with
the field agents. The plan was for the committee to have the aid of
the field agents and superintendent as it might "require and desire,"
but, of course, the degree of input from the OIA would be much
greater and much less dependent on Lakota consent than this euphemistic OIA language suggests.[19]

The committee was still working on the constitution with the
aid of the Lakota and the Laguna field agents in July. The superintendent and Joe Jennings also assisted. In August the constitution committee met with Felix Cohen and Fred Daiker, who had traveled from
Washington. Cohen commented to the committee on a number of
problems with the constitution as drafted: (a) it included no provisions pertaining to the land problems; (b) it did not enumerate the
powers of the council; and (c) it did not provide for a law and order
apparatus. The chairman of the constitution committee explained at
a joint public meeting with Cohen and Daiker, obviously as he was
advised by the OIA, that because the committee members were "not
sufficiently educated in legal terms," it was necessary to "present our
simple views in simple words and let the Washington men word it
in legal language." The committee appointed two representatives to
work in executive session with Cohen and Daiker on the necessary
amendments.[20]

The Oglala Tribal Council met in September to vote on the draft
worked out by Cohen, Daiker, and the two Oglalas. The superintendent addressed the body, saying that he had no right to tell the councilmen how to vote, but admitting that it would give him pleasure to
see the Oglala support Collier's program. He noted that Congress and

the president believed the program was best for Indian people and that surely these great men would not try to trick the Lakota. Referring to the Lakota trickster figure, he said: "I'm sure, my friends, that you do not think John Collier, the President and Congress is [sic] an iktomi." He assured the councilmen that Cohen and Daiker's purpose in getting involved in the drafting had been merely to bring the document up to a standard which would be approved by the secretary of the interior. They made additions which gave the council more power: "Mr. Collier wants you to have more power." He added that additional modifications to the draft could be made by the Oglala, but that would waste valuable time, and he reminded the councilmen that money appropriated for tribal use would be available when "you carry out your part of the law." He explained that as he saw it, John Collier was holding up a good ten dollar bill and saying the Indians could have it for nine dollars, but they were afraid of a trick.[21]

The council deliberations involved concerns that the final draft had not actually been worked out by the Oglala constitution committee but rather by the Washington officials, Cohen and Daiker. The minutes of the August meeting were read and discussed. Some councilmen were confused because they had not previously seen the draft produced in executive session by Cohen and Daiker and the two Oglala committeemen in August. They must have expected it to differ only slightly—and not substantively—from the draft completed by the tribal constitution committee working under the supervision of the OIA field agents. But Cohen and Daiker, working with the two representatives, had later added fifteen powers, among other changes. Some councilmen were clearly shocked at the substantive changes when they saw the new draft in September.[22]

The chairman of the council—who was a member of the constitution committee—was particularly disturbed by this and argued that the council should consider the document drafted by the committee, not the one drafted by Cohen and Daiker. Whether there were specific provisions in the constitution which distressed the chairman and others, or whether they merely resented the fact that Cohen and Daiker, not the Oglalas, had drafted the document, is not clear. The two trust-patented fullbloods who had worked with Cohen and Daiker attempted to defend the procedure, and the council accepted the official draft the next day. However, the council members referred the matter of the community plan—which had been inserted into the Oglala constitution by Cohen and Daiker—to the local district councils for consideration. Indeed, it may well have been the community plan which bothered incumbents on the tribal council because it might— as on Rosebud—imperil their re-election.[23]

Serious resistance to holding the referendum remained. A prominent Oglala mixedblood, who was a Carlisle returned student but who often took up fullblood causes, wrote to Collier and Ickes on 8 October 1935 to protest the action of the September council meeting. "The whole movement leading to the adoption of said constitution and by-laws was the result of the work of propagandists employed by the Indian Office," he said, "who had been conducting an exceedingly active campaign for the new set-up at a large expense to the Indian Office." He insisted that the constitution was not drafted by the Oglala but by non-Indian representatives of the OIA, Cohen and Daiker, and that it was "not representative of the general sentiments of the Pine Ridge Indians." He added that the document was rushed through the council without proper discussion and understanding, and that

> said constitution and by-laws were not truthfully interpreted to
> those present; that they did not have an intelligent understanding of
> their contents; that a large number of those voting did not have suffi-
> cient intelligence or capacity to understand what was being done, as
> they were unable to grasp the meaning of such a document without a
> clear and honest interpretation and an opportunity to ask questions
> to those portions which they did not fully understand; that a large
> number of them did not have a sufficient understanding of English,
> nor did they grasp the importance of the effect upon themselves of
> what was being done.[24]

The idea that the OIA was attempting to move too quickly on the constitution was evidently a general sentiment among the Oglala, as it had been on Rosebud. On 22 October 1935 the field agent for Lakota country reported that the first district meeting in Porcupine to explain the new draft had met with "very little success." The people "used the same old excuse" that the OIA was "trying to move too fast, that more time should be taken." The people were particularly uncertain about the community plan.[25]

By late October 1935 the agency and the field agent reported that after three district meetings to explain the proposed constitution, the community plan was meeting opposition. The plan was to allocate five representatives to each of the districts, and to apportion each representative to a voting precinct composed of a community or group of communities within the district. Besides the resistance of the incumbents on the tribal council who thought reapportionment would harm their chances for re-election, there was also popular resistance to the community plan. Popular resistance stemmed from varying numbers of communities in each district. White Clay District, for example, had nine communities, and since only five representatives would be apportioned to the district, some of the smaller communities would have to share a representative. But the smaller groups were opposed to sharing a representative drawn, naturally, from one community. If the OIA allocated a council representative to each community, however, the council would be too large and unwieldy. Furthermore, the Oglala were, in the words of the OIA examiner of inheritance who worked in the constitution campaign, "district minded"—districts with fewer communities would resent the additional representatives which districts with more would have. The OIA finally dropped the idea of the community plan on Pine Ridge and allocated equal representation to each district.[26]

In November 1935 Collier traveled to Pine Ridge to campaign for the constitution. In two public meetings the commissioner noted the poverty on Pine Ridge and argued that ratifying the constitution would bring the material benefits of the IRA to the Oglala, especially land consolidation (buying up non-Indian land for Indian use within the confines of the reservation) and credit funds. He told an assembly at Allen that "it is important to organize, because by doing so you go along with . . . the plan of getting more land, of providing capital so you can use your own land, and of providing various other benefits that you need, and to me it seems not very important exactly what constitution you adopt to begin with because you can always improve it. You can improve it twice a year if you want to. The thing to do is to get organized."[27]

Collier added that the first tribes to organize were likely to receive a larger proportion of the funds appropriated for credit under the IRA: "Somebody will say, when they read this remark, that John Collier was trying to bribe the Pine Ridge Sioux; that he was holding up and dangling money before them, but I am not doing anything of the sort. But I think that it is my duty to give you the facts to show you that it is better to organize soon, rather than organize late." Collier told a meeting at the agency that the constitution was about as good a job as they could have done with even more time, and "perfectly safe" when they realized that it could always "be amended in a very easy way." No constitution was perfect, Collier told his Allen audience: the federal constitution took years to draft and still had to be amended many times.[28]

It is difficult to ascertain what effect Collier had on Oglala public opinion. At least some Lakota were convinced by Collier's explanation of the constitution. The chairman of the Oglala Council—who had criticized the constitution in September and who would shortly become an old dealer—remarked at the Allen meeting that Indian land was being lost, but "we now realize that if we accept the Wheeler-Howard Bill [that is, the constitution], we will keep the trap from springing; therefore I insist that we accept the Bill." He added: "Mr. Collier is to us what Moses was to the Israelites who delivered them out of the land of Egypt, wherein they were held in bondage; and I believe our future may have been Gypsies, but Mr. Collier has saved us."[29]

By December the OIA campaign to explain the constitution, involving the field agent, day school teachers, and Oglala "educational leaders," was, according to the field agent, "going full swing" in the communities. The *Shannon County News*, published by a fee-patented mixedblood in Martin, lent its voice to the campaign by circulating a flyer which urged the Oglala to "think wisely" and ratify the constitution, since, as Collier had assured them, "they had nothing to fear and everything to gain." The flyer asked: "Who can help you more than yourself if you had credit loans, cattle, horses, a good home, and the powers of organization?" While it may have been unclear exactly how the powers of organization were going to help anybody, the value of loans, cattle, horses, and homes must have been clear enough to Lakota people.[30]

There was, however, still some sentiment for a delay of the referendum. One fullblood opponent of Indian organization from Wounded Knee District reported at a council meeting that he had visited Congressman Werner in Rapid City. Werner had been a staunch opponent of the IRA in 1934, and he now advised his Oglala friends to delay the referendum. The fee-patented mixedblood who had complained to Collier and Ickes about the council's approval of the constitution also called for a delay of the referendum at the same council meeting, but he was ruled out of order by the trust-patented fullblood chair, and the council appointed an election board to oversee the referendum on 14 December.[31]

The constitution was ratified by a vote of 1,348 to 1,041. About 100 more Oglala voted in the constitution referendum than had in the IRA referendum of 1934, and the favorable votes totaled fifty-six percent, compared to fifty-two percent in 1934. There were 179 more favorable votes and 54 fewer opposed votes than in the IRA referendum. There is good reason—based on what we know the Oglala were told about the value of the constitution—to believe that, as with the IRA in 1934, people voted for the constitution not because they wanted Oglala self-government to replace the OIA, but because they wanted the material benefits promised by Collier, the superintendent, and others, if they ratified the constitution.[32]

## The Model of Tribal Government

The constitutions and by-laws of the Rosebud Sioux Tribe and the Oglala Sioux Tribe were not drafted by, nor do they represent the intentions of, the Lakota constitution committees, the tribal councils, or the grassroots. Rather, they were drafted in conformity with the OIA model of Indian self-government. This model was formulated in Washington—and to a lesser extent by the Rosebud superintendent—and imposed on the process of drafting the constitutions through the work of the field agents who supervised the drafting committees and through the work of Cohen and Daiker. I had the opportunity to consult one of the OIA field agents who worked with the constitution committees in 1935. When I asked him if there was any disagreement between the committeemen and the OIA advisors over what should be in the constitutions, he responded: "There wasn't any disagreeing on my part." The procedure in committee work was to go down the list of items in the OIA outline issued from Washington: "For instance, are you going to have a president or chairman? What are you going to name him? . . . I think they decided at Pine Ridge to call him a president. Then, how often do you want to meet? All these things. There are certain things you have to do if you're an organization." It would not be inaccurate to say that the Lakota were presented with boilerplate constitutions and allowed to fill in the blanks.

*Powers*

The enumerated powers set out in both constitutions (see table 4.1) went beyond the powers of the tribal councils before 1935. This is perhaps what the chairman of the old Rosebud Sioux Council had in mind when he called the IRA constitution a "radical departure"; through the new constitution the council could presume *to govern.* The only powers specifically mentioned in the Rosebud Sioux Council constitutions of 1920, 1924, and 1933 were to send delegations to Washington and to amend the constitution. The constitution of the Oglala Tribal Council of 1933 enumerated only the powers to amend the constitution, to assess dues against members, and to use the funds so raised. A 1931 form of the Oglala constitution had provided broadly for the power to "transact any business with the Government involving Tribal Property after securing the consent of not less than three-fourths of all adult members," and to "investigate any matter pertaining to the said band of Indians and report to the Council." These provisions were removed, however, at the behest of the superintendent, who warned in 1932 that if "they are empowered to make investigations, there is danger that they would have things in an unsettled condition; and it would be giving them too much authority." When in 1934 the superintendents were asked to describe the functions which the tribal councils were authorized to handle, they listed only enrollment matters, leases of tribal land, selection of delegations, business with the claims attorneys, advice in formulation of agency programs, and such other matters as the superintendents referred to them.[33]

The new powers in the IRA constitutions were the result of OIA policy, not of an indigenous ideology of self-government. It will be recalled that Cohen and Daiker added fifteen powers to the draft of the Oglala constitution completed by the tribal committee and the field agents. Tellingly, the language of both constitutions where the powers of the tribal councils are enumerated clearly resembles the official OIA outline for constitution discussions used during the drafting. Even the order of the enumerated powers in both constitutions largely matches the order of items in the outline, as if the constitution committees, working with the field agents, and then, later, with Cohen and Daiker, had merely transferred items verbatim from the outline to the constitutions.[34]

Table 4.1    Tribal Council Powers in the Oglala
and Rosebud Sioux Constitutions

---

1. To negotiate with federal, state, and local governments on behalf of the tribe.
2. To employ legal counsel.[1]
3. To lease tribal land.[1]
4. To approve or veto any sale, lease, disposition, or encumbrance of tribal land or other assets by the federal government.
5. To make home assignments on tribal land to tribal members.
6. To accept conveyance of individual trust land in exchange for assignments on tribal land.[2]
7. To advise the secretary of the interior on federal budgets and projects for the reservation.
8. To manage the economic affairs of the tribe in conformity with a charter of incorporation which may be issued by the secretary of the interior.
9. To tax or license non-tribal members[3] doing business on the reservation, and to tax tribal members.
10. To appropriate tribal funds not raised by the council,[2] and to appropriate funds raised by the council for public purposes.
11. To exclude from the reservation those not legally entitled to reside there.[2]
12. To regulate the membership of the tribe.[4]
13. To promulgate a law and order code and to establish a reservation court.[2]
14. To condemn the property of tribal members for public purposes.[5]
15. To regulate trade and the use and disposition of property by non-tribal members,[2] and by tribal members.[6]
16. To cultivate tribal arts, crafts, and culture.
17. To charter and regulate subordinate organizations for economic purposes.
18. To regulate the inheritance of property other than allotted land.[2]
19. To regulate the domestic relations of the tribe.
20. To appoint guardians for minors and mental incompetents.[2]
21. To regulate the procedure of the council, tribal agencies, and tribal officials.
22. To delegate powers to subordinate boards or officers.

Table 4.1 *continued*

---

23. To regulate the manner of nominations and holding elections for tribal offices.[7]
24. To administer charity.[8]

---

[1] Subject to *approval* by the secretary of the interior.

[2] Subject to secretarial *approval* on Rosebud.

[3] Subject to *review* by the secretary of the interior. The superintendent may approve or disapprove of the council action within ten days. An approved action may still be disapproved by the secretary within ninety days. An action disapproved by the superintendent may be referred by majority vote of the council to the secretary, who may approve it within ninety days.

[4] Subject to secretarial *review* on Rosebud.

[5] Subject to secretarial *approval* on Pine Ridge.

[6] Except for non-trust property on Rosebud.

[7] Rosebud only.

[8] Pine Ridge only.

The new powers notwithstanding, the IRA tribal constitutions did not have the effect of reducing the power of the agencies over Lakota people; OIA power was preserved and (some would say) even extended by the constitutions. The constitutions had the effect of creating *additional* government over the Lakota rather than transferring government from the OIA to the Lakota; new levels of domination emerged with which Lakota people had to deal.

*Structure*

The most significant structural change the IRA constitutions brought about in the tribal councils was the abrogation of the Lakota model of three-fourths majority rule. This is another way of saying that the constitutions gave the tribal councils novel—for them, not for the OIA—powers to govern. The New Deal reformers' model of parliamentary/majoritarian democracy on which the constitutions were based envisioned elected officials who would make law and administer public affairs. This model had been, as seen in chapter 2, repudiated on several occasions by the Lakota grassroots which was perennially vigilant regarding the centralization of tribal decision making. This is not to say that the Lakota people were culturally programmed to reject ideologically and to challenge practically any political system not based on three-fourths majority rule. After all, as pointed out in chapter 1, the Lakota people endured the domination of the OIA, a flagrant (one would think) violation of the model of three-fourths majority rule. As will be seen in chapter 7, the underlying problem for the tribal councils was not that they were culturally alien, but that they were—ironically—disempowered by the OIA. Nevertheless, it must be noted that the new IRA tribal councils did violate the model of three-fourths majority rule.

The IRA constitutions also reduced the size of the councils on both reservations. Both superintendents had complained that the pre-IRA councils were too large. Also, in order to keep the council small and streamlined, the two-class system of council representation was scuttled at Rosebud. The solicitor recognized that such a system could be useful in a situation in which "older members of the tribe might want a system of government by chiefs, and the younger members may want government by representatives elected for short terms." The solicitor concluded, however, that the system had "not been very successful." Thus a mechanism which might have insured better representation among the various interest groups on the reservation was eliminated.[35]

The solicitor also decided that the tribal councils should be set up under a system of "unified government." There would be no separation of powers between legislative, executive, and judicial branches. The tribal chairmen would not have veto power. Tribal courts were not established in the constitutions (the constitutions empowered the tribal councils to establish courts, but these were then subordinate to the tribal councils). When the courts were established under tribal law and order codes drafted by the Solicitor's Office and approved by the councils in 1937, they were given jurisdiction only over the enforcement of the tribal penal and domestic relations codes. They were not empowered with judicial review—the power to test the constitutionality of the ordinances enacted by the tribal councils.[36]

The Solicitor's Office was not unaware of the dangers of abuse of power where there is no separation of powers. There were obvious dangers both of oppression of individuals and minorities and of dissipation of tribal property if a tribal council governed without checks and balances. Felix Cohen wrote in 1945 of the inevitable divergence of interest between ruler and ruled, what he called the "principle of political realism," a divergence he said is mediated in democratic systems by the separation of powers; he must have been aware of this principle in 1935. Cohen and Collier told the Lakota in Rapid City in 1934 that the national Court of Indian Affairs proposed in the original draft of the Wheeler-Howard bill would protect tribal minorities against abuse of tribal power. The provisions for this court were struck by Congress, however, and the only protection against abuse of tribal power considered in 1935 were the provisions in the tribal constitutions for *supervision* of council actions by the secretary of the interior and his local representatives, the agency superintendents. This had the effect of leaving ultimate control over some acts of tribal councils with the federal bureaucracy.[37]

Thus, the notion that tribal government was "unified" was a fiction—there *was* separation of powers, not among branches of the tribal government, but between the tribal councils and the United States Department of the Interior. Pursuing the idea of supervision, rather than that of a tribal judiciary, as protection against abuse of tribal power also had the effect that provisions for civil liberties were neglected when the reformers drafted the constitutions; since the secretary of the interior and the superintendents, not tribal courts, would protect tribal members, tribal bills of rights were not necessary—the secretary's and superintendents' wise discretion would suffice.

The stated intent on the part of the OIA and the Solicitor's Office in providing for supervision rather than separation of powers within tribal government was to keep tribal government simple so that it would be workable. It is not at all apparent, however, how supervision over routine tribal council actions by local federal appointees and lawyers and senior government officials in Washington could be less cumbersome than a tribal bill of rights and a tribal court testing the constitutionality of council actions. Indeed, the effect of supervision was not simplicity but disempowerment (see chapter 6). The idea of supervision probably had currency among the Washington New Deal Indian reformers—even though it was an obvious violation of the principle of Indian self-government—because it would allow the reformers to insure that the new tribal councils acted in accordance with *the reformers' model* of Indian self-government.[38]

The disempowerment entailed in supervision was widely recognized outside of the Interior Department. Some Lakota who would come to serve on the councils would resent the supervisory provisions. "There is too much Secretary of the Interior and not enough Indian," the chairman of the Rosebud Sioux Tribal Council told the investigating subcommittee of the Senate Indian Committee that held hearings on the IRA in 1939. The Rosebud Sioux Tribal Council submitted a memorandum to a subcommittee of the House Committee on Indian Affairs in 1944, pointing out: "It is our opinion the Indian Reorganization Act delegates to the Secretary of the Interior too much restrictive power." It is now generally recognized by students of this period that the IRA tribal constitutions did not truly empower tribal councils, relative to the federal bureaucracy, and (some would say) actually *increased* the role of the secretary of the interior in tribal affairs.[39]

The supervisory provisions also had the effect of making the OIA and the secretary of the interior seem *necessary* from the point of view of the grassroots, once the new tribal councils began operating. It was the federal government that would protect the rights of tribal members against abuse of power by the tribal councils (see chapter 6). This adjudicating role of the federal government pushed Lakota political consciousness in the same direction as did its provisioning role (chapter 1): it helped bring about Lakota resignation toward the federal presence on the reservations. As a Lakota consultant put it to me, "The secretary of the interior is our protector." Of course, a tribal supreme court could have been the protector, and tribal governments could have been established with appropriate *internal* checks and balances to correct abuses and excesses. The fact that tribal governments were not empowered by their constitutions to protect civil liberties and to deal effectively with misconduct by tribal officials contributed to the crisis of authority faced by the tribal councils (chapter 7).

## Native Communities

The one area where the Rosebud and Oglala constitutions differed significantly concerned the basis of council representation: representatives were allocated to communities on Rosebud and to districts on Pine Ridge. Collier considered the community plan at Rosebud a model for incorporating native social organization into modern Indian self-government. In September 1935 the OIA issued a circular noting the success of organizing Indians on the basis of "natural" social groups as opposed to arbitrary administrative districts on one reservation (Rosebud), and suggesting the role of ethnologists in working out such an arrangement at other jurisdictions. Collier also reported to Ickes that the Rosebud and Cheyenne River Sioux constitutions incorporated "the very important principle of Sioux organization on the basis of ancient Sioux communities, which even the allotment system has not been able to destroy." This type of arrangement was obviously consistent with Collier's desire to incorporate traditional Indian culture into modern organization, and it also fit well with his admiration for British indirect rule as a mode of administration of native peoples. The community plan was also pushed in the field by the Rosebud superintendent and Scudder Mekeel. It was not an Indian idea.[40]

There is little reason to believe that the communities listed in the Rosebud constitution were "ancient," "natural," or even stable units in Lakota society, or that they commanded people's primordial political loyalties in any consistent way, or that they were characterized by consensus. Even in the nineteenth century, Lakota bands were noncorporate groups with variable personnel. Once the bands settled on the reservation, residence continued to shift because of allotment in severalty, and, in the 1930s, because of the disruptions of the drought and Depression, new day schools, relief employment projects, rehabilitation colonies, and internal politics. The very superintendent who had invented the community plan reported in 1940 that "each tey-osh-pey [tiyośpaye] has two or more factions in it. Every leader is challenged by other would-be leaders."[41]

Internal political pressure to split the supposedly "ancient" and "natural" communities developed as soon as they were formally recognized as permanent groups in the Rosebud constitution. In 1939 some pro-New Deal members of the Grass Mt. community voted to organize a new community—which never materialized—because other members of Grass Mt. were "hopeless and practically all Old Dealers." In 1938 the superintendent disapproved a tribal council resolution to establish Hollow Horn Bear community within the existing Spring Creek community. "From an ethnological standpoint," he commented, "there appears to be no justification for this division in as much as some related families would belong to the Spring Creek Community and others would belong to the new proposed community." Real-life politics apparently did not seem as "natural" to the superintendent as anthropological models of "ancient" kin-based communities, and he advised the council not to allow fission of the communities: "Unless some regulation and limitation is placed upon these divisions there is a possibility that infractionation of communities could continue to the point where you would have no stabilization of community activities nor community life." Of course, this concern had more to do with the agency's need for stable, territorially based administrative units of population than with making tribal government consistent with traditional Lakota social organization.[42]

In 1933 the Rosebud superintendent, reporting on divergent political factions, made no mention of communities but referred to antagonistic small groups resulting from "hereditary chiefs, ancient societies, small disturbances of the past, desire for personal leadership, and the like." The following year the superintendent proposed a plan for organizing grassroots Indian self-government on the basis of the Indian dance hall gatherings. These informal congregations were not local groups but were nonetheless cohesive social units in the superintendent's view. The implication was that the dance hall associations were more stable in membership and solidarity than were neighborhoods, and the superintendent suggested that "those people who voluntarily gather at a given hall should be the representative community so far as organization is concerned."[43]

By 1935 when the constitution was being drafted, the superintendent had replaced his theory of the dance hall as the "natural" grassroots political organization with the *tiyóspaye* theory. The *tiyóspaye*, according to the superintendent, was a local, kin-based, leader-centered, cohesive community, and it was the traditional political community among the Lakota; there were eighteen of them on Rosebud which he located on a map. It was, as already pointed out, much easier for an administrator to identify and formalize the membership of a *local* group, and this explains the superintendent's replacement of the dance hall with the *tiyóspaye* in his community plan for the constitution.[44]

None of this is to suggest that communities were not real social units on the reservation or that extended kinship was not an important basis for solidarity, residence, and cooperation. The point is that communities were no more "natural" units of Lakota political representation than were district councils, tribal councils, or unorganized factions. The Lakota were apparently "district minded" as much as they were community minded. It will be recalled that the Oglala Tribal Council and the Rosebud Sioux Council on the eve of the New

Deal did not have community, but rather district, representation, and that the elderly fullblood chairman of the old council on Rosebud had called the community plan "outrageous."[45]

If communities were not necessarily "natural" units for political representation among the Lakota, why was the community plan so important in the administrative theories of the superintendent, Mekeel, and Collier? The superintendent who invented the community plan had a good reason for insisting that the natural unit of Lakota political loyalty was *below* the level of the tribe. As will be seen in chapter 6, he was a vigorous opponent of empowerment of the tribal councils. He used the argument that *tribal*-level organization was in conflict with traditional Lakota political organization— because Lakota loyalties were to bands, not to the tribe—in order to defend his opposition to tribal council authority. While community representation would not in itself disempower the tribal council, it was consistent with the superintendent's general attempt to bypass the tribal council. He hoped to avoid the outspoken and aggressive Lakota tribal council politicians who were in the mood for anything but cooperation with the agency, and to carry his agency programs directly to the small communities where he was less likely to encounter politically skilled adversaries or organized resistance to his plans.

Mekeel, as an applied anthropologist working for the OIA, had an interest in being the recognized expert on traditional Lakota organization—the more arcane the better for his authority. He sent a memo to Collier in 1934, before he was in the employ of the OIA, suggesting that native bands be taken into consideration in organizing tribes, and he had added: "Anthropology has a distinct contribution to make here." Collier hired him, perhaps on the basis of his memo, and his first job was to use anthropology exactly as he had claimed it could be used: he was detailed to identify the communities on Rosebud for enumeration in the tribal constitution. He was described by the Pine Ridge superintendent as "better qualified to do this than anyone else," apparently, from the OIA's point of view, even better qualified than the Lakota field agent and the Lakota themselves.[46]

For Collier the belief that the community plan incorporated "ancient" forms of social organization must have made it very attractive. Collier's mystical fascination with native culture—the fascination apparent when he first addressed the Rosebud Sioux Council in

1933—was quite real, not a pose. Collier, after all, had long before discovered a "Red Atlantis" at Taos Pueblo, based on a laudable primitivity involving "the earliest statesmanship" and a "complex yet childlike beauty." How could such a mind resist the idea that ancient bands discovered by an anthropologist—and not the existing, pre-IRA tribal council officially recognized by the OIA—were the natural political units of the Lakota, even if few Lakota seemed to agree?[47]

Tribal self-government among the Lakota was constructed not on an indigenous model but on the model worked out by the non-Indian New Deal Indian reformers. While their intentions were humane, the product left much to be desired from the point of view of the Lakota. The constitutions were flawed because they did not effectively transfer OIA power to the Lakota or make the OIA accountable to them, because they did not provide for self-correcting checks and balances in tribal government but rather imposed federal supervision, and because they merely added another layer of government on the reservations which violated the Lakota principle of three-fourths majority rule.

Few Lakota could have seen these documents as results of *their* doing. They knew that the underlying model and the language were Washington's, and most people probably understood little of the constitutions. The refusal of the OIA to postpone the referendums so that the voters could have been more confident in their understandings of the instruments could only have added to the sense among people on the reservations that the documents were not theirs, but were forced on them. The OIA may have euphemistically described the constitutions as "drafted" and "ratified" by the Lakota, but how many on the reservations could have had any faith in such fictions? Most people who voted affirmatively in the referendums—and this group likely included both fullbloods and mixedbloods, trust-patented and fee-patented people, young and old—probably saw access to credit funds, the addition of new lands, access to lands by landless families, and protection of allotments as desirable goals. While most Lakota people would like to have seen the OIA made more accountable to them, it is very unlikely that many voters were contemplating the ethereal "powers of organization" or the fuzzy Washington idea of tribal "self-government" when they went to the polls to vote in favor of the constitutions.

FIGURE 1.   A fullblood couple, Rosebud Reservation, 1923. National Archives and Records Administration.

FIGURE 2.   A mixedblood couple, Rosebud Reservation, 1924. National Archives and Records Administration.

FIGURE 3.   A fullblood husband and mixedblood wife, Rosebud Reservation, 1923. National Archives and Records Administration.

FIGURE 4.   A mixedblood family, Rosebud Reservation, 1923. National Archives and Records Administration.

FIGURE 5. John Collier meets the Oglala, 1933. Buechel Memorial/Lakota Museum.

FIGURE 6. Distributing relief commodities, Pine Ridge Reservation, 1940. National Archives and Records Administration.

FIGURE 7.   Relief work, Rosebud Reservation. National Archives and Records Administration.

FIGURE 8.   A women's sewing project. National Archives and Records Administration.

FIGURE 9.   A women's sewing project. National Archives and Records
Administration.

FIGURE 10.   Mother and daughter at a canning kitchen. National Archives
and Records Administration.

Figure 11.   Working on an irrigation system, Pine Ridge Reservation. National Archives and Records Administration.

Figure 12.   A meeting of the Oglala Sioux Tribal Council. National Archives and Records Administration.

FIGURE 13. A delegation of the Rosebud Sioux Tribal Council meets with John Collier in Washington. National Archives and Records Administration.

FIGURE 14. The Oglala Sioux Tribal Court, 1940. National Archives and Records Administration.

FIGURE 15. A Rosebud couple, 1938. Buechel Memorial/Lakota Museum.

## CHAPTER 5

# The New Deal and the Artificial Economies: Reinforced Dependence

New Deal Indian policy was intended to improve the reservation economies as much as it was intended to grant self-government to reservation populations. There were two dimensions of economic policy under the Indian New Deal. One dimension entailed the provision of relief and relief work as emergency measures which would tide the Lakota over until they could recover from the immediate economic catastrophe of the Great Depression and the drought of the 1930s. The other dimension was intended to attack the long-term structural constraints on Indian agriculture and to foster the development of individual and group enterprises. This was to be accomplished by providing development programs to increase Indian use of Indian land. The New Deal programs did not, however, alter the artificial nature of the reservation economies. In fact, during the New Deal the Lakota became even more dependent on the agencies for resources than they had been in the previous decade.

## Drought and Depression

During the decade of the 1930s, grasshopper infestations, drought, and the agricultural price deflation of the Great Depression began to ravage South Dakota. Crop failures in the state rose from 583,313 acres in 1929 to 9,783,136 acres in 1935, while cropland harvested fell from 17,856,178 acres to 4,863,888 acres during the same period. The value of crops harvested in the state plummeted from $128,082,944 in 1930 to $8,585,390 in 1935. The value of cattle and calves on South Dakota farms was reduced from $97,971,655 in 1930 to $26,315,061

Table 5.1   Combined Values of Crops, Livestock, and
Dairy Products, Pine Ridge and Rosebud Reservations*

| Year | Pine Ridge | Rosebud |
|------|-----------|---------|
| 1920 | $5,231,779 | $25,969,817 |
| 1929 | 7,608,479 | 22,648,534 |
| 1939 | 3,270,007 | 9,806,990 |

*Data are included from all of the original counties of the reservations, including the ceded and fee-patented portions. The Rosebud figures also include all of Gregory County, only part of which was originally included in the reservation.

SOURCE: *Rand McNally Commercial Atlas,* 1930, 61st edition, 397; 1934, 65th edition, 356; 1945, 76th edition, 367.

in 1935. The declines in values of agricultural products on Pine Ridge and Rosebud reservations are presented in table 5.1. While we can assume that these figures primarily reflect the losses sustained by the non-Indian operators who dominated agriculture on the two reservations, the catastrophe was also visited upon small-scale Indian operators and the handfuls of large Indian operators on the reservations. The Pine Ridge Agency reported in 1938 that only two percent of the Oglala stockmen who had formerly owned cattle had survived the depression. What is more, the non-Indian agricultural losses in turn affected the Lakota as reductions in income from leases and land sales.[1]

The decade had opened with optimism for Indian agriculture, among both the Lakota and the agency officials, at least on Rosebud. The superintendent boasted in 1931 about the "remarkable" progress the Lakota had made there, from life as "savages following the hunt for a living," to family farmers producing an average of twenty-five to thirty-five acres of crops, with some farming a quarter section (160 acres) or more. Grasshoppers took enough of those 1931 crops, however, to make it "necessary to feed a large number of people gratuitously to preserve life" in the winter and spring of 1932. Approximately 600 families were issued rations. There was the additional problem that employment was at a "standstill"; there was no government or private sector work available, and many people who had been off the reservation supporting themselves returned because of the economic downturn.[2]

The Pine Ridge superintendent reported crop losses among lessees as early as 1929. In 1930 there were many crop failures among Oglala farmers, and no gardens. In 1931, grasshoppers and the drought caused a "total loss" of crops on Pine Ridge. In the fall of that year, one hundred Oglalas went to Nebraska for seasonal work harvesting potatoes as usual, but because of the deflated agricultural prices reflected in the fee paid per bushel harvested, the Indian families were not able to make their usual grubstakes.[3]

There were precipitous declines in Indian incomes from leases and land sales. Individual income from land sales on Rosebud dropped from $314,430 in 1928 to $38,125 in 1933. On Pine Ridge, land sales declined from $116,828 in 1927 to $18,984 in 1933. By the fall of 1931, non-Indian lessees on Rosebud and Pine Ridge were asking for extensions on or reductions of their payments. The individual lease income on Rosebud dropped from $197,058 in 1928 to $80,594 in 1933. The reduction on Pine Ridge was from $66,000 in 1927 to $57,406 in 1933.[4]

By the mid-1930s, it was clear that any gains made by Indian farmers in self-sufficiency during the 1920s or by Indian landowners in financial independence from the OIA had been crushed by the prevailing crop conditions and by the Great Depression. The Pine Ridge superintendent reported in 1934 that Indian farmers, like their non-Indian neighbors, could not get fair prices for what surplus they could raise. He reported in 1935 that Indian farmers who had raised twenty to fifty acres of corn and oats during the period of 1925 to 1930 had become discouraged and stopped trying. (By this time the OIA no longer forced Lakota people to labor at irrational agricultural enterprises.) Of the more than 1,000 subsistence gardens which had been planted, less than half grew to maturity because of insect infestation, and garden yields were seventy-five percent below normal. In 1936, 997 family gardens were a total failure. Even the wild fruits that were collected by the Lakota—such as wild plums (*Prunus americana*; *k'ata* in Lakota) and chokecherries (*Prunus virginia*; *canpa* in Lakota)—were unavailable because of the drought.[5]

By 1935 more than 225 leases were delinquent on Rosebud. The superintendent reported the same year that the drought had "resulted in practically a total lack of production of crops of any kind" among the Indians. He also reported that 662 families had planted 1,013 acres of garden, and some had replanted a second and third time, but the gardens had failed. Families had liquidated their cattle, horses, and farm machinery to obtain cash for subsistence. "Many even sold the dishes in their houses for subsistence," the Pine Ridge superintendent explained to the investigating subcommittee of the Senate Indian Committee. The economic crisis was being "keenly felt among the Sioux Indians," he reported in 1934.[6]

## Relief and Relief Work .

### Rations and Other Relief

Relief in the form of both direct assistance and work projects became, in the words of the Rosebud superintendent, "the order of the day" under the prevailing economic and crop conditions on the reservations. There were general windfall distributions of food and supplies. The Pine Ridge superintendent issued sheep carcasses from the infamous Navajo stock reductions, as well as flour and canned meats from the Federal Surplus Relief Corporation in 1934. He also issued 12,000 cattle purchased by the South Dakota branch of the Emergency Relief Administration from drought areas. Almost every family received six head of cattle which were butchered and the meat dried, younger women having been given instruction in traditional Lakota meat processing at a training camp sponsored by the agency extension department.[7]

   Rations were the foundation of the relief effort. There was the regular issue of rations to older and/or disabled people who could not work. There was also a great increase in the issue of rations in exchange for labor to able-bodied people who could not provide for themselves. The monthly ration for one person on Pine Ridge in 1940 is presented in table 5.2. A ration for a single individual was valued at $4.11 in 1940, and an able-bodied recipient was required to perform 14 hours of labor for the ration. This ration was increased with the size of the family. A ration for a family of five was valued at $17.42 for 58 hours of labor. On Pine Ridge, the number of rations or cash payments in lieu of rations issued in return for labor increased from 25 in fiscal year 1930 to 1,354 in calendar year 1932. On Rosebud, the

Table 5.2  Monthly Ration for One Person,
Pine Ridge Reservation, 1940

| | |
|---|---|
| 2 lbs. | Dry beans |
| 4 cans | Tomatoes |
| 2 lbs. | Dried fruit |
| 12 lbs. | Flour |
| 5 lbs. | Corn meal |
| ½ lb. | Oat meal |
| ½ lb. | Rice |
| 2 lbs. | Bacon |
| 1 lb. | Oleo |
| 3 lbs. | Sugar |
| ½ qt. | Molasses |
| 2 cans | Fish |
| 8 cans | Milk |
| 1 lb. | Coffee |
| ¼ box | Salt |
| ½ box | Soda |
| ¼ box | Baking powder |
| 2 cakes | Soap |

SOURCE: U.S. Congress, Senate, *Survey of Conditions of the Indians of the United States* (1940), Hearings Before a Subcommittee of the Committee on Indian Affairs, 76th Congress, Pt. 37:21836.

number increased from 54 in fiscal year 1929 to 675 in calendar year 1932, and 615 in calendar year 1933, when the work relief projects began.[8]

*Relief Work*

The most important work opportunities under the New Deal on Lakota reservations were enrollment in Indian Emergency Conservation Work (IECW), more commonly known as the Civilian Conservation Corps–Indian Division (CCC or CCC-ID), work on road construction projects under the agency road departments, and labor on community rehabilitation projects.

Initially funded in 1933, the CCC provided temporary work for Lakota men until its budget was cut in 1942. CCC enrollees earned

$30 per month or $1.50 per day. Enrollees with teams of horses earned an additional one or two dollars per day. The annual wages received by individual enrollees were low because enrollees were called up and furloughed in staggered crews to distribute the work as widely as possible; nonetheless, CCC wages became a critical source of income for many families on the two reservations. A survey of the Rosebud labor force in 1942 found that seventy-five percent of the men had been on CCC payrolls at one time or another since 1933. Projects included constructing dams; drilling wells and improving springs to provide water for reservation pasture lands; constructing truck trails, fire breaks, corrals, telephone lines, and pasture fences; prairie dog eradication; and other improvements.[9]

The agencies set up road departments in 1933, funded with monies from what became known as the Public Works Administration. On Pine Ridge in 1935, road employment paid $4 per day for a man with a team, and $2.40 per day for a man without a team. The Pine Ridge agency road department employed 525 men in 1935, expending $129,000. On Rosebud, 95 were employed, with $52,507 paid in wages. There was also employment on community projects funded through the OIA Rehabilitation Division in Washington, which in turn was funded by the Works Progress Administration (WPA). These community projects included the construction of housing, community gardens, canning kitchens, and other structures. WPA labor was second only to the CCC as a source of income on Rosebud in 1936, and more than $122,000 in wages went to 600 heads of household. Civil Works Administration funds, administered through the agencies, also took up some of the slack in 1933 and 1934, particularly by employing women who were heads of households at making garments and quilts.[10]

Relief work employed a substantial percentage of Lakota men during the New Deal. There were 2,023 families listed in a survey of Pine Ridge in 1933, and a total of 1,225 men—presumably heads of households—were employed in relief work. On Rosebud, where 1,790 families lived, 731 men were employed in relief work in 1933. The vast majority of Lakota relief workers earned small incomes—less than $100. In fact, almost 400 of the 1,225 Oglala workers earned less then $50, and almost 300 of the 731 relief workers on Rosebud earned less than $50 in 1933. Nor was relief work available for every family eligible for it. An inspector traveling through Rosebud in 1936 re-

ported that the funds allotted could provide employment for less than
half of those in need of relief. Yet, relief work was an important
source of income on Lakota reservations. In 1935 CCC wages were
the largest source of individual cash income on Rosebud Reservation (see table 5.3). A 1942 survey of the male labor pool on Rosebud
found that 41 percent of the respondents were working on relief projects, and that 85 percent had been dependent upon such work at
one time.[11]

## The Artificial Economies and Dependence

The significance of relief and relief work during the New Deal is that
these programs reinforced the artificial nature of the reservation
economies and, thus, the dependence of the Lakota upon the OIA. The
Rosebud superintendent estimated in 1935 that of the 1,564 families
on his reservation, 195 were supported by CCC work, 95 by road work,

Table 5.3   Sources of Individual Cash Income,
Rosebud Reservation, 1935

| Source | Amount |
| --- | --- |
| CCC | $132,680 |
| Allotment leases | 100,948 |
| Pro rata shares of tribal funds | 55,651 |
| Agency road work | 52,507 |
| Skilled labor | 42,700 |
| Clerical labor | 32,540 |
| Sioux benefits | 28,461 |
| Livestock sales | 20,140 |
| Pensions | 17,664 |
| Crop sales | 16,889 |
| Rehabilitation labor | 16,441 |
| Trades/professions | 5,585 |
| Timber sales | 4,480 |
| Freighting | 3,000 |
| Beadwork/lacemaking | 436 |

SOURCE: Economic and Social Data on the Rosebud Indian Reservation, 1936, File 19712-1936-259, Pt. 1, Rosebud, CCF.

250 by rations, 83 by existing funds in their IIM accounts, and 134 by their own enterprise. This left 775 families, which we can surmise subsisted on FSA and Social Security checks, state relief, county WPA projects, wind fall issues from the agency, and the generosity, of Lakota friends and relatives. Ninety-five percent of the population received some form of public aid during 1939–40. In 1940 the Pine Ridge superintendent estimated that 90 percent of the Oglala survived directly or indirectly on funds provided by various public assistance agencies. An average of 1,200 families lived on Farm Security Administration (FSA) subsistence grants (funding for these grants was transferred to the OIA for administration in 1940), 300 families depended on CCC work, 200 on agency road work, 300 on WPA employment, and 100 on pensions. It is no wonder that in 1940 a Treaty Council meeting asked that the Indian committees of Congress investigate the rumored discontinuance of "Federal Grants and Reliefs" to the Lakota. They had heard that the government planned to halt relief and force the Indians to "find away [sic] of making living."[12]

## Economic Development

Of course, the OIA did not consider relief or even relief work a solution to the problem of reservation poverty. These programs were thought of as temporary measures, not permanent components of the reservation economy in New Deal policy. New Deal economic development policy had two agendas. One was Indian use of Indian resources—getting Indians, rather than non-Indians, operating on Indian land. Agricultural enterprise on Indian land was dominated by non-Indians. The Rosebud Agency reported that in 1935 non-Indian farmers operated on 146,122 acres of reservation land, while Indian farmers cultivated only 31,841 acres, and more than half of the latter figure was composed of wild hay land. Non-Indian ranchers ran cattle on 440,969 acres of reservation land, while Indian cattlemen used only 107,890 acres. The Pine Ridge Agency reported that non-Indian operators ran cattle on 628,441 acres, while Indian operators used only 294,040 acres. Non-Indian farmers cultivated 1,021,615 acres of Indian trust land on Pine Ridge in 1935, while Indian farmers cropped only 12,109 acres.[13] The other agenda of New Deal economic development policy was to create self-sustaining individual and group ag-

ricultural enterprises which would support the reservation populations and wean them from dependence on artificial flows of federal
relief as much as possible. This, of course, was long a stated agenda
of the OIA, but new methods would be used during the New Deal.

Two structural factors were identified by the New Deal reformers
in Washington as constraints on Indian agriculture, and these factors
were the target both of some of the provisions in the IRA and of OIA
policy during the New Deal. One of the structural factors was heirship infractionation of allotments. The effect of heirship infractionation was to tie up an allotment in multiple interests so that no heir
had sufficient interests in any one estate for viable agricultural operations, although an individual might have substantial interests divided
among numerous scattered allotments. One Rosebud man, for example, had interests in eleven allotments. The assessed value of these
interests ranged from \$.24 for a 648/130,638 interest in one allotment
valued at \$480 to \$65.57 for a 6/84 interest in another allotment valued at \$960.00. On paper he owned \$284 worth of land, but he had no
economically viable tract to operate on or to lease as a unit. One allotment on Rosebud in 1943 had 150 heirs. Sixty percent of the allotted land on Rosebud was in heirship status in 1943.[14]

Undercapitalization resulting from unavailability of credit was
another critical structural constraint on Indian agriculture. The credit
problem was rooted in the trust status of Indian land; because trust
land could not be mortgaged, allottees in effect had no real property
with which to secure loans. This meant that Indians were dependent
upon the government for credit, but available federal credit for Indian
farmers was so insufficient that Indians could not finance their own
operations and had no alternative but to rent their land to non-Indian
operators who had standing capital funds and/or access to commercial credit.

The OIA central office and the agencies aggressively attacked these
structural problems. Three components of OIA New Deal economic
policy will be described: trust land management, credit, and community development.

*Trust Land Management*

One innovation in trust land management during the 1930s was unit
leasing in which trust lands—allotments still owned by the original

allottees, allotments in heirship status, and tribal land—were assembled into range or grazing units. The reservation was partitioned so that each unit had adequate pasture, water, and shelter to make it viable. Units were mapped out in the agency office with these considerations in mind, irrespective of the tenure of land included in units. Grazing permits on the units were then sold by the agency through competitive bid. Permits specified the number of animal units which could be grazed, in conformity with the unit's carrying capacity as determined by the federal government. Prior to the range unit system, a non-Indian lessee could offer an allottee with water on his land a high rent, and could then allow his stock to trespass on surrounding pasture lands for which he did not pay rent; he paid a trespass fee only when his trespassing stock was discovered. The range unit system was designed in 1930 to stop this abuse as well as damage to pasture by overgrazing and to yield the highest return per acre which grass and market conditions would allow for all allottees and heirs with interests in a unit. Under this system, an individual allottee or the heirs holding the majority of the interests in an allotment assigned power-of-attorney to the agency which managed the unit, and the allottee or heirs were not allowed to negotiate individual leases with the livestock operator—almost always a non-Indian—who had previously leased the land.[15]

Besides maximizing the returns for Indian land owners, the range unit system in theory facilitated Indian use of Indian resources because Indian operators were given preference. Indian cattlemen with less than 250 head could be allocated grazing privileges without competitive bidding. Indian cattlemen with 250 or more head were allowed the meet the highest bid at the discretion of the landowners or interest holders in the unit.[16]

Another trust land management innovation implemented by the Rosebud Agency was the Tribal Land Enterprise (TLE). TLE was a complex and ambitious plan designed by the Rosebud superintendent which was, in theory, managed by a Board of Directors of Indian shareholders who formed an interlocking directorate with the Rosebud Sioux Tribal Council. The core of TLE was a procedure for individual owners of trust land or inherited interests in trust land to convey their equities in land, as determined by appraisal, to the tribal corporation in exchange for pro-rated shares in TLE.[17]

The program had three purposes. One was to remove the burgeoning administrative burden on the agency because of heirship infractionation of allotments. When TLE was started, seven full-time agency employees worked on land administration, and fifteen other employees spent part of their time on land matters. TLE was intended to lighten the administrative load by simplifying the probate procedure.

A second purpose of TLE was to realize maximum returns per acre for shareholders via sustained yield management of range resources. Shareholding would eliminate the "desires of individuals toward private negotiations" that plagued the range unit system, and would allow rationalized management by a centralized board.[18]

A third purpose was to allow individuals or families with small inherited interests in scattered allotments to convert these into shares which could be deposited with TLE in exchange for assignment of a consolidated piece of TLE land appraised at a value equal to the deposited shares. This opportunity to convert economically useless interests or tracts into a single, viable holding was "particularly appealing to the Rosebud Indians." By 1945 thirty-four shareholders had received assignments of TLE land.[19]

A fourth purpose of TLE was to facilitate the elimination of checkerboarding of Indian trust land with non-Indian land by purchasing or trading for non-Indian land within what were termed consolidation areas on the reservation.

## Credit

There were existing loan programs—known as reimbursable credit—on both reservations when the New Deal began, and these were continued until 1944. Reimbursable loans were administered by the agencies and were generally made so as to service as many families as possible regardless of prospects for return on investment. As of January 1936, 1,947 reimbursable accounts were open at the Rosebud agency for an amount totaling $87,504; $80,000 of this figure was delinquent. A new reimbursable policy instituted by the Pine Ridge Agency in 1940 entailed fewer loans but at greater amounts in order to create self-sustaining family or cooperative agricultural enterprises. In 1941 thirty-five loans were made from a reimbursable allotment of $26,578. Fourteen of these loans financed fully viable operations. In 1943 more than $100,000 was lent to fifty-four operations, forty of the loans fully capitalizing self-sustaining units. These loans brought total reimbursable indebtedness on Pine Ridge to more than $196,000.[20]

Additional credit sources were made available to the Lakota during the New Deal. One was the repayment cattle program in which cows were issued by the agency to selected Indian operators. The clients returned one heifer from herd increase for each cow issued under the program. Between 1935 and 1938, 2,689 head of cattle had been issued to 335 families on Pine Ridge. An additional source of credit was the rehabilitation funds allocated to loans by the agencies for the construction and repair of homes, barns, chicken coops, toilets, and domestic water sources.[21]

The most important additional source of credit during the New Deal was the IRA revolving loan fund. With the tribal ratification of a corporate charter issued by the secretary of the interior in 1937, the Rosebud Sioux Tribe became eligible for access to this fund. An initial loan of $35,000 from the IRA revolving fund was made to the tribal corporation. The tribe in turn made loans to individuals, partnerships, and cooperative associations, bearing four percent interest. Between 1937 and the close of 1945, the tribe loaned $350,930 to 442 individuals or small partnerships. The loans varied in amount from $25 to more than $7,000. The smaller loans were for harnesses for horse teams, and they were allocated to older people in the hope of defusing opposition to New Deal policy. Larger loans financed livestock operations. Even though some individuals received more than one loan, the credit funds were significantly spread among the population: at least 350 different households received loans over the eight-year period. This figure represents approximately one-fourth of the families on the reservation in 1941. Several livestock cooperative associations were also funded, credit funds thus reaching additional people.[22]

In 1944 Congress made credit funds available to tribes, such as the Oglala, which had not ratified corporate charters under the provisions of the IRA (the Oglala voters rejected the charter at a referendum in 1937 and again in 1938). The OIA administered these funds with the same procedures used in the IRA revolving credit funds for incorporated tribes. The Oglala Sioux Tribal Council organized a credit committee in 1944 and was granted a loan of $150,000 by the

OIA. By the close of the fiscal year ending in 1945, fifty-two loans had been made totalling $91,507. Loans were repayable in six years at three percent interest.[23]

## Community Development

The principal target of Indian New Deal economic development policy was the local communities. The amount of agency attention devoted to local-level development varied from community to community on Pine Ridge and Rosebud and can be described as running along a continuum. At one extreme were simple programs of adult education and community work by the local OIA day school teachers. In many communities, the OIA went further and organized community gardens and livestock cooperatives. At the opposite extreme were ambitious, integrated development projects involving several agency departments and substantial technical and capital input by the federal government. The aim of all these initiatives was to revitalize "natural" Lakota communities, or to create new ones which would be self-supporting.

Adult education carried on by the local day school teachers and home extension work conducted by the agency extension staff were basic community development programs on both reservations. Adult education at Pine Ridge was conceived by the agency to involve the dissemination of "propaganda" in which "diplomatic agents imbued with the missionary spirit" (day school teachers) sought to "indoctrinate the people with a desire for social improvement." Thus, the objectives of adult education on Pine Ridge included inculcating among the Oglala an understanding of the "intelligent expenditure of funds," an "appreciation of property"—in general, "economic intelligence." Other goals were facilitating "cooperation with members of groups and with public officials," "racial harmony," and "public spirit." Also on the list was fostering "family pride and personal pride in assuming family responsibilities," as well as an appreciation of American Indian culture, "moral obligations," and the "worthy use of leisure time"—in short, "character development."[24] Adult education dovetailed with the home extension program, which on Rosebud had as its aim to "Help the Indians to Help Themselves." It emphasized balanced diets and subsistence production for families, production of feed for livestock and poultry, and the provision of clothing and bedding.[25]

Meetings were sponsored by local communities and day schools and involved presentations by agency staff, teachers, tribal officials, and local community members. Topics included development policy, the tribal constitutions and law and order codes, livestock management, health, music, arithmetic, writing for newspapers, spelling, Lakota language, and Lakota crafts, music and dance. Some meetings featured slide shows and films, entertainment—such as performances by a saxophone quartet and a glee club—and refreshments. Farm chapters were organized for men. Beadwork associations were organized for cooperative buying and marketing, and the OIA provided beads, bead looms, and even some buildings on Rosebud. Mothers' clubs were organized by the wives of day school teachers at which such parenting skills as "bathing a baby" were imparted to Lakota women. Extension workers organized women's clubs for yard improvement projects and for training and encouragement in subsistence gardening, poultry raising, canning and drying, household budgeting, and other skills. Each woman answered roll calls at meetings by reciting her garden figures, what was stored in her root cellar, and how she had improved her home. Sewing clubs and sewing centers were organized in which women were provided with materials, sewing machines, patterns, scissors, and other equipment. Four-H clubs and baseball and basketball games were organized. Community agricultural fairs were held. Even dramatic clubs, minstrel shows, and orchestras were organized on Pine Ridge. Some teachers organized community libraries.[26]

Beyond his day school and adult education responsibilities, the day school teacher was also charged with serving as "leader" in organizing community subsistence gardens with the cooperation of the agency Extension Department. On Rosebud, seven community gardens had been organized by 1935, most of approximately thirteen acres and involving fifteen families each. By 1939 eighteen cooperative community irrigated gardens were in operation on Rosebud. By 1939 forty-seven Pine Ridge communities were involved in community garden projects. There were nine irrigated community garden projects on Pine Ridge in 1941 for which the agency provided Extension Department management and funding for irrigation system construction, plowing, and other costs. Harvested produce was apportioned to families on the basis of labor contributed to the community garden, with a fee in kind retained for service. Individual families also gardened on irrigated tracts and paid a fee of one-quarter of produce.[27]

Cooperative livestock associations were also a component of OIA community development. Association members cooperated in breeding and shipping, and they shared range in order to manage pasture resources more efficiently. These associations operated under bylaws drafted by the OIA, and they were eligible for loans from the IRA revolving credit fund and from other sources. Six cooperative livestock associations received IRA revolving fund loans on Rosebud during the New Deal period. Seventeen cooperative associations existed on Pine Ridge during 1941 (including the "Collier Livestock Association"), ranging in size from three to thirty members, with from 10 head of cattle to 467 head of cattle and 111 head of horses. Five cooperatives had received reimbursable loans from the agency in 1940. Most of the cooperatives on both reservations involved individual ownership of stock but joint use and management of range and cooperative breeding and marketing. Some associations involved both individual and joint ownership of stock, and a few involved only joint ownership.[28]

The most ambitious community development projects involved the integration of adult education, cooperative organization, credit, housing and water control programs, and extension services and technical assistance in selected communities. The most well known of these projects were the Grass Mt. Colony on Rosebud and the Red Shirt Table Development Association on Pine Ridge.

The Grass Mt. Colony construction was financed by an OIA Rehabilitation Division appropriation and was completed in May 1937. The dedication ceremony was attended by Xavier Vigeant, director of the Rehabilitation Division. Twelve two-room houses, poultry buildings, and a canning kitchen had been built on fee-patented land bought with Resettlement Administration funds. Nine Lakota families and an OIA day school teacher and his wife were assigned to the houses. New assignees had to be approved by the existing colony members and had to sign a document in which they agreed to participate in cooperative garden and livestock activities. The colony had been designed to benefit landless families or those who were effectively landless because of heirship infractionation.[29]

The intent on the part of the OIA was for rehabilitation colonies to be not just modern housing, but self-sustaining, mixed-agricultural enterprises, based on subsistence gardening, stock crop production, and commercial livestock production. The Grass Mt. Colony had a cooperative irrigated garden, and the members formally organized as the Grass Mt. Development Association and received a loan of $2,500 from the IRA revolving loan fund. This funding and a loan of twenty-six repayment cattle were used to start a cattle operation on an adjacent range unit. As in the community gardens described, records were kept of members' labor contributions in the rehabilitation colonies, and a resident could be expelled for failure to do his or her part. Another major community development project on Rosebud was the Two Kettle Project, also involving livestock and irrigated crop production. There were also less ambitious rehabilitation colonies on Rosebud consisting of a few housing units and sometimes irrigated garden projects.

The showcase project on Pine Ridge was the Red Shirt Table Development Association. The Red Shirt Table community—composed of the descendants of two bands—was described by an OIA staff member in *Indians at Work* as "one of the most backward" on the reservation before the project.[30] Here was an opportunity for the superintendent, who had designed the community plan at Rosebud before he was transferred to Pine Ridge, to demonstrate what could be done by working on the local level. Eighteen families were organized into a cooperative association. The federal government purchased land along the Cheyenne River, and the CCC built a dam and irrigation system. A community garden and crops for winter feed eventually comprised 130 acres of irrigated land. Seventeen houses were built, and some existing houses were repaired. A new day school building, a dairy barn, a poultry house, a root cellar, and a canning kitchen were constructed. A series of loans allowed the development of cattle and poultry production. Cooperative buying and marketing were organized. By 1942, the superintendent reported that the community members "had gotten themselves off the relief rolls, have their obligations and accounts strictly up to date, have their ranges stocked with Indian owned cattle, are managing a promising little irrigation area . . . and have their fences, corrals, and pastures divided according to good range management."[31] Other such integrated projects were launched on Pine Ridge, including the Slim Butte Land Use and Management Association, the Oglala Dam Project, and the Bear Creek Project.

The New Deal period thus witnessed the increasing importance of the OIA in the subsistence of the Lakota because of the increasing role of the OIA in the artificial reservation economies. Drought, insects, the Great Depression, and OIA relief and development programs had a combined and inexorable effect—reinforced dependence on the OIA. Politically, reinforced dependence further solidified the commonsense understanding among the Lakota that continued life on the reservations was not possible without the presence of the OIA. And this, naturally, strengthened the reluctance of the Lakota to challenge the presence of the OIA and its administrative domination.

## CHAPTER 6

# Disempowering Tribal Government

In 1945, the year he left the commissionership, John Collier summarized the Indian New Deal thus: "We tried to extend to the tribes a self-governing self-determination without any limit beyond the need to advance by stages to the goal." Collier's vision involved the Interior Department relinquishing its arbitrary power over Indians and allowing the tribal governments to govern. He saw the New Deal as informed by the British colonial policy of indirect rule, "in which the alien ruler is a minor and, ideally, a disappearing" factor, he wrote in his memoirs, the proper function of whom is "evocation, the opposite of imposition."[1]

Of course, the OIA did not disappear. There were plenty of limits on tribal self-government, and the OIA deployed several technologies of power for shaping the institutional form of the new tribal councils, for regulating their actions, and for retaining control over reservation affairs in the face of demands from the councils for expanded authority and for an attendant reduction of agency authority. These technologies of power ran the full gamut from "evocation" through "imposition." Some of the control might be legitimately interpreted as attempted empowerment: for example, providing technical assistance concerning tribal committee organization, drafting election and impeachment rules, and other procedures of the tribal councils. But much of the control—aggressive, preemptive technical assistance; retention of federal control over economic resources and over agency personnel on the reservations; and supervision of council actions by the secretary of the interior—had the effect of circumscribing the decision making and policy formulating power enjoyed by the tribal councils, and of preserving formidable authority over reservation affairs in the agency offices and in Washington. The net effect of the technologies of power deployed by the OIA was *disempowerment* of the tribal councils relative to the federal bureaucracy on the reservations.

The original draft of the Wheeler-Howard bill declared that it was the policy of Congress "that those functions of government now exercised over Indian reservations by the Federal Government through the Department of the Interior and the Office of Indian Affairs shall be gradually relinquished and transferred to the Indians." The bill also provided for organized tribes to begin the formal transfer of agency administrative functions and of the federal funding budgeted for such functions, to compel the removal of agency personnel for inefficiency or other cause, and to fill vacancies on the agency staffs. The OIA would be required to make regular reports to tribal officials on agency operations, and tribal officials were to be extended "free access to the records and files of the local agency." The Lakota people were advised of these intentions, it will be recalled from chapter 3, during Collier's visit to South Dakota in December 1933, in the OIA Indian self-government circular distributed in January 1934, during the Rapid City congress in March 1934, and during Henry Roe Cloud's campaigns on the reservations in April 1934.

While it is true that probably few Lakota voted in favor of the IRA or the constitutions because of the promises of self-government, when the first council members were elected under the provisions of the IRA constitutions in 1936, some of them looked to the promises made in 1933 and 1934 as a broad model for the development of tribal self-government. Some of the tribal council members had great expectations for Lakota self-government. In his inaugural address in 1936, the president of the new Oglala Sioux Tribal Council referred to Abraham Lincoln, the "great emancipator," and observed: "Today we have another emancipator in the name of John Collier, Commissioner of Indian Affairs."[2] He must have seen the new tribal constitution as an emancipation proclamation from the OIA. However, in practice— because of the technologies of power described in this chapter— organizing tribes did not proceed as anyone had expected in 1934. A mere four months after his inaugural address, the Oglala tribal president called OIA commitment to Oglala self-government "all bunk."[3] The object of this chapter is to demonstrate why Indian self-government in practice was "bunk" as far as the tribal councils were concerned. More specifically, the task is to examine the technologies of power deployed by the OIA and the Interior Department which ultimately disempowered the Lakota tribal councils.

## Technical Assistance

One technology of power which allowed the OIA to shape the form and actions of the tribal councils was technical assistance. From the beginning, the superintendents, their agency personnel, the Organization Division field agent for Lakota country, and others provided advice and instruction in instituting modern procedures to enhance the efficiency of the tribal councils. The Organization Division field agent was the most important provider of technical assistance. Joe Jennings, supervisor of the field agents, described tribal organization as a "tremendous educational program," and he emphasized in a memo to Collier the importance of following up with tribes after the first elections under the IRA. He argued that the ideal would be to have the field agent present at all meetings, and he saw the agent playing a role in assisting the councils in parliamentary procedure, organizing communities, preparing ordinances, organizing law and order schools for tribal judges and policemen, preparing financial records and minutes, explaining the provisions of constitutions and by-laws, and even reconciling the differences between fullblood and mixedblood elements. "In the very nature of the case it is inevitable that the field agent should exert a tremendous influence upon the deliberations and decisions of the councils. In his constant assistance to the councils in their endeavors relating to all the enterprises, law and order codes, etc., etc.—it is apparent that his guidance, intentionally or unintentionally, will go beyond the mechanics into the substance of the council's activities."[4]

Perhaps Jennings exaggerated the influence of the field agents— the Lakota field agent did not attend all meetings. But it is clear that the tribal councils were dependent upon the field agent and other experts. The Solicitor's Office pointed out in 1939 that "many Indian tribes, although they have organized under a constitution and by-laws and have received a corporate charter, are frequently at a loss to understand not only what the provisions of these documents mean, what rights and powers they contain, but how the organizations they have set up can be used by them to develop a healthy tribal community life." When it is recognized that the field agent was a bilingual, college-educated Lakota who was willing to instruct the councilmen in how to organize, it is reasonable to conclude that the field agent's advice was often eagerly sought and that he had a significant role in shaping tribal government in Lakota country. Indeed, it would be difficult to explain why the OIA appointed Indian men to its field agent positions around the country unless it was because these men could serve as more effective intermediaries than could the regular agency or other non-Indian personnel.[5]

There were many instances of tutelage by the field agent among the Lakota. He headed the work of drafting the election rules for the first election of councilmen on Pine Ridge in 1936. He instructed the members of the Rosebud Sioux Tribal Council at their January 1939 meeting in such technical matters as the credentials of voting members, procedures for adopting resolutions, how to achieve a quorum, and how to expel members for cause. In 1941 the field agent and the head community worker at Pine Ridge assisted the Oglala Sioux Tribal Council to draft impeachment rules and to conduct the proceedings for the impeachment of the tribal president. In the same year the OIA directed the field agent to assist a Rosebud tribal delegation to Washington in organizing their business in order to discuss "objectively" and justify their requests with "factual material," as opposed to "rumors, opinions, and desires, unsupported by facts."[6]

The cases of technical assistance described so far might be seen as empowerment since they involved helping the councils to conduct business and to deal effectively with the federal bureaucracy. Sometimes, however, what the OIA saw as technical assistance was aggressive and preempted tribal decision making and policy formulation. One case involved the application of the Rosebud Sioux law and order code. A model code had been circulated to the tribal councils for consideration by the Solicitor's Office in 1936. After drafts were approved by the councils and reviewed by the Solicitor's Office, the codes were formally adopted by the councils and approved by the secretary of the interior in 1937. The codes of the Rosebud and Oglala Sioux tribes were, like the constitutions, almost indistinguishable; they were drafted by the Solicitor's Office (and a private attorney who drafted the domestic relations chapters for the tribal councils) with no significant input from Lakota people. The tribal councils, the

tribal judges, and the tribal police forces, therefore, had trouble understanding the content of the codes.[7]

The codes included an ordinance requiring an annual, five-dollar
license for operating a public dance hall. This ordinance was opposed
in the fall of 1937 by many Lakota, particularly older fullbloods, who
resented the council's authority to tax them for traditional dancing.
The old dealers saw the ordinance as an attack on tribal custom. Because of this outcry, the Rosebud superintendent asked the tribal
council to issue an interpretation of the ordinance on the question of
traditional dancing. The tribal law and order committee was unable
to render an interpretation of the council's own legislative intent in
the matter, however, because the ordinance had been drafted not by
the council but by the Solicitor's Office as part of the model law and
order code. The superintendent and an OIA law enforcement officer
then drafted an interpretation of this ordinance for the council's consideration. They saw the "intent" of the council to be assigning responsibility for the maintenance of order at dances and not the eradication of native custom. They also opined that the ordinance did not
apply to community or tribal celebrations held in arbors, government
buildings, or reservation dance halls (where *omaha, kahomni,* rabbit,
and owl dances—all social dances—were held).[8]

The superintendent reported to Collier that "quite a number of
the council expressed that ordinance number 32 [the dance hall ordi-
nance] is a part of the law and order code as approved by the Department, and that its enforcement and interpretation is a matter for
them to decide." The tribal chairman, however, thought that the
commissioner should have an opportunity to comment before the ordinance was enforced, given the opposition from the old dealers.[9]

The matter received a great deal of attention from the Washington
OIA staff and the Solicitor's Office. The specialists in the Indian Organization Division and Applied Anthropology Unit of the OIA were
decidedly against the ordinance because they saw it as a direct attack
upon Indian custom and individual rights. Evidently, no one in the
OIA realized that the ordinance had been part of the code originally
drafted by the Solicitor's Office for consideration by the council, and
was modeled on dance hall ordinances found in state and municipal
codes.

Joe Jennings of the Organization Division detected an "evident
intent to suppress Indian dances. If Indian dances, ceremonials, or

customs are subject to tribal taxation, it would be entirely possible
for an unfriendly council to suppress or greatly curtail such activities.
As a matter of fact, even so small a tax as five dollars may eliminate
dancing in some homes and communities." Jennings cited Collier's
Indian religious and cultural freedom circular of 1934 (see chapter 3)
and noted:

> Unfortunately the viewpoint of your administration . . . is not uni-
> versally accepted by . . . certain groups of Indians, notably mixed-
> bloods. . . . On many . . . reservations the fullblood Indians are in the
> minority, and Indian culture, ceremonials, and dances are looked upon
> with disdain by a large number of those belonging to the tribe. . . . As
> a matter of fact, several Indian Service people and Indians are taking
> the position that if a majority of Indians through their council wish
> to eliminate Indian customs and ceremonies, this is their privilege.
> There is a danger that Indian Organization might in this manner be-
> come a more effective means of stifling Indian culture than was the
> old Indian Bureau.[10]

Scudder Mekeel, head of the Applied Anthropology Unit, also saw
an intent to suppress native custom in the ordinance, but he argued
that the OIA's reply to the council should be based on federal constitutional or other legal considerations regarding civil liberties: "I do
not believe it would be wise or effective to bring in anything regarding
the protection of Indian customs. I think that the matter is purely
one of individual rights as well as the rights of minority groups, and
the matter should be approached from this angle rather than to bring
in our own viewpoint as to the value of Indian ways."[11]

The staff of the Solicitor's Office took a different tack. Assistant
Solicitor Charlotte Westwood advised Jennings that from the point of
view of federal constitutional law, the tribal council had "large discretion in the regulation of public dances and public dance halls in the
interests of the health and morals of the tribe." Felix Cohen, who may
well have drafted the ordinance, argued that neither the issue of Indian custom nor that of civil liberties should be brought to the attention of the council. He did not see the ordinance as a case of suppression, since it did not discriminate against native dances and was
similar to off-reservation municipal ordinances pertaining to public
dance halls. The interpretation rendered by the superintendent which
exempted traditional dances from the ordinance was an arbitrary ad-

ministrative construction. The Solicitor's Office, thus, argued for protecting tribal council autonomy from intervention by the OIA.[12]

The letter Collier dispatched to the Rosebud Sioux Tribal Council
did not mention civil liberties or Indian custom. Collier did suggest,
however, that a dance hall should be defined more clearly than it was
in the superintendent's interpretation, and he suggested using the
state definition. In conformity with that definition, he pointed out
that the ordinance should not apply to "invitation dances not held for
profit, or non-profit seeking festivals, occasions, dances, etc., which
are matters of tradition or religion."[13]

The only kind of dance hall operated by Indians on Rosebud Reservation was the traditional dance hall, and in pointing out that the
tribal ordinance should not apply to it, Collier would prevent the
council from regulating the most common form of public gathering
on the reservation, next to church assemblies. Regulating dancing
had been a clear policy of the superintendents in Lakota country prior
to Collier's 1934 circular on Indian religious and cultural freedom. On
Rosebud dances had been limited to one per month, and the Rosebud
Tribal Council had been used by the superintendent to regulate dancing (see chapter 2). One concern was that the dances not interfere
with Indian industry or with school attendance. Another concern involved public health: dance hall gatherings were considered opportunities for the spread of infectious diseases.[14]

There was also a concern regarding public morals. The *kahomni*,
rabbit, and owl dances, which appeared in Lakota country in the
1920s and in which men and women danced together, were blamed by
the superintendents and by some Indian people for problems because
of the drinking, sexual license, and fighting associated with them. In
1932 the judges in the court of Indian offenses on Rosebud advised
the superintendent that the "vulgar modern Indian dances" presented
a problem. They reported that "many of the family trouble and adultery cases which go on trial here are found to have propagated from
the immodesty of these dances," and that an alarming number of girls
and boys were "ruined morally" by the rabbit and owl dances.[15]

Later the same year, the Rosebud superintendent pointed out in a
memo to the commissioner the need for a law on the reservations
similar to the state law pertaining to dance hall licensing. He cited as
evidence the fact that rabbit and owl dances were different from the
older *omaha*, were "indulged in for grosser purposes," and "might

compare in purpose and results with the night club dances of ill re-
pute in our cities." Rabbit dancers were "likely to figure largely in
social welfare problems—sex offenses, broken homes, and the like."[16]

The intention of both the superintendent and the tribal judges
here was probably to protect the integrity of the family and to prevent
illegitimate births because of concerns over inheritance of property
and indigents on the ration rolls. One man, who became an old dealer
by 1939, complained to the superintendent in 1933 that the rabbit
dance was responsible for "drinking, taking women not they own
Breaking up family Making a person lazy good for nothing." There
was clearly wide support among both administrators and the Lakota
for regulating at least some dancing on the reservation.[17]

It is impossible to determine if the Rosebud Sioux Tribal Council
members in 1937 were intent on suppressing Lakota tradition or on
protecting the family and public welfare when they contemplated enforcing the dance hall ordinance which had been written for them by
the Interior Department. In either case, the OIA reformers in Washington would not allow tribal regulation of Indian dancing to the extent
that they could impose their interpretation on the ordinance. They
effectively preempted any tribal council decision on the matter via
the issuance of a (nonbinding—although the tribal council may not
have known this) legal opinion.

This is precisely the kind of preemptive technical assistance
which some of the legal staff in the Solicitor's Office believed was an
infringement upon tribal self-government. The Solicitor's Office was
not responsible for the administration of Indian reservations, for formulating or executing policy, or for protecting New Deal legislation
from repeal by a hostile Congress. The staff was therefore much more
prepared than was the senior OIA staff to avoid interference in tribal
government. In a case involving the intention on the part of some OIA
personnel to intervene in the Rosebud Sioux Tribal Council's enact-
ment of the domestic relations chapter of the law and order code—
which was not subject to supervision by the Interior Department—
Assistant Solicitor Kenneth Meiklejohn warned: "if self-government
is to mean anything it seems to me that it should mean that the Indians will themselves attempt to work out their own problems on the
basis of their own experience rather than on the basis of the work
of government personnel or other technical and specialized experts
which necessarily carries with it the voice of authority." Meiklejohn

believed that it was difficult to know exactly who in fact was an "expert" in the extension of modern public administration to Indian communities, and that it was best to allow the new tribal governments to work out their own interpretations and applications, rather than for them to rely on technical advice from the government. This position, protective of the integrity—what is now called the sovereignty—of tribal government, however, did not prevail in the OIA.[18]

## Secretarial Supervision

Another technology of power which limited decision making and policy implementation by the tribal councils is found in the provisions for supervision written into the tribal constitutions. Some acts of the councils were invalid without the approval of the secretary of the interior. Other acts were subject to review by the secretary of the interior. The review procedure was deployed on several occasions to protect what were seen by the OIA and the Solicitor's Office as the civil liberties of tribal members regarding the tribal councils. An additional effect, however, was to remove the power of policy formulation from the tribal councils.[19]

In January 1938 the Rosebud Sioux Tribal Council unanimously enacted an ordinance which required medicine men and practitioners of the peyote religion and of *yuwipi*—a healing ceremony—to obtain a five-dollar license and to submit written descriptions of their ceremonies subject to approval by the council. Violation was punishable by a fine of sixty dollars plus court fees and/or thirty days' labor. The council also passed an ordinance outlawing the use of peyote for purposes other than religion by the Native American Church and limiting the use of peyote by church members to not more than one peyote button or one glass of "peyote soup" per member. The OIA had attempted to suppress the peyote religion before 1934, and the council members probably had this in mind when they enacted these ordinances. The ordinances, as part of the law and order code, were subject to secretarial review.[20]

The two ordinances had been proposed by a council committee in the fall of 1937. Assistant Commissioner Zimmerman had examined the proposed legislation at the time and had expressed to the superintendent his "sincere doubt as to the propriety of either or both of these ordinances." The central question was "the tribe's right to control or interfere with the individual rights and liberties of its members as guaranteed to them by the Constitution of the United States." The proposed legislation was also in conflict with Collier's Indian religious and cultural freedom circular of 1934: "Since this circular lays down the policy of this Office and the Department, it cannot be expected that an ordinance which is in conflict with such policy would be approved by this Office or the Department. I believe the council has gone too far by fixing the number of peyote buttons which may be used." Zimmerman believed that the council had the right to prohibit peyote only where it was not connected with religious activities. He thought that licensing medicine men was appropriate, but that it would be both impractical and unnecessary, given the purposes of the council in the ordinance, for medicine men to provide a full written description of their ceremonies in their license applications.[21]

With the OIA's position in Washington made so clear, the superintendent disapproved the ordinance on peyote when it was enacted by the council in January 1938, contending that it was a violation of OIA policy as outlined in the Indian religious and cultural freedom circular. He approved the ordinance requiring the licensing of peyote men, medicine men, and *yuwipi* men, but warned the council that it must be interpreted in such a way so as not to interfere with religious freedom. That is, it could only apply to practitioners who presumed to cure. The superintendent also quoted to the council from Zimmerman's letter on the inappropriateness of asking practitioners to provide full descriptions of their ceremonies, implying that this provision of the ordinance was not approved. The superintendent's veto of the peyote ordinance and his amendment of the licensing ordinance were not referred by the council to the secretary of the interior for his consideration. The Rosebud Sioux Tribal Council apparently was unaware in 1938 that it could appeal vetoes of its actions by the superintendent to the secretary of the interior.[22]

The OIA used the procedures for secretarial review to intervene in another civil liberties case on Rosebud in 1937. The council had unanimously enacted an ordinance which prohibited meetings of individuals and groups opposed to it without authorization from the chairman. In the preamble to the ordinance, the council pointed out that the old dealers were meeting as an alternative governing body— the Treaty Council. Since the tribal constitution empowered only the Rosebud Sioux Tribal Council to govern, the tribal council deemed the old dealers to be in violation of the provisions in the constitution enumerating the powers of the duly elected council. Violation of the ordinance was punishable by a thirty-dollar fine and/or fifteen days in jail. The ordinance was subject to secretarial review and was rescinded by the superintendent as a "violation of the right of free speech as guaranteed by the constitution of the United States," even though he was in sympathy with the problem caused by the old dealers.[23]

This ordinance was no doubt viewed by the council members, as were the peyote and dance hall ordinances described above, as consistent with the power which the superintendent had wielded in the pursuit of public order on the reservations before the New Deal, and, with all the New Deal rhetoric about transferring administration from the OIA to the tribes, it must have come as a surprise when the superintendent vetoed council control of political assemblies as a violation of the right of free speech. The tribal council was being coerced by the OIA into a stricter adherence to the federal bill of rights than the OIA had previously required of its own agency personnel.

The rescinded ordinance was referred to the commissioner for reconsideration, along with a memo drafted by the tribal secretary. Despite the fact that the IRA constitution in effect dissolved the pre-IRA council, the secretary wrote, "the old gang still continue to hold their meetings about three days of each week, claiming that their council is superior, legitimate, and legally authorized to exist under article twelve of the treaty of 1868." This created the problem of "more than one tribal council" on the reservation. He described the threat posed by the Treaty Council:

> Here are some of their programs: Agitate the abandonment of all mixedbloods and also to include those that fail to declare themselves in favor of the Old Deal. Advocate the immediate payment of all claims now pending and subsequent release of Indians from Bureau control. Eligibility for per capita payments derived from claims to include only those that are on the rolls approved by their council. To circulate a petition to be signed by members of trust land only who thereafter will constitute the Rosebud Sioux Tribe.[24]

The Treaty Council must have seemed seditious indeed to the tribal council, and it is easy enough to imagine any state or local government enacting similar legislation to combat an unauthorized political body which claimed to be the legal seat of government. The response of nation-states to such political activity is, as the American and other civil wars demonstrate, to send troops. The tribal council merely wanted to limit the Treaty Council meetings to one per month, to require open discussion at the meetings, to have tribal council representatives present to answer charges and to correct misinformation, and to provide adult education on treaties, the history of the tribe, and the IRA. The secretary concluded: "Personally I believe that this is within the jurisdiction of the new council to adopt this ordinance without the approval of higher authority as majority rules, and thereby the old council should have been dissolved accordingly." While the wording might not be perfectly concise, the ordinance represented the sentiment of the council. "You will note," the secretary wrote, "that this ordinance was adopted by unanimous vote and was considered more important than many other ordinances acted upon."[25]

The superintendent's disapproval was sustained by the OIA. In a letter to the tribal chairman, Assistant Commissioner Zimmerman pointed out that the ordinance might be used to repress any minority on the reservation unpopular with the council, and that the solution to the Treaty Council agitation was "education work."[26]

A third deployment of the supervisory function in intervening in tribal council actions in order to protect the civil liberties of tribal members took place on Pine Ridge in 1942 and 1943. In January 1942 the Oglala Sioux Tribal Council enacted an ordinance making it illegal "for any Indian to sell, furnish, give away, or offer to sell, furnish or give away; or have in his possession peyote." The impetus in this action had been a petition with over 2,000 signatures circulated by missionaries and others on the reservation opposed to the Native American Church. The ordinance was pigeonholed by the superintendent, and when it was enacted again three months later, he disapproved it. He gave as his reason in a letter to the tribal secretary the fact that the ordinance would in effect outlaw the Native American Church, and thus would constitute a violation of freedom of religion:

> In searching through the constitution and by-laws and the code of Indian offenses [law and order code], I do not find any authorization whereby the Tribal Council is empowered to act in any way which infringes the right of religious liberty. While it may be that the council is not bound by the Bill of Rights of the Federal Constitution,

nevertheless it would appear that some constitutional authorization should exist before the Tribal Council could have the authority to pass an ordinance which in effect is in the nature of a limitation on religious practices.[27]

In 1943 the council again enacted an ordinance prohibiting peyote, carrying a penalty of not more than six months' labor, a fine of not more then $360, or both. The superintendent again rescinded the ordinance and remarked in a report to Collier: "Whether a Tribal Council and a Tribe of Indians is bound in this respect by the Constitution of the United States, I don't know." But he thought the ordinance was questionable on policy grounds because he considered the leaders of the Native American Church to be sincere in their religious convictions; their use of peyote was not for the purpose of intoxication.[28]

The vetoed ordinance was referred to the secretary of the interior by the council. The Solicitor's Office drafted a letter to the council approving the ordinance over the superintendent's veto and circulated this draft in the OIA for comment prior to submitting it to the secretary for his signature. Joe Jennings of the Organization Division was not in agreement with the letter. He concurred with the superintendent that the ordinance infringed upon religious liberty and quoted from the superintendent's report: "if the tribal council can legislate away the right of the Native American Church to use peyote for sacramental purposes, it could do the same concerning the use of wine in the sacrament observed by Christian churches." He also pointed out—as he had in the case of the Rosebud dance hall ordinance—that the ordinance was in conflict with Collier's Indian religious and cultural freedom circular, and it was unconstitutional in terms of the bill of rights. Assistant Commissioner Zimmerman subsequently advised the secretary of the interior that the ordinance was technically within the council's scope of power, but he suggested nonetheless sustaining the superintendent's veto with an explanation that approval of the ordinance would be forthcoming if the religious use of peyote was exempted.[29]

The acting secretary did sustain the superintendent's veto, informing the tribal president: "Although I am reluctant to refuse approval to a unanimous expression of the wishes of the duly elected tribal representatives in a matter of this sort, I find that the ordinance as drafted infringes upon the religious liberties which the Department should be vigilant to protect." He added that the ordinance would meet with approval if it exempted the "bona fide sacramental use of peyote in religious ceremonies." This decision was based upon an Interior Department administrative desideratum—the protection and preservation of native religion—not upon law, since the Solicitor's Office recognized that the guarantee of religious liberty in the federal constitution did *not* apply to tribal governments. It should be realized that, at the time, Arizona, Colorado, Kansas, Montana, New Mexico, North Dakota, South Dakota, Wyoming, Texas, and the Navajo Tribe had anti-peyote laws on the books. The Oglala Sioux Tribal Council thus had considerably less autonomy in regulating its internal affairs, because of supervision by the secretary of the interior, than did the states and a non-IRA tribe.[30]

The Lakota had been told by the New Deal reformers that Indian self-government was about the *transfer* of power from the OIA to the tribal councils and about allowing the tribal councils to operate like local non-Indian governments. The above cases of the use of the supervisory function indicate, however, that the OIA and the Interior Department would not allow the tribal governments to wield the kind of power previously enjoyed by the superintendents or currently enjoyed by state and local governments.

It might be argued that while the execution of the supervisory function described here disempowered the tribal councils, it *empowered* Lakota tribal members. Is it not true that by removing decision making from the tribal governments and retaining it in the OIA and/ or other offices in the Interior Department, secretarial supervision protected Lakota minorities against zealous tribal councils which would infringe on their political, religious, and cultural expression? Certainly the particular tribal members who were the targets of these tribal ordinances must have wanted protection and must have seen the actions of the tribal councils as violations of the Lakota model of three-fourths majority rule. But it must be remembered that it was only the faulty model of tribal self-government devised by the Washington reformers—which did not include a tribal bill of rights or judicial review by a tribal court (see chapter 4)—which made it necessary to go beyond the machinery of tribal government to protect tribal members.

There may actually have been tribal governing machinery in place during the New Deal that could have handled the matters subjected to secretarial supervision. On each reservation there was a superior tribal court composed of three judges nominated by the tribal councils, and paid and appointed by the commissioner. Here were judicial bodies insulated from direct intervention by the tribal legislative bodies. Indeed, the OIA was adamant to protect the superior judges from interference from the tribal councils, refusing to allow the councils to control directly the appointment of judges, much to the consternation of some of the new dealers. The superior courts might have been drafted to execute a supreme court-like function of judicial review (civil liberties amendments might also have been added to the tribal constitutions). The OIA, however, never considered such a possibility. Rather, the Organization Division and the OIA in general were content to expend their energies in scrutinizing and tinkering with—*supervising*—the actions of the tribal councils.[31]

## Administrative Control of Resources via the Federal Budget

Another technology of power by which the OIA maintained its administrative prerogatives and prevented the expansion of the authority of the tribal councils was based on the OIA's control of federal funding. Control by purse strings allowed the agencies—as opposed to the tribal councils—to determine how the critical New Deal resources (discussed in chapter 5) would be administered.

In the IRA revolving loan program on Rosebud, the OIA used its control of funding to dominate the decision making process. An applicant first filed with the local community credit committee, which assisted her or him in completing the OIA forms, explained the regulations and provisions of the OIA loan agreements, and, in theory, either approved or disapproved the application, sending along a confidential report on the approved applicants to the central—tribal council—credit committee. The central credit committee was—also in theory—responsible for acting on applications sent from the community committees, deciding on requests for extensions or modifications of loan agreements, and other matters. Applications approved by the central committee were then forwarded to the agency Extension Department, which worked out operating plans with the applicants. Applications for short-term, fully-secured loans could be approved by the superintendent. Other applications had to be approved by the district credit agent in Pierre.[32]

In actual practice, the OIA had effective control of decision making at all levels of the loan procedure, and it handled all accounting for credit operations. In 1939 a tribal delegation to Washington complained to Collier that the OIA district farm agents actually decided who would and would not receive loans, and that the central credit committee had little authority in managing the loan funds, contrary to what the Rosebud people had been told in the charter campaign about tribal control of credit. There was concern also about the severe backlog of loan applications pending with the OIA; the delegation was convinced that the tribal credit committee could do a better job of expediting loans to borrowers. In the same year the Indian law specialists in the Solicitor's Office issued a memo in which they criticized OIA credit operations: tribal credit programs were tied up in a sea of federal regulations and forms and were administered by OIA personnel, while the understanding in 1934 had been that tribes would administer credit. Collier responded to the tribal delegation, nevertheless, that he did not understand how they could have assumed that disbursement of the credit funds would be turned over to the tribe, since these funds were under the control of the comptroller general. In short, the federal government controlled the money, and it would control the credit program.[33]

In 1940 another tribal delegation complained: "The situation on the Rosebud Indian Reservation under this program is that the tribal council is a figure head." The local agency office dominated the tribal credit committee, and even purchased livestock and equipment for the loan clients, not allowing them any choice in the purchases. In 1943 the council passed a resolution to remove the agency extension agent for "insufficiency"—a reference to the application backlog—and to have the credit committee assume responsibility for the agency extension files. The resolution was beyond the scope of the tribe's constitutional powers, and it was not acted on by the agency. A tribal delegation to Washington that same year also asked for the removal of the extension agent, the complaint being that he attended credit committee meetings without permission or invitation and attempted to influence the decisions.[34]

Rehabilitation and CCC projects were another New Deal economic resource flowing from the federal government over which the

OIA would not delegate decision-making or policy formulation power to the tribal councils. The Rosebud Sioux Tribal Council often complained officially to the OIA about its CCC programs. Too much of the funding was spent on machinery, which replaced Indian labor and required skilled non-Indian operators whose salaries also absorbed much of the funding. Nonmember Indians were given employment on these projects. Projects benefitted the agency or big cattle operators but were of little use to people in the communities, councilmen complained, and they were not consulted in project planning. The projects were sited far apart so that enrollees had to leave their homes for extended periods and stay in the camps. In addition, as a tribal committee pointed out in 1941, CCC enrollees became "wage minded" and bartered away their houses, neglected their crops and livestock, and expected to depend on wages for a living. The problem was that CCC employment was insecure: "The Indian in securing work is led to believe that his problems are solved and his worries are over. But, without due notice all the projects would cease to operate. . . . This leaves the poor Indian poorer than ever and stranded in the agency with no work and no home with bigger problems to worry over and to go on the ration list."[35]

On more than one occasion the Rosebud Sioux Tribal Council would not approve the annual CCC budget because of these issues. In 1939 the council rejected the OIA's annual Rehabilitation budget because red tape allowed the OIA to "control and dominate the council and the whole reservation." It adopted a resolution to use the $38,700 in Rehabilitation funds not for the construction of OIA-planned Rehabilitation colonies but for even distribution across the reservation to pay for the repair and construction of Indian homes. The council voted to put the CCC budget to the same use in 1941. Of course, the council's authority as provided for in the constitution was only "to advise the Secretary of the Interior" on appropriation estimates and federal projects—to rubber stamp federal projects; council approval was not required to expend funds. As William Zimmerman put it to Congressman Francis Case (R., S.D.), the council could "comment on" any proposed project or budget. It had the "right of recommendations," but its opinion was in no way binding on the federal government. On at least one occasion, the OIA simply threatened to remove entirely funding for a Rehabilitation project—the Two Kettle irrigation project—unless the council reconsidered its disapproval of an OIA-drafted budget.[36]

In July 1940 the Rosebud Sioux tribal employment committee adopted a set of recommendations for CCC, Rehabilitation, and agency Road Department work on the reservation. Employees with dependents would be given preference when discharges became necessary, employment of both a man and his wife would be avoided, and nontribal members not married into the tribe were not to be given work. The superintendent disapproved the recommendations, citing the need for "efficiency," as well as the obvious need for relief employment focused on by the councilmen, and admonished: "The employment committee must bear in mind that their activities are limited to cooperative effort [which is to say, an advisory capacity only] and that they do not have power to create and promulgate rules and regulations."[37]

The council referred the vetoed ordinance to the secretary of the interior and pointed out that "the employment situation as it is now in effect on Rosebud Reservation is beyond the control of the Rosebud Sioux Tribal Council and the [agency] Department heads are pretty much in control to the extent that they are dictators when it comes to who shall be employed and who shall not be employed and at times are very arbitrary in their dealings with the affairs of the tribe in general." The agency was giving priority to "efficiency and production" and not the "practical relief situation." The tribal council issued work cards for relief employment, but this procedure did not have any bearing on who worked or for how long. The tribal secretary wrote to Secretary Ickes: "The welfare of the tribe is in such shape that it needs relief assistance. The Tribal Council has taken the stand that all works, CCC-ID, Indian Road Works, and Rehabilitation Program and other works be managed, that the money from such works be earned where it is most needed and where it will do the most good to the most people of the tribe." It is clear that the council members were attempting to influence the expenditure of federal money and the execution of OIA development projects in a way consistent with the desires of their constituents. They were not successful in this endeavor.[38]

The conflict between the tribal councils attempting to expand their power and the agencies attempting to execute OIA policy and protect their power and prerogatives is also clear in a dispute over repayment cattle at Pine Ridge in 1943. The tribal council passed a resolution calling for an "equitable distribution" of the cattle. The superintendent justified his refusal to abide by the resolution to Collier:

> What this resolution purports to do is to make it more or less mandatory on personnel to distribute replacement cattle according to the decision of the Executive Committee [of the council]. A very good example of what happens when the Tribal Council attempts to deal directly with economic affairs is illustrated in the first block of rehabilitation homes that were provided here. The Council parcelled out 52 of these houses over the reservation as a kind of political favor. The results were not good. Repayments lagged. About one-third of them were vacated.

In the opinion of the superintendent, "The Executive Committee does not have the facilities for making the necessary study and the detailed planning relationships with those who are to take care of the cattle." In short, the tribal council, in the view of the superintendent, could not be counted on to identify and funnel resources to good credit risks or, in general, to execute effectively development policy.[39]


## Authority over Reservation Personnel

Closely related to OIA control of resources was control over reservation personnel. Both of these were described by the agencies as "administrative" matters, not matters "in which the tribal council has any authority." The Lakota people had been told by the reformers, however, that they would be given some control over OIA personnel, and the tribal councils sought to make the agencies responsive to the Lakota by having a say in the hiring, firing, and supervision of regular federal personnel.[40]

This issue was apparent from the first meeting of the Oglala Sioux Tribal Council in 1936. Various OIA agency department heads appeared at that meeting to describe their areas of operation. The intent on the part of the OIA Washington office was to allow the councilmen to learn about agency administrative functions in order to facilitate cooperation between the councils and the agencies, and in preparation for transfer of some functions to the tribe—at some unspecified time in the future. The tribal president, however, saw this as an opportunity to make the federal personnel accountable to the Oglala, and he conducted the interviews on the council floor as if he was chairing a congressional investigation, interrogating the federal personnel in an adversarial manner. The physician in charge of the agency hospital was questioned by the council about the qualifications of medical personnel, the danger of x-rays, what kinds of surgery the staff was competent to perform, and whether or not the director was biased against chiropractic. The president informed the physician that the council would examine the mileage records of government cars used by hospital physicians, presumably to uncover waste. The president added toward the end of the meeting, after other OIA personnel had been questioned: "I think that we could compel the various departments to appear whether they want to come or not . . . and if they refuse to open up their books we could demand them to open them up but we don't want to use such harsh methods."[41]

Notwithstanding his earlier promises of Indian control over federal personnel, Collier and the other Washington reformers were probably startled by the tone of the Oglala tribal president. Collier responded to an aggressive letter from the executive committee: "If the council or executive committee endeavors in the very beginning to take over and to deal with every phase of self-government or to go into matters with which it is not familiar or over which it has no control or authority, such as reservation personnel, and so conduct its business as to show a lack of responsibility and a sense of fairness and justice, then the council will not succeed."[42]

With tribal organization begun under such strained relations at Pine Ridge, the superintendent requested that the field agent and Associate Solicitor Charlotte Westwood, who were on the reservation in June 1936 to discuss the charter of incorporation, meet with the executive committee to discuss the powers of the council. The tribal president started by asking about the clause in the IRA requiring the secretary of the interior to establish a procedure for preferential Indian hiring in the OIA. He complained that this procedure had not been carried out on Pine Ridge, and he clearly thought the council should begin filling agency positions with candidates of its own choice. The field agent and Westwood told the executive committee that the council had the power only to recommend candidates for federal appointment. Westwood also advised the executive committee that the supervision of federal employees on the reservation was not within the scope of council powers. There were hostile comments from the executive committee regarding, among other things, an opinion that the OIA should be abolished.[43]

The Oglala Sioux Tribal Council went so far in 1945 as to enact unanimously a resolution to remove the superintendent immediately:

> Whereas: That to retain [the superintendent] would not only be detrimental to his interests, but also detrimental for the best interests of the Sioux people, and the Reorganization Act. That to retain him would only cause disunity and friction among the council members, the Sioux people and the Indian Offices in Washington, D.C. and the Chicago office. The council and people feel that [the superintendent] has not fulfilled the obligations of his office for the best interests of the Interior Dept. controlling the Indian Service. That the council has a right to judge the Indian Service on how well it meets its tasks of readjusting itself in its relation with our tribe.[44]

This conflict with the superintendent derived from the insistence of some of the Oglala tribal council members that they had authority to fill agency vacancies and to transfer agency personnel—as the Lakota had been promised in 1933 and 1934. The council had specifically attempted to remove an agency-appointed superior court judge (a federal position) and replace him with a man chosen by the council, and to transfer from the reservation an employee in the agency Forestry and Grazing Department.[45] The superintendent asserted that the council had become vocal shortly after the tribal president had attended a meeting of the new National Congress of American Indians in Denver in 1944 and had visited at the OIA office now relocated to Chicago. At those places he had met Robert Yellowtail, a Crow who had campaigned for the commissionership before Collier was replaced by William A. Brophy. According to the superintendent, a tribal delegation "came back imbued with the notion that the council has great power, and that it can get personnel removed and replace them with Indians of the Council's selection."[46]

Of course the OIA did not yield to the Oglala agitators. Commissioner Brophy eventually ordered an investigation of the situation by D'Arcy McNickle, a Flathead in the Tribal Operations Division (which had replaced the Organization Division), and by an OIA law enforcement officer. The OIA had no intention, however, of delegating authority over agency personnel to the Oglala Sioux Tribal Council, regardless of the promises in 1934. Senior OIA staff in Washington believed that the Pine Ridge superintendent was doing an exceptional job, even if the Oglala Sioux Tribal Council voted unanimously to remove him. For the period of April 1945 through March 1946, this superintendent received an "excellent" rating from Assistant Commissioner Zimmerman on his efficiency report.[47]

Most remarkable is the rating of "outstanding" the superintendent received for "Effectiveness in developing Indian participation and Tribal Self-Government." This man was clearly hostile in principle to tribal self-government, insisting at a conference in 1938 that it was not the "native Sioux way," and was therefore illegitimate, and that the most that a tribal council could do was to "facilitate the rapprochement of [OIA] employees and Indian populace." When in 1942 the superintendents were asked by the OIA to comment on possibilities for transferring some administrative functions to the Indians, he did not even mention the tribal council. During the furor in 1945, he reported to the OIA: "anyone who knows anything about the Sioux knows that . . . any . . . elected officer cannot truly represent the Sioux people." D'Arcy McNickle, in the report on his investigation of the troubles at Pine Ridge in 1945, described this superintendent as never having "wholly understood or been in sympathy with the idea of self-government for the Sioux people." It is no wonder that the Oglala Sioux Tribal Council unanimously voted to remove him.[48]

But he was not removed and, instead, was given the highest rating by the OIA for his accomplishments in fostering Indian self-government. He was transferred from Pine Ridge with a promotion and pay raise to another jurisdiction the following year. This action was perhaps a partial victory for the Oglala Sioux Tribal Council—the superintendent was gone—but it was also consistent with OIA retention of control over personnel on the reservations. It reinforced the dictum that where the federal government paid the salary, the federal government hired, fired, and supervised the employee.[49]

## The Threat of Empowerment

It was thus through technical assistance, secretarial supervision, and control of critical resources and reservation personnel that the OIA maintained power on the reservations and avoided transfer of its power to the tribal councils. Why were these technologies of power allowed to disempower the tribal councils, especially given the New Deal Indian reformers' stated goals? The purposeful resistance to the empowerment of tribal governments and to the concomitant reduction of OIA power, even in the face of aggressive demands by the tribal councils, was a result of several factors.

One was the OIA reformers' perceived—if unstated—need for central control of the articulation and execution of New Deal Indian policy, if this policy was to come to fruition as hoped for by the reformers. The irony of the Indian New Deal, as is now abundantly clear, is that it was a non-Indian model for Indian self-government. Indians were to govern themselves, but not in ways of their own choosing. Regardless of the reformers' stated intention of local decision making, the senior reformers in the OIA in Washington had a very specific agenda: sustained-yield use of Indian resources by Indians, preservation of native culture, and democratic, civic-minded tribal councils cooperating with the OIA in a gradual transfer of administrative functions—the rate of transfer determined by the OIA, not the tribes. Tribal council members, as Collier and his colleagues quickly came to realize, could not be counted on to accept, understand, or behave in conformity with this agenda—even though it was conceived by the reformers in the supposed best interests of Indians. This was partly because Indian people had their own agenda, based on the perspective from the reservations. It was also because the tribal government machinery, based on the reformers' model, was faulty (although this structural faultiness was not recognized in Washington): there were no local, self-correcting checks and balances to minimize abuses. Tribal governments, therefore (from the perspective of the OIA), could not be allowed to control the administration of the reservations or to operate in the limited areas of jurisdiction allowed them without close scrutiny.

Felix Cohen recalled that the senior OIA staff members in Washington were actually threatened by the notion of Indian self-government. While each division head was prepared to support self-government in principle and in every administrative area other than his own, each argued that his own area of responsibility was too complex to be turned over to an unsupervised and inexperienced tribal council. This resistance was based on a fear among the senior OIA reformers that, if left to their own devices, tribal councils would do some very un-New Deal things—such as ignoring their constitutions, outlawing the Native American Church and political opposition, suppressing native dances, and harassing medicine men. True, the agencies had done such things for years, but this was inconsistent with the reformers' vision of an Indian New Deal.[50]

Truly empowered tribal councils—which is to say, tribal councils transferred power from the federal government as originally planned in Washington in 1933 and 1934—also might do some very unbusinesslike things—such as giving loans to bad credit risks, putting constituents before infrastructure in development projects, and firing or transferring agency personnel who displeased them. Such activities were simply too incongruous with the reformers' agenda, even if they were perfectly consistent with what any non-Indian local or state politician might do.

All these activities would also draw fire from the opponents of the New Deal, both Indian and non-Indian, both on Lakota reservations and nationally, who threatened to bring down the whole program through repeal of the IRA.

For all these reasons, tribal council autonomy could not be countenanced to the extent that the OIA could impose its authority to enforce its non-Indian model of Indian self-government.

At the local level, the superintendents' resistance to the tribal councils' agenda for self-government—the general *supervisory*, indeed, paternalistic, attitude of the superintendents toward the councils—was a function of the same policy imperatives which informed the reformers in Washington. Resistance to tribal empowerment at the local level also derived from the fact that local personnel were not strongly motivated to bring about their own obsolescence. They had more to lose personally than did the reformers in Washington if tribes took over agency functions. As OIA forestry specialist Ward Shepard put it: "It is naive to suppose that, given human nature as it is, any large number of bureaucrats will enthusiastically work themselves out of jobs."[51]

Beyond this structural constraint inherent in the organization of bureaucracies, there were more idiosyncratic factors which contributed to tribal disempowerment at the local level, and these naturally varied from individual to individual. Scudder Mekeel recalled in 1944, long after he had left the OIA, that one of the problems in tribal organization work was old guard OIA field personnel who were committed to the pre-1934 policy of assimilation and, it should be added, paternalistic administration. Mekeel may well have had in mind the Rosebud superintendent who engineered the community plan, and who later was transferred to Pine Ridge, where the Oglala Sioux Tribal Council voted to remove him.[52]

The technologies of power described in this chapter by which the Lakota tribal councils were disempowered had a clear precedent in the technologies for surveillance and control described in chapter 1. OIA paternalism was nothing new to the Lakota. The technical assistance, supervision, control of resource delivery, and stubborn insistence on line authority over reservation personnel which worked to disempower the new tribal councils had a certain generic resemblance to the courts, trust procedures, and ration system which had been—and continued to be (except the courts)—directed at dominating Indian individuals and families. The technologies of power the tribal councils were up against must have seemed very familiar. The difference was that while *wardship* had been the stated policy when the technologies for surveillance and control were established, now—during the New Deal—there was a radical change in the representation of power on Indian reservations. The Indian New Deal was about Indian *self-government,* and the technologies of power deployed by the OIA which disempowered the tribal councils clashed glaringly with the official discourse.

But disempowerment is historically significant not only because it was *ironic* during the Indian New Deal and because it inevitably generated conflict between the Lakota new dealers and the OIA. Disempowerment is also significant because of its effects on Lakota tribal politics. Disempowerment of the tribal councils by the OIA would have the effect of helping to create a crisis of authority for the councils among their own would-be constituents. The *inefficacy* of the tribal councils—brought about largely by the federal government's refusal to transfer decision-making and policy formulating power as described in this chapter—made them *intolerable* from the perspective of the Lakota grassroots, the situation to which we now turn.

## CHAPTER 7

# The Crisis of Authority in Tribal Government

The new IRA tribal councils in Lakota country not only faced challenges to their authority from the OIA. From the beginning, some Lakota—the old dealers—refused to recognize the IRA tribal councils as the legal tribal governments on the reservations. While the official tribal councils were meeting and transacting tribal business, the old dealers held meetings of their opposition organization, the Treaty Council. The English term "Treaty Council"—a neologism—first appeared in the records in 1931 (see chapter 2), but the customary Lakota term was *okaśpe yamni*. Treaty Council referred to the whole pre-New Deal organization of three-fourths majority rule involving district (local) councils in which all people—or at least all men— could participate, as well as tribal councils in which representatives from the districts conveyed the sentiments of the grassroots. During the New Deal the term implied and could apply to: (1) local community or district general councils (some but not all of the local councils espoused *okaśpe yamni* rather than the IRA tribal councils; in some areas there may have been rival local councils); (2) reservation-wide councils; and (3) inter-reservation assemblies variously known as the Eight Reservation Treaty Council, Great Sioux Nation Black Hills Claim and Treaty Council, the Sioux Nation Tribal Council, and by other names—not to be confused with the officially recognized Black Hills Council organized by the IRA tribal councils in 1938. The term usually was used to refer to reservation-wide assemblies of representatives from the districts (it was in these reservation-wide councils that the old dealers were most conspicuous from the point of view of the new dealers and the OIA), but all of the above assemblies were thought of as connected in a continuum through the principle of three-fourths majority rule; the more inclusive assemblies, in theory, expressed the will of the less inclusive assemblies, and ultimately of the people in the districts.[1]

Understood in this way, the Treaty Council constituted a serious challenge to the authority of the tribal councils on the reservations. "The controversy of the old tribal council and the new tribal council under the Indian Reorganization Act," the chairman of the new Rosebud Sioux Tribal Council wrote to Collier in 1936, "is the question as to who has the legal authority to act as the representative of the tribe. The three-fourth majority clause in the Act of April 19, 1868, is misconstrued and the wrong interpretation of it has caused the tribe to cling to the old tribal council." In 1937 a member of the Rosebud Sioux Tribal Council complained to Collier that the Treaty Council, under the leadership of the man who had been chair of the Rosebud Sioux Council in 1935, was meeting three days weekly, and that he had counted fifty tents at the camp assembled for its meeting in Soldier Creek.[2]

The puzzle of Lakota politics, however, is this *insubordination* of the old dealers regarding the IRA tribal councils, *given the resignation of the Lakota regarding the OIA bureaucracy and the agencies*—a resignation which has already been described. When Oglala old dealers gave testimony hostile to, among other things, the Oglala Sioux Tribal Council and the IRA at a Senate hearing in 1939, the Pine Ridge superintendent accounted for it in this way:

> There are many Indians who would prefer to entrust their affairs . . .
> directly in the hands of the superintendent. The common term
> which the older Indians use in speaking of or to the superintendent
> is 'father.' The old ladies of the tribe frequently use the term 'papa'
> and it is undoubtedly an expression of affection or respect or both.
> One of the greatest concerns of this group of Indians in the Reorgani-
> zation Act was the feeling that the authority of the superintendent,
> the father, was reduced and that of some elective officer increased.[3]

The superintendent described some of the older members of the Treaty Council to the commissioner in 1938 in these terms: "While they might reserve the right to criticize the Commissioner of Indian Affairs or the Superintendent in their hearts, they depend on these officials, and they do not want any disturbance of the power or authority of the Great White Father in Washington or the local Tun-ha-sla (father) [t'unkaśila, grandfather]." He described another old dealer to the commissioner in 1940: "He likes to come to the office and call me 'papa' and to have me personally settle all his affairs for him. He gets mad as a range bull when you suggest the Tribal Council to him."[4]

The question at hand is why a Lakota tribal member would get as mad as a range bull regarding the tribal council, but not regarding the OIA. This chapter will draw out the critique of the tribal councils in the political discourse of the old dealers. It will then go on to describe the structural predicament of Lakota tribal governments. The aim is to account for the remarkable alignment of political loyalties among the Lakota in which they disowned their "own" tribal governments while appearing to welcome the continued presence of the federal government on the reservations.

## The Old Dealers

### Personnel

Who were the old dealers? They were primarily, but not exclusively, trust-patented fullbloods. Of twenty Rosebud old dealers who were politically active during the period, twelve were trust-patented fullbloods, three were fee-patented fullbloods, and three were fee-patented mixedbloods. Of nine Oglala old dealers chosen for analysis, six were trust-patented fullbloods, one was a fee-patented fullblood, and two were fee-patented mixedbloods. The old dealers ranged in age from men who had been born before the 1868 treaty—before the establishment of the Great Sioux Reservation—to men who were born in the twentieth century and had known nothing but reservation life. At least some of the old dealers were also chiefs; they were descended from chiefs and were recognized as chiefs when the New Deal began.[5]

Data on the educational backgrounds of the old dealers are fragmentary and not available for Rosebud, but they suggest a wide range in level of education. Of seven Oglala old dealers for whom education data are available, six had some schooling, and one had never been to school. Of the educated, four had been to Carlisle Indian School in Pennsylvania—the most educated man had nine years of school—and two had spent a few years at a day school or agency boarding school.[6]

What *all* the old dealers had in common was that they were not members of the IRA councils. Some of these leaders did not even run for office in the IRA council elections, and they and their followers may actually have boycotted elections. Some of the old dealers, however, had been active on tribal councils before the New Deal. The chairmen of both the Rosebud Sioux Council and the Oglala Tribal Council in 1935, for example, became prominent old dealers in 1936. Other old dealers had not been involved in tribal councils before the New Deal.[7]

There is no evidence that IRA tribal council members *became* old dealers when out of office, but there is good evidence that, when not in office, IRA tribal council members were sympathetic to the cause of the old dealers and also challenged the tribal councils. Three people who had previously served on the Rosebud Sioux Tribal Council, for example, responded on a questionnaire in 1941 that Indians should not be in charge of *any* of the administrative areas listed on the questionnaire—land use, work projects, health work, education, or running the agency. Clearly these people no longer had faith in New Deal tribal government. A former president of the Oglala Sioux Tribal Council—the first president elected in 1936—met with a group of "special delegates" as an "independent council for Indians" in 1943. The delegates included, besides the former president, another fee-patented mixedblood who would become tribal president and a prominent new dealer in 1944, a former councilman who was a trust-patented fullblood, and two trust-patented fullbloods who were principals in the Treaty Council. They complained that the IRA was "throwst [sic] down the throats of the red man against their wishes," and they adopted a resolution that the "peace treaty of 1868 as ratified by Congress be now carried out as was intended." Both of these assertions were central in the political discourse of the old dealers. It is clear that people who were supporters of the IRA councils when they served on them could be opponents—along with the old dealers—when out of office.[8]

There is also suggestive evidence that the old dealers benefitted less from OIA employment and economic development programs during the New Deal than did members of the tribal councils. Of the eight Oglala old dealers for whom data are available, for example, not one had an income of more than $15 from agency or tribal employment in 1939. Of the thirty Oglala Sioux Tribal Council members for

whom data are available, in contrast, seven (23 percent) had 1939 incomes from OIA relief work, regular agency employment, or tribal employment, ranging from $152 to $1,200. Regarding the IRA revolving
credit program, only three of twenty Rosebud old dealers chosen for
analysis received loans. The five loans made to these individuals
(some received more than one loan) ranged from $36 to $271. In contrast, of the ninety-six different individuals who served on the Rosebud Sioux Tribal Council during the New Deal period, twenty-eight
received IRA revolving credit loans. The forty-two loans made to these
tribal council members ranged from $26 to $3,474, with a median
of $113.[9]

### Traditional Decision Making and Modern Abuses

One of the claims repeatedly made by the old dealers to the OIA, to
congressmen, and to others was that the IRA and the new tribal councils were a violation of the principle of three-fourths majority rule
provided for in article twelve of the Fort Laramie Treaty of 1868. As
will be recalled from chapter 2, that article provided that no cession
of tribal land could take place without the approval of three-fourths
of the adult males. The Lakota developed an indigenous interpretation of this provision as a model for tribal decision making in general,
not just for land cessions. This was the model under which the Rosebud Sioux Council and the Oglala Tribal Council, and the district
councils on both reservations, operated on the eve of the New Deal.
The IRA and the tribal councils were seen to violate the treaty provision because the IRA, the constitutions, and the charter on Rosebud,
had not received the approval of three-fourths of the adult males. Furthermore, the tribal councils were departing widely from the model
of three-fourths majority rule by making important decisions without
the approval of the people, such as ratifying the law and order codes,
controlling the use of tribal land, and using tribal funds.[10]

Violation of three-fourths majority rule was most severe on Pine
Ridge where the new tribal president represented a type of leadership
which, as the head community worker put it, sought to "run away
with the bit in its mouth." The same man who interrogated agency
personnel at the first meeting of the new Oglala Sioux Tribal Council
in 1936 (see chapter 6), conducted council meetings without standard
parliamentary procedure. At the same meeting, for example, a motion
was made and seconded that he be authorized to appoint a commit-

tee. He told the council: "There is no use to vote on this as I have been empowered through a motion made that I appoint a committee." He also repeatedly refused to entertain motions from the council floor. In 1937 an Oglala councilman wrote to Collier asking for help in drafting rules of order "that will hold a check to the arbitrary actions of the President and also to the Executive Committee." According to a report prepared by Joe Jennings in 1944, the president had even intimidated the treasurer and other council members with physical threats. Such abuses were made more pressing by the absence of provisions for checks and balances in the constitutions (see chapter 4).[11]

The use of tribal funds without three-fourths approval was one of the more common violations of article twelve in the view of the old dealers. Shortly after the IRA tribal councils were set up, they began to receive revenue from the lease of tribal lands, taxes on the lease of individual allotments, license fees for businesses, and other sources. This income was expended, among other purposes, to pay per diem and mileage expenses for council members attending council meetings or otherwise conducting tribal business, and to pay salaries to tribal officers. Examples of tribal council budgets are presented in tables 7.1 and 7.2. In 1937 the Treaty Council on Pine Ridge adopted a resolution to "abolish the new Indian Reorganization . . . for the reason the officers of the Oglala Sioux Tribal Council every time calls for monthly meeting they receiving a great deal of Tribal funds without consent from the Pine Ridge Indians." In 1939 the Treaty Council on Rosebud adopted a resolution to protest all appropriations submitted by the tribal council (or the agency) not in accordance with the 1868 treaty. In 1943 it adopted a resolution stating that the members withdrew—under the provisions of the 1868 treaty—from the TLE (Tribal Land Enterprise) and the "New Organization Council," since through these bodies tribal trust funds had been "embezzled." The actions in question were probably not arguably embezzlement in terms of any official criminal code, but they violated the terms of the old dealers' interpretation of article twelve of the 1868 treaty.[12]

There was also bitterness about the fact that the tribal councils collected a tax on leases and permits on trust land owned by individuals. This was particularly disturbing because some of the councilmen and officers who received per diem or salaries were landless (because they had been fee patented), yet were benefitting from the

Table 7.1    Budget of the Oglala Sioux Tribal Council,
Fiscal Year 1945

| Items | Amounts |
|-------|---------|
| RECEIPTS | |
| Dance hall license fees | $30 |
| Leases of tribal land | 40 |
| Taxes on individual allotment leases | 800 |
| Traders' license fees | 806 |
| Lease of tribal land to War Department | 2,800 |
| Grazing permits on tribal land | 3,000 |
| Total Receipts | $7,476 |
| EXPENDITURES | |
| Per diem and mileage for critic | 62 |
| Office supplies | 100 |
| Vice president's salary | 120 |
| Salary for executive committee member | 120 |
| Per diem for loan committee members | 320 |
| President's salary | 1,200 |
| Treasurer's salary | 1,200 |
| Secretary's salary | 1,320 |
| Per diem for council members | 2,083 |
| Contingent funds | 899 |
| Total expenditures | $7,424 |

SOURCE: Minutes of the Oglala Sioux Tribal Council, 11–13 July 1944, File 9684–E–1936–054, Pt. 2, Pine Ridge, CCF.

meager lease incomes of allottees who had retained their lands. A Rosebud old dealer complained in a letter to Congressman Karl Mundt (R., S.D.) in 1943 that he had formerly collected fees directly from his lessee every month. Now the money went through the agency office, which collected a tax for the "New tribal council."[13]

Table 7.2    Budget of the Rosebud Sioux Tribal Council,
Fiscal Year 1945

| Items | Amounts |
|---|---|
| **RECEIPTS** | |
| Yuwipi license fees | $30 |
| Commercial license fees | 170 |
| Leases of and grazing permits on tribal lands | 2,000 |
| Taxes on leases of and grazing permits on individual allotments | 2,300 |
| Total receipts | $4,500 |
| Balance on hand | 597 |
| **EXPENDITURES** | |
| Janitor | $12 |
| Treasurer's bond and deposit box | 17 |
| Telephone | 25 |
| Office supplies | 50 |
| Delegation expenses | 150 |
| Vital statistics fee | 200 |
| Per diem for executive committee | 480 |
| Treasurer's salary | 780 |
| President's salary | 1,200 |
| Per diem for councilmen | 1,620 |
| Total expenditures | $4,534 |

SOURCE: Minutes of the Rosebud Sioux Tribal Council, 10–12 April
1945, File 5951-1944-054, Pt. 2, Rosebud, Box 262, Accession 56A-
588, Record Group 75, NA.

Again, the situation was worse on Pine Ridge. In February 1939
Fred Daiker, head of the OIA Organization Division, wrote to the
tribal president, informing him of the findings of an audit in which it
was disclosed that the president had retained without proper accounting $210 of tribal funds. The audit also disclosed—and this was prob-

ably much more damaging from the standpoint of the grassroots—
that between September 1937 and November 1938, the president had
been issued checks totalling $2,918.32, and the treasurer had received
$744, for per diem and expenses. This letter and the auditor's report
were sent to the president through the superintendent, a common
procedure on reservations, but before passing on the letter, the superintendent made the contents available to the executive committee
and to the Treaty Council.[14]

The Treaty Council responded to this disclosure by seeking action on a petition filed with the federal government during the previous fall requesting the secretary of the interior to call a tribal referendum on revocation of the Oglala constitution. This procedure was
provided for in the tribal constitution. The petition had 1,061 signatures, but the Interior Department had not called the referendum because the petition did not fully meet the requirements set out in the
constitution. In March 1939 a Treaty Council delegation met with the
OIA and insisted on a referendum. They wanted, as Zimmerman advised the superintendent, "to see everything wiped from the books"—
the council, the constitution, and the acts, leases, and permits exe-
cuted by the council. A referendum was never called, but both the
superintendent and the agency head community worker warned in
April 1939 that the Oglala people would vote to revoke the tribal constitution if a referendum was held. The tribal president was finally
impeached in 1941 on the basis of the 1938 charge that he committed
a "technical embezzlement" by retaining $210 of tribal funds without
properly accounting for same.[15]

Another abuse of power alleged by the old dealers pertained to the
new tribal law and order apparatus—particularly the junior courts
where penal cases originated. There were no provisions for trial by
jury at the time. The junior judges and the tribal police officers were
elected to two-year terms and were remunerated on the basis of fees
assessed against convicted perpetrators. The junior judges were reported to be less competent than the superior judges appointed and
paid by the OIA, probably because their tenure was more temporary
and they therefore benefitted less from the law and order schools held
occasionally by the OIA.[16]

What is more, the junior judges were generally believed by the
Lakota people to be new dealers—that is, to be partial in cases regarding old dealers. In the words of the Pine Ridge superintendent, they

were "a bit more zealous than has heretofore been the case with the Federally appointed Indian judges."[17] In January 1938, the investigating subcommittee of the Senate Committee on Indian Affairs began to hear complaints from Oglala witnesses that opponents of the New Deal were subjected to arrest for their political views. An Oglala old dealer who had been arrested under the law and order code on a charge of fraud for "misrepresenting, false interpreting and obtaining money from the Indian people"[18] in pursuit of Treaty Council business alleged the political use of the police and court: "You know if you talk to anybody up there . . . 'This Howard-Wheeler Act is no good,' then if they hear that, they want you arrested."[19] The superintendent in fact believed that the man "obviously had not committed an offense under the code,"[20] and the OIA Washington office was concerned about "possible evident disregard [of] civil liberties" in this case.[21] The arrest was apparently a response to the old dealer's collection of travel money and his allegedly fraudulent circulation of petitions.[22] In 1939, another Oglala old dealer complained to the Senate subcommittee that he had been arrested at the direction of the tribal president because he had a copy of the letter Fred Daiker had written to the president about fiscal improprieties.[23] The superintendent reported that in one tribal court case, the tribal president sat in the courtroom and "virtually heckled and admonished [the judge] into a decision favorable to his views."[24]

Many Oglala, according to the Pine Ridge superintendent, also believed that because of the fee system for compensating junior judges and tribal policemen, people were "brought into court merely in order for a judge and officer to obtain a fee. They feel that the officers are out in the interest of drumming up business rather than policing public places or otherwise attending the duties usually ascribed to an officer." The superintendent reported that investigation had confirmed the suspicion that the "officers are more interested in a conviction than in strictest fair play."[25] A petition was circulated on the reservation in 1939 calling for the abolition of the junior court system because of abuses inherent in the fee system. Even a Rosebud Sioux Tribal Council delegation complained to the OIA in Washington of the abuses of the fee system in the junior courts in 1940.[26]

The old dealers claimed that the legal and customary tribal government of the Lakota was the tribal and district council organization based on article twelve of the 1868 treaty, not on the IRA. While the new IRA councils met at the agencies, the old dealers met in loosely-organized groups covered by the term Treaty Council, which they claimed was continuous with tribal organization before the New Deal. The old dealers pointed out that the Treaty Council had been in place when the New Deal appeared, and that it had deep historical roots. The chairman of the pre-IRA Rosebud Sioux Council, who had organized resistance to the constitution referendum in 1935 (see chapter 4), wrote to attorney Ralph Case in 1936 as the chairman of the "Original Rosebud Sioux Council." In 1937 he told the House Indian Committee through an interpreter: "Years ago our forefathers made the treaties and had an organization at the same time with *three-fourths majority*." An Oglala old dealer told the Pine Ridge superintendent that the "Treaty Council started over forty years ago" (he was probably referring to the Oglala Council organized in 1891; see chapter 2), and that the new tribal council, the tribal president, "and his bunch never did meet with us before, . . . and what he has started is something new." Another Oglala old dealer complained in 1945 that "the treaty council was a functioning organization at the time of the election of the new council in the spring of 1936. That no consideration was given the treaty council and no provision made for merging its function into the new organization. That the treaty council was ignored during the campaign for the adoption of the organization act and the subsequent election."[27]

Some of the old dealers also sought legitimation of the Treaty Council by reference to the fact that they were chiefs and that this special status had been ignored in tribal organization under the IRA. Some signed letters and petitions with the title chief and were introduced at congressional hearings with that title. The role of chiefs in the pre-New Deal tribal councils will be recalled from chapter 2.[28]

The old dealers also insisted that because the New Deal in general was inconsistent with both treaty law and Lakota custom, they did not understand it. An Oglala old dealer told the Senate subcommittee through an interpreter in 1939: "the New Deal . . . probably would fit into your way of living and style of thought, but it does not fit us at all; we do not understand it; it is not the proper thing for us to work under." A Rosebud old dealer told the same assembly through an interpreter:

We feel that this reorganization scheme is something that is probably more adaptable to our white people [the white people? mixedbloods?]. Our Indians do not understand it and have not been able to
understand its operations. Therefore they dislike it . . . it just does
not fit us.

It is probably significant to mention the fact that when we talk Indian here, speaking in our own Indian tongue, the committee members here do not understand our language and they do not know what
we mean. In like manner, we are not able to understand this act that
we are objecting to. We are quite determined that as long as we live
we do not want this Wheeler-Howard Act and we want to get out
from under it.

The delegitimating implications for the tribal councils are clear.[29]

### Social and Cultural Aliens

The old dealers insisted that the supporters of the IRA councils and
the beneficiaries of the Indian New Deal in general were largely
mixedbloods (ieska), and that mixedbloods were not real Indians. (It
is likely that mixedbloods with more than one-half degree of Indian
blood were often categorized by Lakota people as fullbloods.) One old
dealer complained in 1945 about the alien nature of the new election
procedures and of the people who thereby benefitted: "The tech-
niques of propaganda and voting were new and different than what
the Indian way had been, consequently the election was captured by
the mixedbloods." "Half blood people run everything," a Rosebud old
dealer wrote to Senators Elmer Thomas (D., Ok.) and William J. Bulow (R., S.D.) in 1938.[30]

Who were the new council members? The elections under the IRA
constitutions beginning in 1936 brought about a change in the composition of the tribal councils. There was some replacement of personnel who had been active on the councils before 1936, at least on
Rosebud. Three-quarters of the council members who attended the
December 1934 (pre-IRA) meeting of the Rosebud Sioux Council had
attended previous meetings since 1929; there was clearly a stability
in the personnel of the pre-IRA council. By 1938, however, a substantial majority of the new Rosebud Sioux Tribal Council members
had not answered the roll call at any council meeting between 1929
and 1936, during the pre-IRA period. This pattern of new personnel
on the IRA council became more pronounced in subsequent years.

The new men—and one woman in 1936—came from all social categories—mixedblood and fullblood, fee-patented and trust-patented, young and old. The new personnel probably appeared because of the new election system: council representatives were no longer selected by an open poll at district council meetings as they had been prior to 1936; they were now elected by secret ballot and in new election precincts—"communities"—partitioned by the Rosebud constitution. There was also a new constituency—women—which had been enfranchised by the IRA constitutions.

There was also a change in the proportions of holders of different social statuses in the councils. As can be seen from tables 7.3 and 7.4, there was an increase in the proportion—and on Pine Ridge in the absolute number—of mixedbloods on the tribal councils on both reservations in 1936, with the first election under the IRA constitutions. There was also a sizeable increase in the proportion of fee-patented allottees on the Rosebud Sioux Tribal Council. This was not the case on Pine Ridge, but there was a slight increase in the absolute number of fee-patented allottees on the tribal council (see tables 7.5 and 7.6). Importantly, however, both fullbloods and trust-patented allottees continued to predominate on both councils during the New Deal period. There was some replacement of older men by younger people on the IRA tribal councils, as can be seen in tables 7.7 and 7.8.

Changes in the educational level of council members are more

Table 7.3   Blood Quanta of the Oglala Sioux Tribal
Council Members

| Year of Election | Fullblood | Mixedblood | Unknown |
|---|---|---|---|
| 1935 (pre-IRA) | 16 | 6 | 2 |
| 1936 | 17 | 15 | 0 |
| 1938 | 20 | 13 | 0 |
| 1940 | 22 | 13 | 0 |
| 1942 | 19 | 8 | 1 |
| 1944 | 23 | 9 | 0 |

SOURCE: 1937 Census, Roll 444, ICR; personal communication, U.S. Department of the Interior, Bureau of Indian Affairs, Pine Ridge Agency, Pine Ridge, S.D.

Table 7.4    Blood Quanta of the Rosebud Sioux
Tribal Council Members

| Year of Election | Fullblood | Mixedblood | Unknown |
|---|---|---|---|
| 1934 (pre-IRA) | 57 | 19 | 4 |
| 1936 | 16 | 9 | 1 |
| 1938 | 16 | 18 | 0 |
| 1940 | 19 | 12 | 0 |
| 1942 | 17 | 12 | 1 |
| 1944 | 17 | 5 | 1 |

SOURCE: Reports of Industrial Surveys, Record Group 75, NA; 1934 Census, Roll 383, ICR; Report of Council Election, 1940, File 9712–1936–055, Rosebud, CCF; Superintendent to Commissioner, 11 November 1943, File 9712–1936–055, Rosebud, CCF; personal communication, U.S. Department of the Interior, Bureau of Indian Affairs, Rosebud Agency, Rosebud, S.D.

Table 7.5    Allotment Statuses of the Oglala Sioux
Tribal Council Members

| Year of Election | Trust-Patented | Fee-Patented * | Other | Unknown |
|---|---|---|---|---|
| 1935 (pre-IRA) | 14 | 7 | 1 | 2 |
| 1936 | 20 | 10 | 0 | 2 |
| 1938 | 25 | 7 | 0 | 1 |
| 1940 | 23 | 10 | 1 | 1 |
| 1942 | 16 | 4 | 0 | 8 |
| 1944 | 22 | 9 | 0 | 1 |

* Includes only allottees whose allotments were completely fee-patented.

SOURCE: Personal communication, U.S. Department of the Interior, Bureau of Indian Affairs, Pine Ridge Agency, Pine Ridge, S.D.

Table 7.6    Allotment Statuses of the Rosebud Sioux
Tribal Council Members

| Year of Election | Trust-Patented | Fee-Patented * | Unknown |
|---|---|---|---|
| 1934  (pre-IRA) | 50 | 21 | 9 |
| 1936 | 13 | 12 | 1 |
| 1938 | 18 | 14 | 2 |
| 1940 | 18 | 13 | 0 |
| 1942 | 15 | 13 | 2 |
| 1944 | 14 | 7 | 2 |

* Includes only allottees whose entire allotments were fee-patented.

SOURCE: Reports of Industrial Surveys, Record Group 75, NA; 1934 Census, Roll 383, ICR; Report of Council Election, 1940, File 9712–1936–055, Rosebud, CCF; Superintendent to Commissioner, 11 November 1943, File 9712–1936–055, Rosebud, CCF; personal communication, U.S. Department of the Interior, Bureau of Indian Affairs, Rosebud Agency, Rosebud, S.D.

Table 7.7    Ages of the Oglala Sioux Tribal Council Members

| Year of Election | 39 or Younger | 40–49 | 50–59 | 60–69 | 70 or Older | Unknown |
|---|---|---|---|---|---|---|
| 1935  (pre-IRA) | 3 | 3 | 6 | 6 | 4 | 2 |
| 1936 | 3 | 13 | 8 | 6 | 2 | 0 |
| 1938 | 6 | 10 | 9 | 7 | 1 | 0 |
| 1940 | 3 | 10 | 15 | 6 | 1 | 0 |
| 1942 | 3 | 8 | 5 | 9 | 2 | 1 |
| 1944 | 5 | 3 | 10 | 11 | 2 | 1 |

SOURCE: 1937 Census, Roll 444, ICR; personal communication, U.S. Department of the Interior, Bureau of Indian Affairs, Pine Ridge Agency, Pine Ridge, S.D.

Table 7.8    Ages of the Rosebud Sioux Tribal Council Members

| Year of Election | 39 or Younger | 40–49 | 50–59 | 60–69 | 70 or Older | Unknown |
|---|---|---|---|---|---|---|
| 1934 (pre-IRA) | 3 | 15 | 24 | 26 | 8 | 4 |
| 1936 | 7 | 7 | 3 | 9 | 0 | 0 |
| 1938 | 8 | 10 | 4 | 9 | 2 | 0 |
| 1940 | 5 | 15 | 5 | 3 | 3 | 0 |
| 1942 | 3 | 8 | 6 | 9 | 3 | 1 |
| 1944 | 1 | 8 | 5 | 5 | 3 | 1 |

SOURCE: Reports of Industrial Surveys, Record Group 75, NA; 1934 Census, Roll 383, ICR; Report of Council Election, 1940, File 9712–1936–055, Rosebud, CCF; Superintendent to Commissioner, 11 November 1943, File 9712–1936–055, Rosebud, CCF; personal communication, U.S. Department of the Interior, Bureau of Indian Affairs, Rosebud Agency, Rosebud, S.D.

difficult to ascertain from the fragmentary record. While data are not available for many of the council members, the existing data from Pine Ridge suggest that there was a decrease in the proportion and absolute number of council members with no education and an increase in the proportion and absolute number of members with at least some education beginning with the IRA council in 1936 (see table 7.9). It is reasonable to assume that council members with no formal education were less fluent or literate in English than those with schooling. The rational bureaucratic procedures of modern public administration and intergovernmental affairs had come to the Lakota, and those who spoke English and understood bureaucracies would have a distinct advantage in getting things done, and this would certainly be recognized by those Lakota who went to the polls to vote.

To summarize, it would be quite imprecise to say that all or even most of the council members were mixedbloods or fee-patented allottees. It would likewise be inaccurate to say that all trust-patented fullbloods were opposed to the IRA councils. Even though mixedbloods did not predominate numerically on the councils, however, fee-patented mixedbloods were prominent during the New Deal. This was both because their proportional (and, on Pine Ridge, their ab-

Table 7.9   Educational Backgrounds of the Oglala
Sioux Tribal Council Members

| Year of Election | No Education | Some Education | Unknown |
|---|---|---|---|
| 1935  (pre-IRA) | 5 | 11 | 8 |
| 1936 | 2 | 22 | 8 |
| 1938 | 0 | 22 | 11 |
| 1940 | 1 | 26 | 8 |
| 1942 | 0 | 19 | 9 |
| 1944 | 0 | 17 | 15 |

SOURCE: Reports of Industrial Surveys, Record Group 75, NA; Competency Commission Reports, Roll 12, Major James McLaughlin Papers, microfilm copy, Assumption Abbey Archives, Richardton, N.D.

solute) numbers on the councils had increased, and because they were very prevalent among the officers (see tables 7.10 and 7.11). All the tribal chairmen elected from 1936 were mixedbloods, usually fee-patented, and often relatively successful ranchers.

The change in the kind of individual filling the chairman's position after the IRA was, in fact, quite dramatic. In 1935, on the eve of the formation of the IRA tribal councils, the chairmen of the Rosebud Sioux Council and the Oglala Tribal Council were elderly, trust-patented fullbloods. They had long been involved in tribal politics. The Rosebud chairman had received no education and did not read or write English or speak it very well, and the Oglala chairman had only three years of education in a reservation day school. Council meetings were conducted in Lakota. The first chairman elected by the Rosebud Sioux Tribal Council in 1936 was a thirty-three-year-old, landless, bilingual mixedblood. He grew up in a traditional community (Ring Thunder) and was associated with fullblood people, but he had never been involved with the tribal council before 1936. He was also fairly educated—"self-educated," as a consultant put it—and he had even been considered by the OIA for an Organization Division field agent position. By 1938, the chairman of the Rosebud Sioux Tribal Council was a forty-six-year-old, fee-patented rancher of very little Indian ancestry, who had red hair, was "raised white" in the

Table 7.10    Blood Quanta and Allotment Statuses
of the Oglala Sioux Tribal Officers

|  | Year of Election | | | | | |
|---|---|---|---|---|---|---|
| Office | 1935* | 1936 | 1938 | 1940 | 1942 | 1944 |
| President | FB/TP | MB/FP | MB/FP | MB/FP | MB/UK | MB/FP |
| Vice President | FB/TP | MB/FP | FB/TP | FB/TP | FB/TP | MB/FP |
| Secretary** | FB/TP | FB/TP | FB/TP | FB/FP | MB/FP | FB/TP |
|  | MB/FP | | | | MB/FP | MB/FP |
| Treasurer | | MB/FP | MB/FP | MB/FP | MB/FP | FB/TP |

Symbols: FB Fullblood; MB Mixedblood; TP Trust-patented; FP Fee-patented; UK Unknown

* Pre-IRA.

** The tribal council often had more than one secretary, or an assistant secretary in addition to the secretary.

SOURCE: 1937 Census, Pine Ridge, Roll 383, ICR; personal communication, U.S. Department of the Interior, Bureau of Indian Affairs, Pine Ridge Agency, Pine Ridge, S.D.

words of one of my Lakota consultants, spoke no Lakota, and conducted council meetings in English (with translations into Lakota). The first president of the Oglala Sioux Tribal Council, who served in three consecutive terms, was a fifty-three-year-old, fee-patented, bilingual mixedblood and a successful rancher. He had never been active in tribal politics before, and in fact had been involved in the Republican party off reservation.

The old dealers also believed that mixedbloods were getting the "cream" of federal benefits or otherwise profiting at the expense of fullbloods during the New Deal. This belief was fostered in part by the predominance of mixedbloods among the Indian range unit permittees. Of the twenty-nine individual Indian permittees on Rosebud between 1936 and 1941, twenty-four were mixedblood men—almost all of less than one-half degree of Indian blood—and one was a white man married to a mixedblood woman (the pejorative but common English term among the Lakota was, and is, *squawman*). All the individual Indian permittees operating on Pine Ridge range units be-

Table 7.11   Blood Quanta and Allotment Statuses
of the Rosebud Sioux Tribal Officers

|  | Year of Election | | | | | |
|---|---|---|---|---|---|---|
| Office | 1934* | 1936 | 1938 | 1940 | 1942 | 1944 |
| Chairman | MB/FP | MB/FP | MB/FP | MB/FP | MB/TP | MB/FP |
| Vice Chairman | FB/FP | FB/TP | FB/TP | FB/FP | FB/TP | FB/FP |
| Secretary** | MB/FP | FB/TP | MB/FP | MB/TP | MB/FP | MB/FP |
| Treasurer | FB/TP | FB/TP | MB/TP | MB/FP | MB/FP | MB/TP |

Symbols: FB Fullblood; MB Mixedblood; TP Trust-patented; FP Fee-patented
* Pre-IRA.
** The same man served as chairman and secretary in the 1944–46 term.

SOURCE: 1934 Census, Rosebud, Roll 444, ICR; personal communication,
U.S. Department of the Interior, Bureau of Indian Affairs, Rosebud Agency, Rosebud, S.D.

tween 1937 and 1939 were mixedblood men or white men married to
Indian women. Some allottees resented the new unit leasing program
which prevented individuals from signing leases with non-Indian lessees, who were perceived as more reliable rent payers, and which gave
preference to Lakota (in effect, almost always mixedblood) ranchers,
who were perceived as less reliable. A handful of allottees also had
their lease incomes reduced by the unit leasing program (because each
allotment in a unit was assigned an equal share of the unit income
regardless of the value of the particular allotment), and they perceived
this as exploitation by mixedblood ranchers.[31]

The perception that mixedbloods were skimming New Deal cream
at the expense of fullbloods was also fostered by mixedblood participation in the revolving tribal credit programs. Mixedbloods, who
comprised approximately 60 percent of the Pine Ridge population
in 1944, received 55.7 percent of the tribal credit funds (fullbloods
41 percent, unknown 3.3 percent) and 45.5 percent of the individual
loans (fullbloods 45.5 percent, unknown 9 percent). On Rosebud
mixedbloods, who comprised approximately 56 percent of the population in 1940, received 36.2 percent of the credit funds loaned to

individuals (fullbloods 46.5 percent, unknown 17.4 percent) and 23 percent of the loans made to individuals (fullbloods 54.5 percent, unknown 22.5 percent) during the New Deal period.[32]

Mixedbloods were thus under-represented in the tribal credit programs. To many Lakota, however, mixedbloods of little Indian ancestry who had been fee-patented were not real Indians. Mixedbloods—or at least those with little Indian ancestry who had been fee patented (recall that mixedbloods with high Indian blood quanta may have been categorized as fullbloods)—were not legitimate Indians in the political discourse of the old dealers because they had been transformed from "wards" into "citizens" or "taxpayers," and, more pointedly, from "Indians" into "white people," by fee patenting. An Oglala told the Senate subcommittee through an interpreter in 1938:

> Historically speaking I wish to bring out the point at this time that the mixed-blood element, the most of them, if not nearly all of them, have secured patents in fee to their lands, and under the Allotment Act [Great Sioux Agreement of 1889] the trust period was designated for a certain number of years, and as long as that land was held in trust they were considered as wards of the Government and as Indians. But when the patent was issued it was with the understanding that *they became citizens, or became taxpayers, or became white people* so to speak. Now that they have secured their patents and squandered their lands, when the reorganization act was passed they turned right around, and today the landless element are dominating the reservation, and they are getting all the benefits, or the cream, out of Indian reorganization.
>
> When *they have decided to become whites,* they should let them remain as whites instead of giving them all the benefits that the Indians, who have retained their allotments, should have.

The old dealers remembered that the stated Interior Department goal under the policy of Indian citizenship through fee patenting had been the absorption of "competent" Indians into the larger society. They remembered that allottees could apply for fee patents, that fee patents had been given by the competency commission on Pine Ridge, and that all allottees of less than one-half degree of Indian blood had been declared competent. They also recalled the bureaucratic lexicon of the previous decade: one was classified as either a citizen/taxpayer (fee-patented) or a ward (trust-patented) in OIA records. Even the idea that mixedbloods "squandered" their land was drawn from the OIA discourse.[33]

In short, according to the old dealers, the mixedbloods had lost whatever Lakota rights (treaty rights) they had when they were fee patented; they "became white people." Now, they had failed, had "squandered" their land and the proceeds from land sales, and were eating up benefits under the New Deal—loans, employment, Rehabilitation housing—and getting control of tribal land and funds and even individual allotments and allottees' and heirs' lease money. As one old dealer put it: "Half blood people like Grasshopper eat us up pretty soon." They were not real Indians and were certainly not entitled to receive benefits intended for Indians, to have access to tribal land or funds, to control allotments or leasing, to speak for the Lakota, or to run tribal government—at least according to some of the more vocal old dealers.[34]

From the perspective of many fullbloods, this historical representation was very effective at delegitimating the tribal councils and legitimating the Treaty Council. As an interpreter for an Oglala explained in 1945: "The lease fees [for tribal land] which are paid here go to the tribal council fund; the Chief says the old dealers own most of the land, that it is improper and wrong for the tribal council officers, many of whom have squandered their land, to have authority to spend the money as they see fit." The Treaty Council was—according to minutes of a 1937 meeting—composed of "only full bloods & Land Holders." As one Oglala put it in 1945: "Most of the land is owned by fullbloods; we want our own representation."[35]

## The Puzzle of Lakota Politics

Thus the old dealers called into question the existence of the New Deal tribal councils. It would be easy enough to stop the analysis of Lakota politics here and to interpret the old dealers' opposition to the tribal councils simply as the opposition of the grassroots to a new-fangled and oppressive organization based on non-Indian ways and staffed with wily social and cultural aliens. Indeed, the old dealers themselves saw it this way to some extent. This would not, however, account for the puzzle of Lakota politics, the fact that while the old dealers called for—and came close to bringing about—the abolition of the IRA tribal councils, they were prepared to let the OIA and the agencies stand. Why were the tribal councils opposed, but not the OIA and the agencies? The answer has to do with reservation "political ecology"[36]—the distribution of niches within a structured power field.

In the historical representation which was part of the political discourse of the old dealers, tyranny began not with the establishment of the reservations and the imposition of the OIA's administrative technologies for surveillance and control beginning in the 1880s, but with the coming of the New Deal. In fact, in the old dealers' historical representation, the agencies were not construed as an imposition at all before the New Deal. They were not represented as interfering with Lakota politics or Lakota custom. It was the New Deal which was the tragic watershed in Lakota history. Note how "the [U.S.] Government" before 1934 on the one hand and traditional Lakota ways on the other were assumed to be entirely harmonious—the presence of the OIA was *unremarkable* before 1934—in this old dealer's testimony to the Senate subcommittee through an interpreter in 1938:

> The Indians would like to have their own way of taking care of their affairs.
>
> They were brought up under a system which they had prior to the passage of that act [the IRA]. This land upon which you people live today and upon which the Indians live had their own language and their own way of communicating with each other.
>
> The old time form of government which the Indians had was well understood by themselves, and they were law-abiding among themselves, and listened to each other's words, and got along nicely.
>
> Then came along this change of policy on the part of the Government, referred to as the New Deal. It was the thing that brought trouble among our Indians.
>
> The Indians are of different blood from the white men. You have your ways of living and you understand these. And the Indians have their way that they understood; and it is rather difficult for us to understand yours, and it is hard for us to follow some of these things that are the white man's ways.[37]

A Rosebud old dealer wrote to Congressman Karl Mundt in 1944: "I feel as many others, that in order to survive as human beings, the old Indian way of living is our only salvation."[38] What is crucial to recognize is that this "old Indian way"—or what Lakota people called *oun t'anni*,[39] or old deal in English—*did not refer to life before the reservations were established.* The term old deal referred retrospectively to the arrangement in which individual property owners lived on their allotments and/or received income therefrom, enjoyed the delivery of services, goods, and other resources—understood as treaty rights—from the United States government through the OIA, and made tribal decisions on the basis of three-fourths majority rule. What the old dealers called for was a return to pre-New Deal arrangements, *not the abolition of the OIA.* Indeed, in 1940 and 1941, 55.7 percent of 185 Rosebud fullbloods surveyed believed the Lakota lived best under the old deal; only 23.2 percent believed Indians lived best before the coming of the white man (21.1 percent believed life was better under the New Deal).[40]

This is not to suggest that the old dealers did not challenge particular OIA policies—such as the Indian New Deal—or criticize particular OIA personnel. The comments by the Pine Ridge superintendent at the beginning of this chapter regarding the friendliness of the Lakota toward OIA officials was not the whole story. As pointed out in chapter 1, *reformist* criticism was the form Lakota resistance to OIA domination took, and the old dealers continued to dish it out during the New Deal. In April 1938, for example, the Treaty Council on Pine Ridge adopted a resolution to authorize four delegates to proceed to Washington to appear before the committees of Congress in order to bring about a halt of appropriations for the OIA until such time as certain Interior Department employees were removed from their positions. The list included fourteen employees—and one employee's wife—and it ran the gamut from John Collier and Solicitor Nathan Margold, through the Pine Ridge superintendent, the agency social worker, right down to the level of an assistant farmer.[41]

What must be borne in mind, however, is that this was not a call to *abolish* the OIA, but rather to replace personnel while leaving the structure of the OIA bureaucracy in place. As one of the more vocal Oglala old dealers put it in 1944 and 1945, the aim, at its most radical, was to "weed out the Indian Bureau officials," to "clean out the hacks," and fill the positions with qualified Indians. The demands were thus reformist, not abolitionist, as were the old dealers' demands regarding the tribal councils.[42]

Some old dealers did eventually come to articulate a demand for the abolition of the OIA, but they retracted the demand when they realized what it would mean. In 1943 the Senate investigating sub-committee issued Senate Partial Report 310, recommending a sweeping curtailment of the operations of and funding for the OIA, leading eventually to its liquidation. When Congressman Karl Mundt held hearings on Indian affairs in South Dakota in 1944, talk of liquidating the OIA was in the air because of the Senate report. At the hearings, one Oglala old dealer called for abolition, another for freeing Indians from the OIA, and there were apparently other Lakota who felt similarly. But the old dealers did not intend abolition of the flow of resources and services—what they perceived as treaty rights—from the federal government. The termination drive behind the Senate partial report, of course, did not entail the idea of turning over OIA funding to Indians, but of abolishing special federal resources and services for Indians altogether. Thus, the old dealers—and, indeed, all the Lakota—were trapped into opposing any major reduction of OIA authority, since it was only the preservation of the OIA which would preserve treaty rights.[43]

The Treaty Council, therefore, opposed the Senate partial report when many specific measures to do away with OIA administrative functions—and, thus, resources for Indians—were at issue. At a joint meeting of the executive committee of the Oglala Sioux Tribal Council and representatives of the Treaty Council in 1943, it was unanimously resolved to work to defeat the aims of the Senate subcommittee as set out in the partial report—"to free Indians from federal wardship, to eliminate rehabilitation of Indians as Indians" and other agenda. In January 1944 three representatives of the Treaty Council appeared at an Oglala Sioux Tribal Council meeting and encouraged the tribal council to act to discourage the Senate subcommittee from sponsoring legislation based on the report.[44]

In short, the OIA as an institutional structure was never the main target of the old dealers, not because the old dealers were satisfied with the situation, but because they realized that Congress only meant to remove the OIA in order to remove the costs of underwriting the reservations.

The resignation of the Lakota people with respect to the presence of the OIA is plain enough. As argued in chapter 1, the OIA's political domination of individuals, of families, and of the tribes—a domination which was *not* ameliorated during the New Deal period—was endured because of Lakota *dependence.* Challenging the presence of the agencies or the general structure of reservation administration, of the OIA, or of Indian affairs in the United States, would have meant endangering the flow of resources which allowed the physical, social, and cultural survival of the Lakota and their communities on the reservations. This dependence was *reinforced* during the New Deal period, when relief, relief work, credit, development projects, and other new resources administered by the agencies underwrote continued reservation life among the Lakota. The danger of throwing out the baby with the bath water if the presence of the OIA was challenged must have been particularly apparent to the Lakota during the drought and Depression. There was also the critical role of the federal government in protecting civil liberties in the absence of tribal supreme courts.

## The Inefficacy of Tribal Government

If it is largely OIA control over crucial resources in reservation political economy which explains the resignation of the Lakota regarding the presence of the OIA and its domination, it is the *lack of control* over resources which explains the crisis of authority experienced by the tribal councils, a crisis manifested, in part, as the resistance organized by the old dealers. Because the IRA tribal councils were not extended control over most OIA programs on the reservations, and were certainly not empowered to have control over agency operations (see chapter 6), they were not able to deliver resources to their would-be constituents. Nor were the tribal councils able even to represent effectively their would-be constituents to the OIA or to influence OIA procedures in resource delivery, for the agencies were staffed by federal bureaucrats who took orders from Washington, not from tribal councils. Furthermore, without appropriate *internal* checks and balances written into the constitutions, tribal councils could not effectively correct their own excesses and abuses.[45]

The tribal councils *attempted* to deliver benefits to the people, or at least to influence OIA administration and the delivery of federal resources. The Rosebud Sioux Tribal Council, for example, sought to expedite credit procedures, and both councils wanted to spread relief employment equitably among Indian people, as seen in chapter 6. The tribal councils also went to bat for their constituents over unit leasing. In 1941, the Rosebud Sioux Tribal Council sought to raise the grazing rate for tribal and individual land to a level which was considered exorbitant by the OIA, which feared it might put small Indian operators out of business. The argument of the council was that market rates had risen, and landowners should thereby benefit. The council finally approved a compromise rate. In 1944, the Oglala Sioux Tribal Council discussed allocating higher returns to watered lands within range units and voted to circulate a petition to revoke power-of-attorney for unit leasing. Obviously, the councils were interested in protecting what the allottees viewed as private property rights.[46]

Disempowered as they were by the OIA, however, the tribal councils could not deliver in any systematic way for their constituents. This essential *inefficacy* with respect to the real life concerns of the grassroots only served to highlight the extent to which the tribal councils were an imposition and to foreground the apparent abuses of power by the tribal governments. In addition to being useless, the tribal governments violated treaties, operated according to culturally alien principles, oppressed people with the tribal law and order apparatus, spent and misspent tribal monies, taxed individual lease incomes, and were run by social and cultural aliens who stood to gain personally from the New Deal but who had no right to speak for the Lakota people or to access to resources allocated for the Lakota. Such was the discourse of the old dealers.

But—and this is the essential point to recognize—*each of these criticisms—except, critically, uselessness—could just as easily be directed at the OIA agencies.* Was the OIA's imposition of wardship, and the technologies for surveillance and control this legal status entailed, arguably any less a treaty violation than elective tribal councils? The 1868 treaty certainly did not establish wardship; in fact, it would later be argued by some Lakota—during and after the 1973 Wounded Knee incident—that the 1868 treaty actually recognized the Lakota as an independent nation. It might be argued that the Great Sioux Agreement of 1889 established some of the procedures for trust restrictions, but certainly the wardship status and administrative surveillance and control established by the OIA were not what the Lakota had in mind when they signed the agreement.

It is hardly necessary to point out that the administrative procedures of the agencies were culturally alien. It would be difficult indeed to argue that the operations of the tribal councils during the

New Deal were more alien than the operations of the OIA agencies.

Regarding oppression via the tribal law and order apparatus, it should be remembered that on the eve of the New Deal, the agencies routinely jailed Lakota people for illicit cohabitation. OIA policemen were also used before the New Deal to break up peyote meetings and other "illegal" gatherings.[47]

The agencies also interfered with access to individual funds, and they arguably misspent those funds since they could apply individual funds to satisfy defaulted individual loan accounts. The agencies also historically expended tribal funds without permission of the tribes to defray expenses of administration, and Collier even pointed this out to the Lakota at the Rapid City congress in 1934. Before the IRA, the secretary of the interior had the statutory authority to expend at his discretion specified amounts from the tribal funds established by the Great Sioux Agreement of 1889 and by the sale of Tripp County by the Rosebud Lakota in 1907. Congress also appropriated additional monies from tribal funds in its annual appropriation acts. Between fiscal year 1919 and fiscal year 1932, Congress appropriated for the "support," "civilization," "education," and "administration of Indian property," $604,000 of Rosebud tribal funds for use by the Rosebud Agency, and $30,800 of Oglala tribal funds for use by the Pine Ridge Agency.[48]

The Lakota in general and the old dealers in particular were, of course, aware of the historic access of the agencies to tribal funds. In 1937, for example, the Medicine Root District Council on Pine Ridge adopted a resolution regarding the "misappropriation and diversion of Pine Ridge Indian trust funds for the support of the Indian Bureau, use of Indian trust monies without the consent of the Pine Ridge Sioux Indians to support the Indian Bureau." The resolution asked "the Government to give us back the full amount, since the Government first misappropriated funds in 1900." But such awareness notwithstanding, the old dealers did not call for the abolition of the agencies.[49]

The OIA even taxed Lakota allottees who leased their land. Beginning in 1941, the OIA assessed a tax of one percent of annual rental in order to cover the costs of drawing up the leases, collecting and distributing rentals, and bookkeeping. The Rosebud Treaty Council was well aware of this and even circulated a petition objecting to the tax.[50]

In short, the OIA agencies engaged in activities which, other things being equal, one could reasonably expect to be as compromising, if not more so, than the activities of the Lakota tribal councils during the New Deal. Yet, the old dealers did not work for the abolition of the OIA or claim that the Treaty Council and not the OIA was legally entitled to run the reservation. The agencies, as seen, had a degree of security among the Lakota based on their control over resources in the artificial reservation economies. Challenging the presence of the agencies would have put the continued flow of those resources at risk, something we can well imagine to be unwise among a people made dependent as the Lakota had been. Nothing, however, prevented the grassroots from challenging the tribal councils. Their abolition would not be a loss to anyone except those who happened to be in office in any one term. All things considered, many Lakota people believed the price asked by their tribal governments was too high for what they got in return. The same balance, however, tipped in favor of retention of the OIA agencies.

## Cooptation and Displacement

The crisis in tribal council authority was made worse by the fact that the tribal councils not only earned the hostility of many of their would-be constituents through their own operations and excesses. They also took political heat for the OIA agencies. The tribal councils were held accountable by the grassroots for OIA operations in which they were extended a formal, puppet role, but not substantive authority. As will be recalled from chapter 6, the tribal councils rubber stamped federal projects and budgets for the reservations. The Rosebud Sioux Tribal Council issued relief employment eligibility cards, but without actually deciding who was and who was not eligible for work. The council also officially passed on applications for revolving loan funds. The old dealers who held it accountable for the IRA credit program complained, for example, that the tribal council was not providing loans to the old people. The council credit committee, of course, was forced to comply with OIA regulations regarding credit (see chapter 6). What is noteworthy is that the old dealers blamed the tribal council—which acted on applications in conformity with OIA regulations—and not the OIA.[51]

The chairman of the Rosebud Sioux Tribal Council recognized that the council served the role of "goat"—in the sense of scapegoat—for the OIA because it had a *formal*, but not substantive, role in some critical OIA operations. He complained to Francis Case in 1939 regarding the OIA's refusal to allow tribal council control of credit operations: "Ask the men who got up this Re-Organization act for self Gov't to point out to us just where the self-gov't is. After all these years try as hard as we can we still fail to see where we are given any self gov't or a very small voice in our affairs except in being *made the goat when it comes time to pay for all the [OIA] employees playing around in our affairs.*"[52]

The tribal councils actually came to *represent*—in the sense of "to stand for"—the OIA in the thinking of the grassroots. The Lakota term *oun t'eca* or *oun lecala* (New Deal) referred to a new way of life based on the IRA tribal councils, range units, relief employment, revolving loans, and other components of New Deal Indian policy. The native category did not distinguish between the tribal bureaucracy and the federal bureaucracy. On at least one occasion, both tribal officers and the Pine Ridge superintendent were described as new dealers by an old dealer. The Treaty Council called a 1940 Oglala Sioux Tribal Council delegation to Washington an "Indian Bureau Delegation." While a distinct boundary existed as far as the new dealers and OIA personnel were concerned, from the standpoint of the grassroots the boundary was blurred at best, and the IRA tribal councils could easily stand for the OIA.[53]

The association of the IRA tribal councils with the OIA by the grassroots was almost inevitable given the history of tribal organization. The puppet role extended the tribal councils has already been noted. What is more, tribal organization was pursued not from the bottom up but from the top down; it was *an OIA agenda,* aggressively implemented with little or no local input. The tribal councils were the result of the OIA's doing, not the grassroots'.

Such a situation in which an effectively powerless organization is publicly associated with and held accountable for the actions of a superordinate organization that holds effective power has been called *formal cooptation* by Philip Selznick—"the sharing of the public symbols or administrative burdens of authority, and consequently public responsibility, without transfer of substantive power." In Selznick's analysis the critical significance of cooptation is that a "front" organization (in this case, the tribal council) lends an "aura of respectability" to the penetrating bureaucracy (here, the OIA), thereby enhancing the bureaucracy's legitimacy among the grassroots. Is Selznick's analysis applicable, and did the tribal councils somehow serve the authority of the OIA?[54]

While it is doubtful that the tribal councils lent an "aura of respectability" to the OIA, the cooptation of the tribal councils did help to secure the authority of the agencies. The tribal councils represented the OIA, but at the same time everyone knew that—unlike the OIA agency departments—tribal councils did not deliver critical resources. They could therefore safely be vilified and even abolished. Calling for the abolition of the tribal council must have felt from the vantage point of the Lakota like calling for the abolition of a particularly oppressive and useless OIA agency department. The existence of the tribal councils thus served to compartmentalize the historic Lakota political ambivalence toward the OIA. Political ambivalence toward the OIA was compartmentalized into (1) hostility toward the IRA tribal councils (representing the OIA) on the one hand, and (2) resignation toward the OIA agencies on the other hand. The hostility, or at least a good part of it, embedded in the ambivalence of the Lakota toward the OIA was thus *displaced* away from the OIA agencies and directed toward the tribal councils which represented the OIA. This displacement of hostility facilitated a less hostile, less ambivalent acquiescence regarding the continued presence of the OIA—which continued to deliver critical resources—in the lives of Lakota people. The implications of this compartmentalization of ambivalence for the security of OIA authority is apparent: by giving the Lakota a safe target to absorb resistance, the IRA tribal councils protected the authority of the OIA on the reservations. They indeed played the role of "goat."

In 1939 Felix Cohen mused in *Indians at Work* on how long Indian tribal governments would survive. He predicted that tribal governments would last as long as "the Indians themselves feel that tribal governments satisfy important human wants." He saw providing for economic development, delivering municipal services, enriching recreational life, and pressing tribal claims against the government as some of the important human wants which could potentially be served by tribal governments. Cohen recognized that OIA personnel would be unwilling to transfer their control over reservation administration—and, thus, their ability to serve the most important human wants on the reservations—to tribal governments. Transfer would not take place by "gifts of delegated authority from the Federal bureau," he insisted, "but rather as a result of insistent demands from the local community that it be entrusted with increasing control over its own municipal affairs." Without such transfer, he warned, tribal government would be "barred from the hearts of its people." "Government," after all, "is an affair of human loyalties," loyalties which must be won by serving real human wants.[55]

As has been seen, however, despite the insistent demands of the tribal councils for substantive empowerment of tribal government, the OIA bore out Cohen's prediction by jealously guarding its administrative control of crucial resources and federal personnel and by preventing the tribal councils from effectively representing constituents or governing the reservations. The tribal constitutions established largely figure-head organizations which were indeed barred from the hearts of many Lakota people. Tribal councils were propped up by the OIA, but not empowered by the OIA. Had the Lakota people been left to their own devices, their tribal governments would not have survived long. Where the OIA stood with respect to the hearts of the Lakota is more complicated, but the OIA clearly enjoyed the resignation of the Lakota regarding its presence. This resignation was reinforced by the displacement of the normally "backstage" Lakota resentment of the OIA into open hostility toward the tribal councils.

## Conclusion

In February 1973 armed members of the American Indian Movement (AIM) occupied the little community of Wounded Knee on Pine Ridge Reservation. The seizure was mounted to protest oppression of Oglala Lakota people by the Oglala Sioux Tribal Council and by the Bureau of Indian Affairs (BIA; the name was changed in the 1940s). AIM had been asked to intercede by the Oglala Sioux Civil Rights Organization. The site of the infamous 1890 massacre of Lakota people was purposefully chosen for symbolic effect, and as the occupiers and federal law enforcement personnel—the latter armed with military assault weapons and armored personnel carriers—dug in on the prairie in South Dakota, the world watched on television and in newspapers and wondered if there would be a second massacre at Wounded Knee.

With a standoff between the government and the occupiers, AIM, the Oglala Civil Rights Organization, and a group of Oglala chiefs jointly declared the Independent Oglala Nation, based on the Fort Laramie Treaty of 1868. The Independent Oglala Nation announced its intention to send a delegation to the United Nations, and it called upon the Iroquois Six Nations—another sovereign native nation—to send emissaries to Wounded Knee. The standoff with federal forces, which witnessed much gunplay and two gunshot deaths, was brought to a negotiated close after seventy-one days, but it wasn't until a year later that the Independent Oglala Nation was specifically recognized by the First International Indian Treaty Council held on Standing Rock Reservation.[1]

Do the events at Wounded Knee in 1973—the declaration of national independence by armed militants and their traditionalist Lakota allies—indicate that the Lakota had finally become *insubordinate* regarding the presence of the United States government? This book has argued that Lakota people have historically submitted to the presence of the United States government and its oppressive administrative gaze. This submission has been engendered by Lakota dependence upon the artificial reservation economies, which have been underwritten by the federal government and which have allowed Lakota communities and a modified traditional Lakota way of life to survive in the changing agrarian landscape of rural South Dakota. Resignation to the federal presence has also been facilitated by the federal role in protecting tribal members against abuse of tribal council power.

While OIA and other federal functionaries have enjoyed a relative acquiescence on the part of the Lakota regarding their presence and activities—which is to say, their domination of Lakota people—functionaries of the tribal governments organized during the Indian New Deal have enjoyed no such resignation on the part of the population. Because the OIA actively disempowered tribal governments and prevented them from controlling the critical resources in the artificial reservation economies or from truly representing the people or guaranteeing civil liberties with appropriate courts, tribal governments appeared as oppressive and parasitic to their would-be constituents in ways that the OIA did not. What is more, tribal councils were held accountable for OIA actions over which they had no control. They were associated with the OIA from the perspective of the grassroots and served as political lightning rods, discharging some of the political electricity generated in the domination by the federal government, thus securing the authority of the OIA among the Lakota.

But had things become so oppressive—or so obvious—by 1973 that the presence of the federal bureaucracy could no longer be endured by Lakota people? The history narrated in this book suggests that the Wounded Knee takeover and the declaration of the Independent Oglala Nation was, from the perspective of Oglala people, less about independence from the United States and the removal of the federal bureaucracy and more about abolition of the Oglala Sioux Tribal Council.

It is telling that an Oglala occupier shot and killed by an FBI sharpshooter at Wounded Knee was buried—at a much-publicized funeral—by his family and comrades *in his United States Army uniform*, hardly what one would expect from an independent nation. Pride in armed forces veterans is obvious among Lakota people, even among the people who were sympathetic with the occupiers of Wounded Knee. The irony of this funeral, which could not have been lost on Lakota people, was that this man was an American citizen who had fought for his country but who had been gunned down by his own government while protesting oppression.[2]

It is also noteworthy that a grassroots Lakota plan for the "Oglala Lakota Oyate Nation"[3] that was submitted to the Senate Subcommittee on Indian Affairs investigating the Wounded Knee occupation in 1973 stated: "The judicial system of the new Nation will, of course, revert back to the jurisdiction of the Secretary of the Interior. It is hoped that a Court of Indian Offenses can be established in each Tiyospaye [district]."[4] What exactly was the *independence* that was being declared?

The 1973 Wounded Knee incident was arguably only a more militant version of the resistance organized by the old dealers in the 1930s and 1940s. While the BIA came in for as much criticism as did the Oglala Sioux Tribal Council during the Wounded Knee incident, the occupation and the declaration of the Independent Oglala Nation was not so much a separatist movement as it was an action against the IRA tribal government and its support by the BIA. There were no *specific* proposals during the Wounded Knee incident for abolition of the federal bureaucracy on the reservation or for a severance of ties with the United States—eventualities which would, of course, have put into question the $23,336,000 in federal expenditures estimated for Pine Ridge in 1973. There was, however, a direct and specific action against the Oglala Sioux Tribal Council: a petition with 1,400 signatures was presented to the Pine Ridge superintendent calling for a referendum to revoke the IRA constitution of the Oglala Sioux Tribe. The Interior Department did not act on the petition, citing procedural defects, much as it had in 1939. Wounded Knee was the legacy of the contradictions of reservation politics and economy set into place during the New Deal and with which this book has concerned itself.[5]

How then can we characterize the Indian New Deal? What changed and what did not? Certainly federal domination of Indian affairs—both personal and tribal—did not disappear. All the technologies of power for surveillance and control instituted between 1880 and the New Deal period continued to be deployed by the OIA, except that some of the law enforcement apparatus was turned over to the tribal governments. While tribal governments with a statutory basis were established during the New Deal, they had been invented and designed by non-Indian federal functionaries, not by the Lakota. The Lakota people who were elected to tribal office, many of whom had visions of Lakota self-government, were routinely frustrated by the administrative and procedural disempowerment of the new tribal governments by the federal government; tribal governments, which ostensibly had "inherent powers" of self-government, were given few powers relative to those of the federal officials. Most authority over both personal and tribal affairs, thus, was not turned over to individuals or to the tribal governments, but remained with the OIA and the Interior Department.[6]

The artificial nature of the reservation economies did not disappear either. In fact, because of the Depression and drought and OIA relief and economic development programs, the reservation economies became even more artificial, which is to say, more dependent on the flows of federal resources. This economic situation reinforced the resignation of the Lakota regarding the OIA bureaucracy on the reservations.

What *did* change during the Indian New Deal was the *representation of power.* Indian policy was no longer talked about in terms of civilizing Indians or in terms of the incompetence of wards. True, the OIA continued to dominate both individuals and tribes through various technologies of power, but the discourse, the symbols, the models, the performances, and the rituals of power were radically revised. OIA personnel were now expected to "consult" with Indian people, to "cooperate" with Indian people, and to respect and—when possible—preserve Indian culture.

Let it not be thought that the new discourse, symbols, models, performances, and rituals were "only symbolic," without material reality. They had a distinct *materiality* because they opened up political space for Lakota people of all political stripes and elicited their demands—newly defined as not only legitimate but as necessary—for representation and empowerment. As Stephen Cornell puts it: "the IRA facilitated and legitimated Indian political mobilization," even if "it did not fundamentally increase federal accountability to Indians."[7] The new culture of Indian affairs could even be used *against* the federal functionaries who invented it, one of the great ironies of the New Deal: both the new dealers and the old dealers used the OIA's

New Deal discourse on Indian self-government to articulate and authorize their own agendas, agendas clearly divergent not only from each other's but also from the OIA's. One wonders if tribal politics in Lakota country would have been so intense during the period—if Lakota politicians would have been so outspoken and so active—if they had not repeatedly been told by the OIA that the New Deal meant that Indian people, and not white administrators, would determine the future of the reservations.

This new representation of power remained after Collier left office, and the postcolonial culture of Indian affairs is as important a legacy of the Indian New Deal as is the IRA. Once the pluralist idea of Indian people having a right to self-determination had become respectable in the political dialogue of Indian affairs in the United States, there could be no going back to the old representation of power in which Indian people were neither competent nor authorized to speak for themselves. This postcolonial culture of Indian affairs surely had a role to play in the Wounded Knee incident—in eliciting Lakota resistance on Pine Ridge Reservation, and in making the resistance meaningful to the powerful non-Indians who helped decide the fate of the occupiers. And the postcolonial culture of Indian affairs invented during the New Deal continues to be important in the present for Lakota people—in helping to legitimize the legal and political demands of the tribal governments for empowerment and territorial sovereignty. We have yet to see the legacy of the New Deal among the Lakota fully played out.

# Abbreviations Used in the Notes

AED     Archives of the Episcopal Diocese of South Dakota. The Center for Western Studies, Augustana College, Sioux Falls, S.D.

BCIM     Bureau of Catholic Indian Mission Records. Archives, Marquette University Library, Milwaukee, Wis.

CCF     Central Classified Files. Record Group 75, National Archives, Washington, D.C.

GRCIO     General Records Concerning Indian Organization. Record Group 75, National Archives, Washington, D.C.

ICR     Indian Census Rolls, 1885-1940. Record Group 75, Microfilm Publication M595, National Archives, Washington, D.C.

MDF-PR     Main Decimal File, Pine Ridge Agency Records. Record Group 75, National Archives, Kansas City.

MDF-RB     Main Decimal File, Rosebud Agency Records. Record Group 75, National Archives, Kansas City.

NA     National Archives and Records Administration, Washington, D.C.

NL     The Newberry Library, Chicago.

PI     Procedural Issuances: Orders and Circulars, 1854–1955. Record Group 75, Microfilm Publication M1121, National Archives, Washington, D.C.

PR     Pine Ridge Agency Records. Record Group 75, National Archives, Kansas City.

RA     Richardson Archives. I. D. Weeks Library, University of South Dakota, Vermillion.

RB          Rosebud Agency Records. Record Group 75, National Archives, Kansas City.

RC          Reports of the Commissioner of Indian Affairs.

RCWHA       Records Concerning the Wheeler-Howard Act. Record Group 75, National Archives, Washington, D.C.

RI          Reports of Inspection of the Field Jurisdictions of the Office of Indian Affairs, 1873–1900. Record Group 75, Microfilm Publication M1070, National Archives, Washington, D.C.

RST         Rosebud Sioux Tribe, Rosebud, S.D.

SAR         Superintendents' Annual Narrative and Statistical Reports from Field Jurisdictions of the Bureau of Indian Affairs, 1907–1938. Record Group 75, Microfilm Publication M1011, National Archives, Washington, D.C.

SFM         St. Francis Mission Records. Archives, Marquette University Library, Milwaukee, Wis.

SSC         Records of the Investigating Subcommittee of the Senate Committee on Indian Affairs. Record Group 46, National Archives, Washington, D.C.

# Notes to Chapters

## Introduction

1. Minutes of the Rosebud Sioux Council, 11 December 1933, File 11255–1934–054, Rosebud, CCF.

2. Ibid.

3. *Statutes at Large of the United States*, vol. 48:984.

4. Fullblood and mixedblood are terms employed by the Lakota and OIA personnel to classify putative ancestry and assumed social and cultural orientation. See Macgregor 1946:25; Wax, Wax, and Dumont 1964:ch. 3; Daniels 1970; Wax 1971:75–77; Powers 1975:117–19.

5. Wolf 1990:586.

6. Ibid., 587.

## Chapter 1

1. RC, 1893, 293; RC, 1895, 294.

2. Useful references on early Lakota history are Mekeel 1943 and Hyde 1975. Many Lakota people take issue with anthropologists on the assertion that the Lakota were recent arrivals in their homeland.

3. *Statutes at Large of the United States*, vol. 7:250, 252, 257. Useful histories of the Oglala and Sicangu in the nineteenth century are Hyde 1956, 1975; Olson 1975; Hyde 1974.

4. *Statutes at Large of the United States*, vol. 11:749.

5. Ibid., vol. 15:635.

6. Ibid., vol. 19:254.

7. RC, 1878, 1879.

8. RC, 1877, 1878, 1879.

9. *Statutes at Large of the United States,* vol. 25:888.

10. Ibid., vol. 33:254.

11. Ibid., vol. 34:1230.

12. Ibid., vol. 36:448.

13. Ibid., vol. 36:440.

14. This analysis of administrative apparatuses has benefitted from readings of Michel Foucault 1979, 1980; and Anthony Giddens 1987.

15. RC, 1888, xxix; RC, 1892, 27; U.S. Department of the Interior, Office of Indian Affairs, *Regulations of the Indian Office* (1904), 101–5. See Hagan (1966) on the courts of Indian offenses. Major crimes on reservations were placed under the jurisdiction of the federal courts by the Major Crimes Act of 1885.

16. McGillycuddy 1941:121, 125.

17. The records maintained by the agencies may not have distinguished between crimes under the jurisdiction of the federal courts as provided for in the Major Crimes Act and crimes under the jurisdiction of agency courts or courts of Indian offenses. For present purposes, it is assumed that the crimes listed in tables 1.1 and 1.2 which legally were under the jurisdiction of the federal courts (assault with intent to kill, burglary, larceny, rape, and robbery) were heard in the agency courts because there was insufficient evidence to bring a federal case. The cases of rape listed probably pertain to statutory rape. The actual labels for cases listed in the OIA records have been edited for tables 1.1 and 1.2. The intention in the tables is only to show the range of cases and the prominence of cases pertaining to illicit relationships, adultery, bastardy, and related offenses.

18. But apparently the Pine Ridge court did grant divorces in 1905; see table 1.1.

19. RC, 1901, 42; RC, 1904, 330–31; Order, 5 April 1901, Roll 1, PI; Narrative Report, 1911, Pine Ridge, Roll 106, SAR; Narrative Report, 1930, Rosebud, Roll 119, SAR; Narrative Report, 1935, Rosebud, Roll 119, SAR.

20. *Statutes at Large of the United States,* vol. 25:888. Additional legislation affecting allotment on Rosebud and Pine Ridge was subsequently enacted, primarily to allot children born after allotment had begun.

21. U.S. Department of the Interior, Office of Indian Affairs, *Regulations of the Indian Office,* 99.

22. Circular 561, 31 August 1911, Roll 9, PI; Narrative Report, 1924, Pine Ridge, Roll 106, SAR; Narrative Report, 1927, Pine Ridge, Roll 106, SAR.

23. Statistical Report, 1921, Pine Ridge, Roll 106, SAR.

24. Narrative Report, 1921, Rosebud, Roll 118, SAR; Narrative Report, 1922, Pine Ridge, Roll 106, SAR; Ponca District Council to Commissioner, 14 January 1925, File 4971–1925–054, Rosebud, CCF; Superintendent to Commissioner, 12 February 1925, File 4971–1925–054, Rosebud, CCF; Superintendent to Commissioner 30 January 1931, File 312, MDF-RB; Superintendent to Winner Advocate, 5 September 1934, File 312, MDF-RB. By the 1920s allottees were allowed to collect their rentals directly from the lessees.

25. Narrative Report, 1911, Rosebud, Roll 118, SAR; Narrative Report, 1914, Rosebud, Roll 118, SAR; Report, 1 May 1918, File 40953–1918–150, Rosebud, CCF; Report, 30 July 1919, File 15903–1920–150, Rosebud, CCF; Report, 16 June 1930, File 32661–1930–150, Rosebud, CCF. Allotments fractionated by heirship status into multiple interests not economically viable were also liquidated through supervised sales. Because many Lakota allottees died intestate, their property descended according to the probate laws of the State of South Dakota, and many allotments were partitioned into multiple inherited interests. Sale was the only practical course of action until the Tribal Land Enterprise was established on Rosebud in 1943 (see chapter 5).

26. *Statutes at Large of the United States*, vol. 34:182.

27. Report, 4 September 1907, File 75225–1907–150, Rosebud, CCF; Narrative Report, 1914, Rosebud, Roll 118, SAR; A Report on the Bureau of Indian Affairs Fee Patenting and Canceling Policies, 1900–1942, Institute of Indian Studies, University of South Dakota, Vermillion, 8, 9, 11; McDonnell 1991.

28. Declaration of Policy in the Administration of Indian Affairs, 17 April 1917, Ordinances and Resolutions, RB; Economic and Social Survey, File 059, MDF-PR; Economic and Social Survey, box A–1381, RB; McDonnell 1991.

29. Pine Ridge Competency Commission Records, 1920, Roll 12, McLaughlin Papers, microfilm copy, Assumption Abbey Archives, Richardton, N.D.; Narrative Report, 1921, Pine Ridge, Roll 106, SAR; McDonnell 1980; A Report on Fee Patenting; McDonnell 1991.

30. Superintendent to Farmers, 4 October 1930, File 6948–100–1923, Rosebud, CCF.

31. IIM procedures were liberalized by 1929, when the OIA authorized the agencies to disburse cash in limited amounts to able-bodied adults deemed competent, to be spent without supervision. Access to cash still required, however, the approval of the agency. Circular 2558, 7 March 1929, Roll 14, PI.

32. Inspection Report, 27 August 1926, File 40973–150–1926, Rosebud, CCF; Narrative Report, 1927, Pine Ridge, Roll 106, SAR.

33. Inspection Report, 27 August 1926, File 40973–150–1926, Rosebud, CCF; Narrative Report, 1927, Pine Ridge, Roll 106, SAR; Circular 2558, 7 March 1929, Roll 14, PI. The farmers were authorized to issue purchase orders in amounts of $100 or less without permission from the superinten-

dent, at least on Rosebud in 1926. Minutes of The Rosebud Tribal Council, 2–4 December 1926, File 17583–1927–054, Rosebud, CCF.

34. Report, 16 June 1930, File 32661–1930–150, Rosebud, CCF.

35. *Statutes at Large of the United States*, vol. 19:256.

36. RC, 1882, 96.

37. Correspondent to Commissioner, 3 January 1917, File 2043–1917–155, Rosebud, CCF; Superintendent to Commissioner, 25 January 1917, File 2043–1917–155, Rosebud, CCF.

38. Assistant Commissioner to Correspondent, 6 February 1917, File 2043–1917–155, Rosebud, CCF.

39. Report, 17 May 1884, Rosebud, Roll 43, RI; Dragenett 1907:25.

40. Sally Falk Moore (1988:160) has noted that state ideologies of "legitimation" may function less to dupe the powerless and more "as a comfort to the political sensibilities of the relatively powerful."

41. This is not to suggest that the Ghost Dance was primarily resistance to the OIA's administrative apparatuses per se. It was a complex movement indeed, with multiple causes. See James Mooney 1965.

42. RC, 1891, 411; Report, 9 January 1891, Rosebud, Roll 43, RI; RC, 1902, 337.

43. I am aware of only one other case of a threat to use violence against federal personnel in the conduct of their legitimate duties, and one case of arson involving an OIA building, on the two reservations during the period under consideration. The former involved a mounted war party threatening an allotment survey crew on Rosebud Reservation in 1903. The latter was the burning of a slaughterhouse in White Clay District on Pine Ridge Reservation in 1899 to protest the issue of beef on the block, rather than on the hoof. Members of the district took up a collection to reimburse the OIA for the destruction caused by the malcontents. RC, 1899, 335; Allotting Agent to Commissioner, 1 March 1903, Special Cases File 147, Rosebud, Record Group 75, NA.

44. Scott 1985:284.

45. Report, 10 July 1880, Pine Ridge, Roll 36, RI; Superintendent to Commissioner, 8 April 1940, File 076, MDF-PR; Feraca 1964:19.

46. Scott 1985.

47. RC, 1881, 106–7; RC, 1886, 249, 296. Ernest Schusky (1970:143) describes "gossip, apathy, and ridicule" as another weapon of the weak by which Lakota people can defeat administrative initiatives.

48. Census, 1885, RB; Report, 30 March 1886, Rosebud, Roll 43, RI; Report, 3 September 1887, Rosebud, Roll 43, RI.

49. This is not to suggest that abuses could not or did not take place. In the nineteenth century the OIA was notoriously plagued by the spoils system and corrupt and inept personnel. Eventually, however, OIA personnel were brought under the civil service system. Corruption and malfeasance did not disappear from the OIA, of course, but the rationalization brought on by civil service reform had some effect and gave Indian people some protections. See Prucha 1984:250–51.

50. Clark Wissler (1971:ch. 3) describes how he was mistaken for a "big cat" on a plains reservation, probably Pine Ridge.

51. U.S. Congress, Senate, *Survey of Conditions of the Indians in the United States* (1930), Hearings before a Subcommittee of the Committee on Indian Affairs, 71st Cong., 2d sess., pt. 7.

52. Scott 1985. On the effect of channels defusing potential resistance, see Lacy 1982.

53. Buecker 1984:315, 316, 322; 1987:92.

54. Annual Reports, Pine Ridge, Rolls 118 and 119, SAR; Annual Reports, Rosebud, Rolls 106 and 107, SAR; Mekeel 1932b:95–100; 1936:8–11.

55. Report, 9 January 1891, Rosebud, Roll 43, RI; RC, 1900, 7; RC, 1901, 6.

56. RC, 1901, 6, 367, 371; RC, 1906, 11–12.

57. The agencies bought cattle from Indian ranchers for distribution as rations. The income from cattle sales was monopolized by a handful of mixedblood families.

58. Report, 8 April 1882, Rosebud, Roll 43, RI; RC, 1884, 82; RC, 1890, 59; Report, 9 January 1891, Rosebud, Roll 43, RI; RC, 1892, 461; RC, 1893, 295; RC, 1894, 295; RC, 1895, 295–96. Freighting was also done for the private traders on the reservations.

59. RC, 1902, 337; RC, 1904, 336.

60. RC, 1905, 337; Acting Superintendent to Commissioner, 26 November 1910, File 91634–09–211, Rosebud, CCF.

61. *Congressional Record* (1920), vol. 59., pt. 2:1130–35; *Statutes at Large of the United States*, vol. 42:995; Narrative Reports, 1925, 1926, 1927, Pine Ridge, Roll 106, SAR; Narrative Reports, 1925, 1927, Rosebud, Roll 118, SAR; Narrative Report, 1930, Rosebud, Roll 119, SAR.

62. Narrative Report, 1925, Pine Ridge, Roll 106, SAR; Meriam et al. 1928:200; Mooney 1965:71. The Nebraska and North Dakota death rates are used for comparison because death statistics were not collected by the United States Census Bureau for South Dakota, and a 1925 death rate for the state is not available.

63. Leacock and Lurie 1988.

64. On dependence see Prucha 1988:ch. 2.

65. U.S. Congress, Senate, *Rosebud Indians of South Dakota* (15 January 1904), 58th Cong., 2d sess., Doc. 158; Hoxie 1984:ch. 5; McDonnell 1991.

66. Narrative Report, 1916, Pine Ridge, Roll 106, SAR; Narrative Report, 1919, Pine Ridge, Roll 106, SAR; Narrative Report, 1921, Pine Ridge, Roll 106, SAR.

67. Superintendent to Commissioner, 22 June 1916, Finance File, box 4, Rosebud Records, RA; Narrative Report, 1916, Rosebud, Roll 118, SAR; Narrative Reports, 1918, 1919, Pine Ridge, Roll 106, SAR.

68. Castile 1974; Hoxie 1979. The resignation of the Lakota has some obvious affinities to *hegemony*, particularly with respect to the presence of OIA domination being endured in the common sense understandings of the Lakota. Nevertheless, the resignation of the Lakota regarding the presence of the OIA is *not* best seen in terms of the concept of hegemony. Hegemony is most useful when it refers, not to "consent" based on economic or political necessity, but to a more insidious form of *cultural* domination based on control of the institutions of cultural production and reproduction—schools and the news media, for example—by a dominant group. Hegemony loses its conceptual potency if it is applied to situations—such as that among the Lakota—in which subaltern groups acquiesce to the presence of subordinating arrangements because of their immediate and obvious *material* interests. Williams 1977:108–14; Gramsci 1971:12; Lears 1985; Scott 1985:ch. 8; Comaroff and Comaroff 1991:ch. 1.

69. Scott 1985:324. Several writers have commented on the profound *ambivalence* in the attitude of the Lakota toward government authority. Erik Erikson (1963:114, 132) spoke of "passive resistance," Gordon Macgregor (1946:120) of "wards who resent wardship," and Everett Hagen (1962:475, 496, 500) of "hostile dependency." Predictably, none of these writers, who wrote before social power became interesting to social scientists, located the source of the ambivalence in the combination of dependence and domination. Of course, as Wax, Wax, and Dumont (1964:34) point out, the OIA employees were just as hostilely dependent on the Lakota, as were the Lakota on the OIA.

Jorgensen (1972:233) has noted the ambivalence of the Ute and Shoshone regarding the Bureau of Indian Affairs: "Indians cannot live with the BIA, and they cannot live without the BIA."

70. U.S. Congress, *Survey of Conditions*, 71st Cong., 2d sess., pt. 7:2824.

71. RC, 1882, 96; U.S. Congress, Senate, *Message from the President of the United States Transmitting Reports Relative to the Proposed Division of the Great Sioux Reservation, and Recommending Certain Legislation* (10 February 1890), 51st Cong., 1st sess., Exec. Doc. 51, 81; Mekeel 1936:6; U.S. Congress, Senate, *Survey of Conditions of the Indians of the United*

*States* (1940), Hearings before a Subcommittee of the Committee on Indian Affairs, 76th Cong., pt. 37:21833; Hagen 1962:496; Erikson 1963:119.

72. U.S. Congress, Senate, *Survey of Conditions,* 76th Cong., pt. 37: 21785. Many Lakota people continue to think of food stamps, health care, and other benefits received on the reservations as based on either the letter or the spirit of the treaties by which their ancestors ceded land to the United States. For another discourse involving a special claim among the Quechan, see Bee 1981:163–64.

73. U.S. Congress, Senate, *Survey of Conditions,* 71st Cong., 2d sess., pt. 7:2958.

74. This does not mean that it is necessary to accept Foucault's (1979: 176) assertion that power is "automatic" and "anonymous," that it operates as much from "bottom to top" and "laterally," as from "top to bottom," that supervisors are as supervised as much as they supervise. *Who* controls power— and who does not—and *for what purposes,* is clear enough in the case of the Lakota on the reservations.

## Chapter 2

1. Moore 1986:10.

2. Parkman 1946:123. References on Lakota sociopolitical organization—which by no means agree with each other—are Wissler 1912:7–11; Feraca 1964; Hassrick 1964:11–13, 26–27; Feraca 1966; Howard 1966:3; Mirsky 1966:390–92; W. Powers 1975:30–36, 40–41; Schusky 1975:23–6; DeMallie 1976:80–82, 1978:240–48; Standing Bear 1978:ch. 5; Walker 1982; E. C. Deloria 1983:27–28.

3. See Wissler 1912: 7–11; Feraca 1964:2, 5–9; Hassrick 1964:25–28; Feraca 1966:2–3; DeMallie 1982a, 1982b; Walker 1982:25, 29–32, 35–39, 58–61.

4. Wissler 1912:11.

5. *The Missouri Republican,* 2 November 1851; *Statutes at Large of the United States,* vol. 11:749; Chiefs' certificates, 1873, South Dakota State Historical Society, Pierre; U.S. Congress, House, *Right of Way to Dakota Central Railway Through Sioux Reservation, Dakota* (11 December 1883), 48th Cong., 1st sess., Exec. Doc. 11; U.S. Congress, Senate, *Message from the President of the United States* (19 December 1883), 48th Cong., 1st sess., Exec. Doc. 20; U.S. Congress, Senate, *Letter from the Secretary of the Interior* (23 January 1884), 48th Cong., 1st sess., Exec. Doc. 70; Account of a Council of Pine Ridge and Rosebud Indians, 29–24 February 1892, PR; DeMallie 1988:xviii.

6. RC, 1881, 112–13.

7. *Revised Statutes of the United States*, vol. 18, sec. 2090.

8. Poole 1988:47, 55, 120.

9. RC, 1882, 87, 97–8 (emphasis in original).

10. RC, 1879, 144 (emphasis in original).

11. Red Cloud to the Great Father and our Great Chiefs, 4 September 1880, Pine Ridge, Roll 36, RI; Superintendent to Commissioner, 6 December 1881, Rosebud, Roll 43, RI; Chiefs of the Rosebud Agency to Our Great Father, 14 December 1881, Roll 43, RI; RC, 1885, 267. The "deposing" of Red Cloud notwithstanding, many Lakota and non-Indians continued to recognize him as head chief until his "abdication" in 1903 (Walker 1980:137–40).

12. RC, 1880, 163; RC, 1882, 98.

13. Report, 20 July 1880, Pine Ridge, Roll 36, RI; RC, 1880, 168–69; RC, 103; RC, 1888, xxviii. Compare the statements of the two agency policemen with an Oglala Kit Fox (*tokala*) society song (Wissler 1912:15):

I am a fox.
I am supposed to die.
If there is anything difficult,
If there is anything dangerous,
That is mine to do.

14. U.S. Congress, Senate, *In the Senate of the United States* (7 March 1884), 48th Cong., 1st sess., Rept. 283; U.S. Congress, House, *To Divide a Portion of the Reservation of the Sioux Nation of Indians in Dakota in Separate Reservations* (31 May 1884), 48th Cong., 1st sess., Rept. 1724.

15. U.S. Congress, Senate, *Message from the President of the United States* (10 February 1890), 51st Cong., 1st sess., Exec. Doc. 51, 16.

16. The flyer provided by the Indian Defense Association was Dakota on Wiwicaygapi kte cin, Dakota Item 47, Ayer Indian Linguistic Collection, NL.

17. U.S. Congress, Senate, *Message from the President*, 59.

18. Ibid., 49.

19. Ibid., 48.

20. Ibid., 35.

21. Ibid., 111.

22. Ibid., 35.

23. U.S. Congress, House, *To Divide a Portion of the Reservation*, 2.

24. RC, 1891, 412.

25. U.S. Congress, House, *Agreements with Rosebud and Lower Brule Indian for Cession of Lands in South Dakota* (3 May 1898), 55th Cong., 2d sess., Doc. 447, 18.

26. Mekeel 1932a:277; Grass Mt. Indian Dance Hall, *Indians at Work* 2, no. 22 (1 July 1935): 32–33; Macgregor 1946:66–67; Feraca 1964; Feraca 1966; Tiyospaye, 1974, Red Cloud Indian School, Pine Ridge, S.D.

27. U.S. Congress, Senate, *Message from the President*, 50–51, 106–12; U.S. Congress, Senate, *Agreement with Indians of Rosebud Agency, S. Dak.* (9 December 1901), 57th Cong., 1st sess., Exec. Doc. 31; Council, 18 December 1906, Roll 27, Major James McLaughlin Papers, microfilm copy, Assumption Abbey Archives, Richardton, N.D. It is apparent that chiefs did not merely think of themselves as spokesmen. They were *chiefs* of bands, and they had signed the old treaties themselves, or were the sons of men who had signed the treaties. At a 1901 Rosebud council on the opening of Gregory County, one of the chiefs told McLaughlin: "My friend we have sung the 'Big Belly' song right here to-day—the song we always sing when we are going to make a treaty." The reference, of course, was to the chiefs society (*naca ominicia*) and to the days before 1889 when the chiefs made treaties. U.S. Congress, Senate, *Agreement with Indians of Rosebud Agency*, 18.

28. McLaughlin to Secretary, 9 April 1898, Roll 23, McLaughlin Papers.

29. Minutes of a Council, 7 August 1903, Roll 26, McLaughlin Papers.

30. Report on Pine Ridge Council, 17 March 1909, Roll 29, McLaughlin Papers.

31. Proceedings of Council, Pine Ridge, 5 April 1909, Roll 19, McLaughlin Papers.

32. Superintendent to Commissioner, 23 November 1920, File 62245–1920–054, Rosebud, CCF.

33. Narrative Report, 1911, Rosebud, Roll 118, SAR; Superintendent to Commissioner, 6 January 1922, File 064, MDF-PR.

34. Superintendent to Education Division, 15 February 1938, File 9684–C–1936–057, Pine Ridge, GRCIO; Wax 1971:77.

35. Narrative Report, 1911, Rosebud, Roll 118, SAR.

36. Narrative Report, 1915, Rosebud, Roll 118, SAR.

37. Superintendent to Commissioner, 3 April 1916, File 38194–16–054, Rosebud, CCF.

38. Constitution and Bylaws of the Rosebud Tribal Council, 1 March 1916, File 38194–16–054, Rosebud, CCF.

39. Superintendent to Commissioner, 13 September 1915, File 100647–1915–057, Rosebud, CCF; Chief to Commissioner, 27 March 1916, File 21330–14–054, Rosebud, CCF; Superintendent to Commissioner, 18 April 1916, File 35556–16–054, Rosebud, CCF; Commissioner to Correspondent, 5 May 1916, File 35556–16–054, Rosebud, CCF; Superintendent to Commissioner, 11 October 1917, File 95673–1917–054, Rosebud, CCF; Commis-

sioner to Superintendent, 12 October 1917, File 95673−1917−054, Rosebud, CCF.

40. Superintendent to Commissioner, 4 March 1916, File 38194−16−045, Rosebud, CCF. On the role of government−fostered tribal councils in eliminating the influence of chiefs see Hoover 1980.

41. Superintendent to Commissioner, Ibid. On the Omaha Dance see Wissler 1912:48−52, 1916; Howard 1951.

42. Superintendent To All Farmers, 12 November 1919, in *Wassaja* 10, no. 4 (January 1920): 2−3, File 064, MDF-PR.

43. Superintendent to Commissioner, 3 November 1920, File 28135−1922−054, Rosebud, CCF.

44. Constitution of the Rosebud General Council, 20 December 1920, File 101910−1922−054, Rosebud, CCF; Revised Constitution and By-Laws of the Rosebud General Council, 5 December 1924, File 101910−1922−054, Rosebud, CCF; Constitution and By-Laws of the Rosebud Sioux Council, 8 April 1933, File 40494−1930−054, Rosebud, CCF; Questionnaire on Tribal Organization, 1934, File 9712−A−1936−068, Rosebud, CCF.

45. Superintendent to Commissioner, 26 August 1933, File 40494−1930−054, Rosebud, CCF; Questionnaire on Tribal Organization, 1934, File 9712−A−1936−068, Rosebud, CCF.

46. Superintendent to Commissioner, 26 August 1923, File 40494−1930−054, Rosebud, CCF; Superintendent to Commissioner, 28 October 1929, File 35682−1929−054, Rosebud, CCF; Superintendent to Secretary, 29 October 1929, File 35682−1929−054, Rosebud, CCF; Superintendent to Secretary, 4 January 1930, File 35682−1929−054, Rosebud, CCF; Superintendent to Commissioner, 26 August 1933, File 40494−1930−054, Rosebud, CCF; Questionnaire on Tribal Organization, 1934, File 9712−A−1936−068, Rosebud, CCF.

47. Minutes of the Rosebud General Council, 1−2 December 1922, File 101910−1922−054, Rosebud, CCF; Minutes of the Rosebud General Council, 7−8 December 1923, File 97988−1923−054, Rosebud, CCF; Minutes of the Rosebud General Council, 4 May 1928, File 25963−1928−057, Rosebud, CCF; Minutes of the Rosebud General Council, 12−14 December 1929, File 35682−1929−054, Rosebud, CCF; Minutes of the Rosebud General Council, 6−8 April 1933, File 40494−1930−054, Rosebud, CCF.

48. Constitution and By-Laws of the Rosebud Sioux Council, 8 April 1933, File 40494−1930−054, Rosebud, CCF.

49. Constitution and By-Laws of the Rosebud General Council, 5 December 1924, File 101910−1922−054, Rosebud, CCF.

50. RC, 1885, 263; Superintendent to Commissioner, 23 October 1900, File 48952−1909−054, Pine Ridge, CCF; Superintendent to Commissioner,

28 March 1907, File 48952–1909–054, Pine Ridge, CCF; Superintendent to Commissioner, 24 June 1909, File 48952–1909–054, Pine Ridge, CCF; Mc-Laughlin to Secretary of the Interior, 23 September 1909, Roll 27, Mc-Laughlin Papers; Standing Committee to Superintendent, 25 October 1910, File 069, MDF-PR.

51. Narrative Report, 1911, Pine Ridge, Roll 106, SAR; Narrative Report, 1913, Pine Ridge, Roll 106, SAR; Narrative Report, 1914, Pine Ridge, Roll 106, SAR.

52. Constitution and By-Laws of the Oglala Council, 1916, File 064, MDF-PR.

53. Superintendent to All Indians, 27 February 1918, File 062, MDF-PR. Each voter was required to sign his name and affix his allotment number on the ballot, probably intended as a registration procedure rather than a technique of intimidation, but, of course, it is impossible to know what effect this had on the polling. Ballot, 1918, File 062, MDF-PR.

54. Superintendent to Commissioner, 9 February 1918, File 062, MDF-PR; Superintendent to President, 10 May 1918, File 064, MDF-PR; Superintendent to Any Member, 6 September 1919, File 064, MDF-PR; Superintendent to Chairman, 26 July 1923, File 062, MDF-PR.

55. Constitution and By-Laws of the Oglala Tribal Council, 26 April 1921, File 064, MDF-PR; Chief to Commissioner, 21 July 1921, File 61020–1921–054, Pine Ridge, CCF; Meeting of Delegates, 1 November 1921, File 062, MDF-PR; Superintendent to Commissioner, 6 January 1922, File 064, MDF-PR; Narrative Report, 1922, Pine Ridge, Roll 106, SAR; Williamson to Commissioner, 28 February 1923, File 064, MDF-PR; Commissioner to Superintendent, 22 March 1923, File 064, MDF-PR; Superintendent to Chairman, 26 July 1923, File 062, MDF-PR; Correspondent to Attorneys, 28 December 1923, File 064, MDF-PR; Case to Commissioner, 5 January 1924, File 064, MDF-PR; Superintendent to Commissioner, 12 February 1924, File 064, MDF-PR.

56. Narrative Report, 1924, Pine Ridge, 1924, Roll 106, SAR; Minutes of the Wakpamni District Council, 20–21 March 1925, File 064, MDF-PR; Proceedings of the Oglala Council, 21–23 January 1926, File 064, MDF-PR; Wanblee District Committee to Superintendent, 26 February 1926, File 064, MDF-PR; Minutes of the Oglala Council, 23 November 1926, File 064, MDF-PR; Corresponding Secretary to Superintendent, 7 February 1927, File 064, MDF-PR; Correspondent to Commissioner, 15 August 1927, File 064, MDF-PR.

57. Narrative Report, 1926, Pine Ridge, Roll 106, SAR.

58. Superintendent to Case, 24 September 1926, File 064, MDF-PR.

59. Superintendent to Commissioner, 16 January 1928, File 1131–1924–054, pt. 1, Pine Ridge, CCF; Superintendent to Commissioner, 31 July 1928, File 1131–1924–054, pt. 1, Pine Ridge, CCF; Constitution and By-Laws of the

Oglala Tribal Council, 30 November 1928, File 1131−1924−054, pt. 1, Pine Ridge, CCF; Superintendent to Commissioner 3 December 1928, File 1131−1924−054, pt. 1, Pine Ridge, CCF; Minutes of the Oglala Business Council, 5−6 April 1929, File 1131−1924−054, pt. 1, Pine Ridge, CCF; Minutes of the Oglala Business Council, 17 May 1929, File 1131−1924−054, pt. 1, Pine Ridge, CCF; Minutes of the Oglala Business Council, 2−3 April 1930, File 19969−1930−057, Pine Ridge, CCF; Minutes of the Oglala Business Council, 15 July 1930, File 42631−1930−057, Pine Ridge, CCF; Minutes of the Oglala Business Council, File 5671−1931−057, Pine Ridge, CCF; Field Agent to Commissioner, 9 September 1931, File 51571−1931−054, pt. 1, Pine Ridge, CCF.

60. Minutes of the Oglala Business Council, 15 January 1931, File 5671−1931−057, Pine Ridge, CCF.

61. Minutes of a Council at Porcupine, 20 February 1931, File 1131−1924−054, pt. 1, Pine Ridge, CCF.

62. Field Agent to Commissioner, 15 April 1931, File 1131−1924−054, pt. 1, Pine Ridge, CCF.

63. Minutes of a Council at Porcupine, 20 February 1931, File 1131−1924−054, pt. 1, Pine Ridge, CCF.

64. Field Agent to Commissioner, 15 April 1931, File 1131−1924−054, pt. 1, Pine Ridge, CCF.

65. Superintendent to Commissioner, 12 January 1929, File 1131−1931−054, pt. 1, Pine Ridge, CCF.

66. Minutes of a Council at Porcupine, 20 February 1931, File 1131−1924−054, pt. 1, Pine Ridge, CCF.

67. Field Agent to Commissioner, 15 April 1931, File 1131−1924−054, pt. 1, Pine Ridge, CCF.

68. Correspondent to Williamson, 3 April 1931, Pine Ridge Reservation File, box 4, Williamson Papers, RA; Correspondent to Commissioner, 3 April 1931, File 1131−1924−054. pt. 1, Pine Ridge, CCF.

69. Treasurer to Commissioner, 6 March 1931, File 1131−1924−054, pt. 1, Pine Ridge, CCF.

70. Treasurer to Williamson, 9 March 1931, Pine Ridge Reservation File, box 4, William Williamson Papers, RA; Williamson to Commissioner, 10 March 1931, Pine Ridge Reservation File, box 4, William Williamson Papers, RA; Correspondent to Williamson, 7 August 1932, Pine Ridge Reservation File, box 4, William Williamson Papers, RA. One of the chiefs involved in the opposition also wrote to Williamson, pointing out that he had helped him with votes, and that now it was time for Williamson to help the Oglala in their squabble with the Business Council. Chief to Williamson, 7 March 1931, Pine Ridge Reservation File, box 4, William Williamson Papers, RA.

71. Secretary to Commissioner, 8 March 1931, File 1131–1924–054, pt. 1, Pine Ridge, CCF.

72. Minutes of General Council, 13–14 November 1931, File 51571–1931–054, pt. 1, Pine Ridge CCF; Minutes of General Council, 11–12 December 1931, File 1131–1924–054, pt. 1, Pine Ridge, CCF; Constitution and By-Laws of the Oglala Treaty Council, 1931, File 1131–1924–054, pt. 1, Pine Ridge, CCF; Articles of Incorporation of the Oglala Tribal Council, 1933, File 9684–A–1936–068, GRCIO.

## Chapter 3

1. *Sioux Falls Argus Leader*, 2 and 4 March 1934.

2. Superintendent to Commissioner, 2 June 1933, File 40494–1930–054, Rosebud, CCF.

3. Assistant Solicitors to Commissioner, 28 December 1933, File 3395–1934–066, General Service, CCF.

4. Minutes, 8 December 1933, File 12021–1034–054, Pine Ridge, CCF; Superintendent to Commissioner, 27 December 1933, File 150, MDF-PR.

5. Circular 2970, 3 January 1934, Roll 14, PI.

6. Commissioner to Hughes, 4 December 1933, Folder 2, box 217, BCIM; Plan of Cooperation, Folder 9, box 226, BCIM; Regulations, 15 January 1934, General Correspondence, SFM.

7. Circular 80426, 20 January 1934, box 7, pt. 8, RCWHA.

8. Superintendent to Commissioner, 18 December 1933, File 150, MDF-PR.

9. Superintendent to Commissioner, 27 December 1933, File 150, MDF-PR; Holy Rosary Mission Superior to Hughes, 26 February 1934, Folder 2, box 217, BCIM; Holy Rosary Mission Superior to Ryan, 14 March 1934, Folder 14, box 223, BCIM; Missionary to Cardinal, 20 April 1937, Folder 3, box 241, BCIM; Philp 1977:148. The Lakota concern in the boarding school furor may not have been Catholic education for their children, but regular meals and other support for their children provided by the boarding schools.

10. Superintendent to Commissioner, 31 January 1934, Unlabeled File, box 2, RCWHA.

11. Minutes of the Rosebud Sioux Council, 1 February 1934, Unlabeled File, box 2, RCWHA; Superintendent to Commissioner, 8 February 1934, File 3919–50–066, Pine Ridge, GRCIO; Commissioner to Superintendent, 9 February 1934, File 020, MDF-PR.

12. Correspondent to Commissioner, Folder 14, box 223, BCIM; Missionary to Hughes, 2 April 1934, Folder 14, box 223, BCIM.

13. St. Francis Mission Superior to Hughes, 3 February 1934, Folder 15, box 1, BCIM.

14. U.S. Congress, Senate, *To Grant Indians Living under Federal Tutelage the Freedom to Organize for Purposes of Local Self-Government and Economic Enterprise* (27 February 1934), Hearings Before the Committee on Indian Affairs on S. 2755, 73rd Cong., 2d sess.

15. U.S. Department of the Interior, Office of Indian Affairs, *Minutes of the Plains Congress* (1934), Haskell Institute, Lawrence, Kan.

16. Ibid., 11.

17. Ibid., 12.

18. Ibid., 10. Such a "crazy plan" was, in fact, implied in a Solicitor's Office memo to Collier in December 1933. The memo advised Collier on the inequality of land holdings among allottees: "Plainly, such inequality must be eliminated as quickly as possible." However, "To state these objectives in statutory terms is perhaps politically inadvisable." Assistant Solicitors to Commissioner, 28 December 1933, File 3395−1934−066, General Service, CCF.

19. U.S. Department of the Interior, Office of Indian Affairs, *Minutes of the Plains Congress*, 19.

20. Ibid., 20.

21. Ibid., 116.

22. Ibid., 27−31.

23. Ibid., 33.

24. Ibid., 110.

25. Ibid., 99.

26. Ibid., 99.

27. Ibid., 100, 101.

28. Ibid., 131−32.

29. Correspondent to Director, 3 March 1934, File 35, box 224, BCIM. See also Correspondent to Director, 3 and 6 March 1934, File 35, box 224, BCIM.

30. *The Word Carrier*, March-April 1934, Ayer Collection, NL.

31. To All Missionaries, 6 June 1934, General Correspondence, SFM.

32. Superintendent to Commissioner, 19 April 1934, File 020, MDF-PR.

33. *South Dakota Churchman*, March-April 1934, AED.

34. General Referendum, 26 April 1934, File 076, MDF-PR.

35. Chairman to Commissioner, 27 March 1934, box 3, Part II-B, RCWHA.

36. Discussion of the Howard-Wheeler Bill by Dr. Henry Roe Cloud, 11 and 13 April 1934, pt. II-B, box 3, RCWHA.

37. Ibid.

38. Correspondent to Norbeck, 19 April 1934, Collier Indian Bill File, box 170, Norbeck Papers, RA; Superintendent to Commissioner, 4 May 1934, pt. II-B, box 3, RCWHA; Minutes of Meeting of Permittees, 12 December 1934, File 312, MDF-RB.

39. Assistant Director of Taxation to Werner, 22 February 1934, Collier Indian Bill File, box 170, Norbeck Papers; Superintendent to Commissioner, 16 March 1934, pt. II-B, box 3, RCWHA; Schell 1975:284−85.

40. Superintendent to Commissioner, 27 April 1934, pt. II-A, box 4, RCWHA.

41. Discussion of the Wheeler-Howard Bill by Dr. Henry Roe Cloud, 11 April 1934, pt. II-B, box 3, RCWHA; Pine Ridge Superintendent to Commissioner, 23 April 1934, File 065, MDF-PR; Report to the Sioux Nation, 30 April 1934, File 064, MDF-PR; Jennings to Commissioner, 13 September 1934, File 9684−1936−066, Pine Ridge, GRCIO.

42. Jennings to Commissioner, 16 September 1934, File 9684−A−1936−068, Pine Ridge, GRCIO; Superintendent to Commissioner, 28 September 1934, File 9684−1936−066, Pine Ridge, GRCIO; OIA to Rosebud Superintendent, 30 September 1934, Allotment Folders, Realty Office, Bureau of Indian Affairs, Rosebud Agency, Rosebud, S.D.; Superintendent to Commissioner, 4 October 1934, File 076, MDF-PR; Superintendent to Commissioner, 12 October 1934, File 076, MDF-PR; Ralph Case Report, Under Cover Commissioner to Superintendent, 18 October 1934, File 076, MDF-PR; Attorneys' Flyer, File 065, 1935−1937, MDF-PR; Educational Leaders, File 9684−1936−066, Pine Ridge, GRCIO.

43. Zimmerman to Secretary, 28 October 1934, File 9712−1936−068, Rosebud, GRCIO; Commissioner to Superintendent, 6 October 1934, File 9684−A−1936−068, Pine Ridge, GRCIO; Zimmerman to Superintendent, 20 October 1934, File 065, MDF-PR; Notice to Election Boards, 25 October 1934, File 065, MDF-PR; Indian Ballot, *Indians at Work* 2, no. 7 (15 November 1934): 9.

44. Haas 1947. The national average voter turnout based on the presidential election in 1932 and the congressional elections in 1934 was 60 percent (Taylor 1980:59).

45. U.S. Department of the Interior, Office of Indian Affairs, *Minutes of the Plains Congress*, 105.

46. Superintendent to Commissioner, 5 April 1934, File 9712−1936−068, Rosebud, GRCIO.

47. *The Word Carrier,* September-October 1934, Ayer Collection, NL; Mekeel 1944:213.

48. U.S. Congress, Senate, *Survey of Conditions of the Indians of the United States*, Hearings before a Subcommittee of the Committee on Indian Affairs, 76th Cong., pt. 37:21503.

49. Instructions Governing the Holding of the Referendum, File 076, MDF-PR.

50. Superintendent to Road Employee, 6 November 1934, File 076, MDF-PR; Superintendent to Commissioner, 22 January 1935, File 633338–1934–054, Rosebud, CCF.

51. General Referendum, File 065, MDF-PR; Vote on the Indian Reorganization Bill, File 9684–1936–066, Pine Ridge, GRCIO; Mekeel 1936:85.

52. Statement, 2 June 1934, File 29035–1934–054, Pine Ridge, CCF; Superintendent to Commissioner, 22 November 1934, File 9684–1036–066, Pine Ridge, GRCIO.

53. *The Word Carrier*, May-June 1934, Ayer Collection, NL.

54. Ballots and Results of Voting on the Wheeler-Howard Bill, RB; Correspondent to Bonnin, 14 December 1934, Allotment Folders, Realty Office, Bureau of Indian Affairs, Rosebud Agency, Rosebud, S.D.

55. Indian Vote Favorable to Wheeler-Howard Bill, *Mellette County Pioneer*, 2 November 1934.

56. Jennings to Commissioner, 1 December 1934, File 020, Wheeler-Howard Act, MDF-PR; Rosebud Tribal Chairman to Brenner, 1 November 1935, File 9712–066, Rosebud, CCF; U.S. Congress, Senate, *Survey of Conditions*, 21467.

57. Correspondent to Norbeck, 15 March 1926, Indian File, 1921, 1925, box 157, Norbeck Papers; Correspondent to Norbeck, 24 January 1927, Rosebud Indian Reservation File, box 3, Williamson Papers; Indian File, 1930, box 157, Norbeck Papers; Correspondent to Williamson, 14 January 1932, Pine Ridge Reservation File, box 4, Williamson Papers; Burnette and Koster 1974:116–17; Taylor 1980:59.

## Chapter 4

1. U.S. Congress, Senate, *Survey of Conditions of the Indians of the United States* (1940), Hearings before a Subcommittee of the Committee on Indian Affairs, 76th Cong., pt. 37:21808; Haas 1947:2; Collier 1963:177.

2. Deloria and Lytle 1984:15.

3. Minutes of the Rosebud Sioux Council, 6–8 December 1934, File 113–1935–054, Rosebud, CCF; Superintendent to Commissioner, 9 January 1935, File 076, MDF-PR; Superintendent to Commissioner, 10 January 1934, File 9712–A–1936–068, Rosebud, GRCIO.

4. Circular 96589, File 4894–34–066, pt. 8, box 7, RCWHA; Holst to Commissioner, 23 June 1935, Faris File, Correspondence with Officials, Records of the Indian Organization Division, Record Group 75, NA.

5. Jennings to Commissioner, 2 July 1935, File 020, MDF-PR; Superintendent to Commissioner, 24 July 1935, File 9712–A–1936–068, Rosebud, GRCIO.

6. Field Agent to Commissioner, 25 August 1935, File 9712–A–1936–068, Rosebud, GRCIO; Interview 28, American Indian Research Project, Dorris Duke Oral History Project, University of South Dakota, Vermillion.

7. Minutes of the Rosebud Sioux Council, 9–12 September 1935, File 4610–1936–054, Rosebud, CCF.

8. Minutes of the Rosebud Sioux Council, 10–11 October 1935, File 4610–1936–054, Rosebud, CCF; Rosebud Superintendent to Commissioner, 12 October 1935, File 9712–A–1936–068, Rosebud, GRCIO.

9. Zimmerman to Superintendent, 23 October 1935, File 9712–1936–068, Rosebud, GRCIO; Jennings to Superintendent, 6 November 1935, File 9711–1936–066, Rosebud, GRCIO; Commissioner Collier Visits Reservation, *Mellette County Pioneer*, 22 November 1935; Annual Report of the Extension Division, Rosebud, Records of the Division of Extension and Industry, Record Group 75, NA.

10. Chairman to Commissioner, 14 October 1935, File 9712–C–1936–057, Rosebud, CCF. The superintendent insisted that a quorum had been present at the October meeting. If a quorum meant a majority, however, a quorum had not been present. Only twenty-five councilmen were in attendance. While the precise size of the pre-IRA council was variable, in 1933 it had fifty-six official members. In one roll call in 1934, eighty councilmen were present. Superintendent to Commissioner, 18 October 1935, File 9712–C–1936–057, Rosebud, CCF; Minutes of the Rosebud Sioux Council, 11 December 1933, File 11255–1934–054, Rosebud, CCF.

11. Chairman to Werner, 1 November 1935, File 9712–066, Rosebud, GRCIO; Norbeck to Commissioner, 11 November 1935, File 9712–066, Rosebud, GRCIO; Commissioner to Norbeck, 16 November 1935, File 9712–066, Rosebud, GRCIO.

12. Petition, 28 October 1935, File 9712–066, Rosebud, GRCIO.

13. Ibid.; Secretary to Werner, 2 December 1935, File 9712–066, Rosebud, GRCIO.

14. Superintendent to Commissioner, 27 November 1935, File 9712–1936–068, Rosebud, GRCIO.

15. Minutes of the Rosebud Sioux Council, 13–14 December 1935, File 4610–1936–054, Rosebud, CCF.

16. Superintendent to Commissioner, 17 January 1935, File 076, MDF-PR; Superintendent to Commissioner 4 February 1935, File 9684–A–1936–068, Pine Ridge, GRCIO; Minutes of the Oglala Tribal Council, 25–26 January 1935, File 9684–E–1936–054, pt. 1, Pine Ridge, CCF.

17. Draft of the Constitution and By-Laws of the Oglala Sioux Tribal Council, File 9684–A–1936–068, Pine Ridge, GRCIO.

18. Superintendent to Commissioner, 4 February 1935, File 9684–A–1936–068, Pine Ridge, GRCIO; Zimmerman to Tribal Chairman, 13 February 1935, File 9684–C–1936–057, pt. 1, Pine Ridge, GRCIO.

19. Plan of Campaign, 24 June 1935, File 9684–1936–068, Pine Ridge, GRCIO; Minutes of the Oglala Tribal Council, 25 June 1935, File 46886–1935–054, Pine Ridge, CCF.

20. Jennings to Commissioner, 2 July 1935, File 020, MDF-PR; Joint Public Meeting, 8 August 1935, File 076, MDF-PR; Field Agent to Commissioner 28 August 1935, File 9684–A–1936–068, Pine Ridge, GRCIO.

21. Speech of Superintendent, 27 September 1935, File 9684–A–1936–068, Pine Ridge, GRCIO.

22. Minutes of the Oglala Tribal Council, 27–28 September 1935, File 9684–A–1936–068, Pine Ridge, GRCIO.

23. Ibid.

24. Correspondent to Commissioner and Secretary, 8 October 1935, File 9684–A–1936–068, Pine Ridge, GRCIO.

25. Field Agent to Commissioner, 27 October 1935, File 9684–A–1936–068, Pine Ridge, GRCIO.

26. Field Agent to Commissioner, 22 October 1935, File 9684–A–1936–068, Pine Ridge, GRCIO; Superintendent et al. to Commissioner, 24 October 1935, File 9684–A–1936–068, Pine Ridge, GRCIO; Examiner of Inheritance to Commissioner, 28 October 1935, File 9684–A–1936–068, Pine Ridge, GRCIO.

27. Meeting Held at Allen, South Dakota, 19 November 1935, File 9684–E–1936–054, pt. 1, Pine Ridge, CCF; Meeting Held at Pine Ridge Agency, 19 November 1935, pt. 2, ser. 2, Collier Papers, Microfilm copy, Manuscripts and Archives, Yale University Library, New Haven, Conn.

28. Meeting Held at Allen, South Dakota, 19 November 1935, File 9684–E–1936–054, pt. 1, Pine Ridge, CCF; Meeting Held at Pine Ridge Agency, 19 November 1935, pt. 2, ser. 2, Collier Papers. The Pine Ridge superintendent also dangled money before the Oglala at a council meeting after Collier left: "There is money laying in the Treasury Department waiting to be loaned to your people. Collier explained this to you and explained he wants to get even

more money." Minutes of the Oglala Tribal Council, 25 November 1935, File 9684–E–1936–054, pt. 1, Pine Ridge, CCF.

29. Meeting Held at Allen, South Dakota, 19 November 1935, File 9684–E–1936–054, pt. 1, Pine Ridge, CCF; Meeting Held at the Pine Ridge Agency, 19 November 1935, pt. 2, Ser. 2, Collier Papers.

30. Flyer, File 065, MDF-PR; Field Agent to Dear Sir, 4 December 1935, File 9684–C–1936–057, pt. 1, Pine Ridge, GRCIO.

31. Minutes of the Oglala Tribal Council, 3 December 1935, File 67446–1935–054, Pine Ridge, CCF.

32. Pine Ridge Superintendent to Commissioner, 21 December 1935, File 9684–A–1936–068, Pine Ridge, GRCIO. It was later claimed by opponents of the IRA that the referendum was held during a blizzard and that those favorable to ratification were transported to the polls by the OIA. There was a blizzard in South Dakota west of the Missouri on 14 December, and the OIA did use buses to transport voters, but it denied that the transportation was purposely selective. Diary of Father Eugene Buechel, 14 December 1935, SFM; U.S. Congress, Senate, *Survey of Conditions*, 21467, 21826.

33. Constitution and By-Laws of the Rosebud General Council, 20 December 1920, File 101910–1922–054, Rosebud, CCF; Constitution and By-Laws of the Rosebud General Council, 5 December 1924, File 101910–1922–054, Rosebud, CCF; Constitution of the Oglala Treaty Council, January 1932, File 1131–1924–054, pt. 1, Pine Ridge, CCF; Superintendent to Commissioner, 2 February 1933, File 51571–1931–054, pt. 1, Pine Ridge, CCF; Constitution and By-Laws of the Rosebud Sioux Council, 8 April 1933, File 40494–1930–054, Rosebud, CCF; Articles of Incorporation of the Oglala Sioux Tribal Council, 2 May 1933, File 51571–1931–054, pt. 1, Pine Ridge, CCF; Questionnaire on Tribal Organization, 17 July 1934, File 9684–A–1936–068, Pine Ridge, GRCIO; Questionnaire on Tribal Organization, 14 August 1934, File 9712–A–1936–068, Rosebud, GRCIO.

34. Circular 96589, File 9894–34–066, pt. 8, box 7, RCWHA.

35. Basic Memorandum, October 1935 File, Correspondence of the Office of the Solicitor, Record Group 48, NA.

36. Ibid.

37. Ibid.; Cohen 1960a.

38. Basic Memorandum.

39. U.S. Congress, Senate, *Repeal of the So-Called Wheeler-Howard Act* (2 August 1939), 76th Cong., 1st sess., Rept. 1047, 3; U.S. Congress, Senate, *Survey of Conditions*, 21873; U.S. Congress, House, *Investigate Indian Affairs* (1945), Hearings before a Subcommittee of the Committee on Indian Affairs, 78th Cong., 2d sess., pt. 3:176; Schusky 1975:192–93, 223; Jorgen-

sen 1978:17; Garbarino 1980; Bee 1981:95–96; Talbot 1981:70, 75; Hauptman 1984:141, 1986:369; Clow 1987:132; Cornell 1988:95, 193.

40. Circular 3095, 8 September 1935, Roll 15, PI; Commissioner to Secretary, 12 September 1935, Weekly Reports to the Secretary of the Interior, pt. 2,
ser. 2, Collier Papers; Collier 1963:346.

41. U.S. Congress, Senate, *Survey of Conditions*, 21820.

42. Superintendent to Tribal Chairman, 26 January 1938, Correspondence
File, Tribal Records, Lakota Archives and Historical Research Center, Sinte
Gleska College, Rosebud, S.D.; Grass Mt. Correspondent to Chair, 3 June
1939, Correspondence File, Tribal Records, Lakota Archives and Historical
Research Center.

43. Superintendent to Commissioner, 2 June 1933, File 40494–1930–054,
Rosebud, CCF; Program for the Development of Indian Self-Government and
Leadership, 21 May 1934, File 25688–1934–066, Rosebud, CCF.

44. Superintendent to Mekeel, 22 August 1935, File 9712–1936–066,
Rosebud, CCF; Administration at the Rosebud, 22 August 1935, File 9712–
1936–066, Rosebud, CCF.

45. William K. Powers (1975:109) and Marla N. Powers (1986:146) have
pointed out that it is the farm districts on Pine Ridge, not small communities, that have some correspondence with the nineteenth-century *tiyośpaye*
divisions.

46. A Memo on the Wheeler-Howard Bill, File 4894–1934–066, pt. 10-A,
box 8, RCWHA; Superintendent to Commissioner, 4 October 1935, File 9712–
A–1936–068, Rosebud, GRCIO.

47. Collier 1922:18.


## Chapter 5

1. Annual Extension Report, 1938, File 6687–1939–031, Pine Ridge,
CCF; U.S. Bureau of the Census, *Agriculture* (1942), Sixteenth Census of the
United States, 1940, vol. 1, pt. 2:468; ibid., vol. 2., pt. 1:718.

2. Narrative Reports, 1931, 1932, Rosebud, Roll 119, SAR.

3. Narrative Reports, 1929, 1930, 1931, 1933, Pine Ridge, Roll 107, SAR.

4. Narrative Reports, 1927, Roll 106, and 1933, Roll 107, Pine Ridge, SAR;
Narrative Report, 1928, Rosebud, Roll 118, SAR; Economic and Social Survey,
File 059, MDF-PR; Economic and Social Survey, box A–1381, RB; Indian Land
Leases File, box 3, William Williamson Papers, RA.

5. Narrative Reports, 1934, 1935, Pine Ridge, Roll 107, SAR; Annual Extension Report, 1935, File 13396–1936–031, Pine Ridge, CCF; Annual Exten-

sion Report, 1936, File 4589−1937−031, Pine Ridge, CCF; Resolutions of the Black Hills Treaty and Claim Council of Kyle, South Dakota, 19 January 1940, S2103 File, 76th Cong., Record Group 46, NA.

6. Narrative Report, 1934, Pine Ridge, Roll 107, SAR; Superintendent to Commissioner, 15 March, 1935, File 312, MDF-RB; Narrative Report, 1935, Rosebud, Roll 119, SAR; U.S. Congress, Senate, *Survey of Conditions of the Indians of the United States* (1940), Hearings before a Subcommittee of the Committee on Indian Affairs, 76th Cong., pt. 37:21818.

7. Narrative Report, 1934, Pine Ridge, Roll 119, SAR; Narrative Report, 1935, Rosebud, Roll 119, SAR; Reinstating an Ancient Tribal Craft on the Pine Ridge Indian Reservation, *Indians at Work* 2, no. 19 (15 May 1935): 21−25.

8. Statistical Report, 1929, Rosebud, Roll 119, SAR; Statistical Reports, 1930, 1932, Pine Ridge, Roll 107, SAR; Statistical Report, 1932, Pine Ridge, Roll 107, SAR; Annual Extension Report, 1933, Rosebud, Records of the Division of Extension and Industry, Record Group 75, NA; Superintendent to Commissioner, 9 August 1938, File 9711−1936−066, Rosebud, CCF; U.S. Congress, Senate, *Survey of Conditions,* 21836, 21925−27, 21931, 21933, 21936; Social Services Department to No. 16 Day School Teacher, 18 December 1941, File 749, MDF-PR. In addition to these sources, many Lakota families were eligible for relief not administered by the agencies. Agricultural Adjustment Administration (AAA) payments, Farm Security Administration (FSA) subsistence grants, and Social Security payments and commodities all played a role. As many as 1,400 Oglala families received FSA grants at one point. U.S. Congress, Senate, *Survey of Conditions,* 21818.

9. An IEWC Report from Rosebud Made at the Request of the Indian Workers, *Indians at Work* 2, no. 4 (1 October 1934): 22; The IEWC on Pine Ridge Reservation, South Dakota, *Indians at Work* 2, no. 6 (1 November 1934): 18−19; Special Agent to Commissioner, 22 October 1935, File 59819− 1935−054, Rosebud, CCF; Narrative Report, 1935, Pine Ridge, Roll 107, SAR; Narrative Report, 1936, Rosebud, Roll 119, SAR; Economic and Social Data on the Rosebud Indian Reservation, File 19712−1936−259, pt. 1, Rosebud, CCF; Useem, Macgregor, and Useem 1943:2; Parman 1971; Bromert 1978, 1980:ch. 6.

10. Employment under the Civil Works Administration, *Indians at Work* 1, no. 8 (1 December 1933): 5; The Emergency Employment Programs and the Sioux, *Indians at Work* 1, no. 12 (1 February 1934): 27−28; Narrative Report, 1935, Pine Ridge, Roll 107, SAR; Narrative Report, 1935, Rosebud, Roll 119, SAR; Economic and Social Data on the Rosebud Indian Reservation, File 19712− 1936−259, pt. 1, Rosebud, CCF; Minutes of the Rosebud Sioux Tribal Council, 5−7 January 1937, File 9712−E−1936−054, Rosebud, pt. 1, CCF; Memo to

Cooley, 5 December 1942, Extension 1941−46, Rehabilitation Garden Project File, box 6, Pine Ridge Records, RA; Bromert 1980:122.

11. Economic and Social Survey, 1934, Pine Ridge Reservation, File 059, MDF-PR; Economic and Social Survey, 1934, Rosebud, box A−1381, RB; Useem, Macgregor, and Useem 1943:2.

12. Narrative Report, 1935, Rosebud, Roll 119, SAR; Resolutions of the Black Hills Treaty and Claim Council of Kyle, South Dakota, 29 January 1940, S2103 File, 76th Cong., Record Group 46, NA; U.S. Congress, Senate, *Survey of Conditions,* 21818; Useem, Macgregor, and Useem, 1943:1.

13. Annual Extension Report, 1935, File 13396−1936−031, Pine Ridge, CCF; Annual Extension Report, 1935, File 13401−1936−031, Rosebud, CCF.

14. Reservation Program Data, 1943, RB; Rosebud's Tribal Land Enterprise, *Indians at Work* 11, no. 6 (March-April 1944): 15.

15. General Grazing Regulations, 28 December 1935, File 301, MDF-RB; Grazing, Reservation Program Data, 1940, RB; U.S. Department of Agriculture, Soil Conservation Service, Range Management of the Pine Ridge Indian Reservation, 1940, Pine Ridge Agency, Bureau of Indian Affairs [copy in possess. of author]; U.S. Congress, Senate, *Survey of Conditions,* 21823, 21916−17.

16. General Grazing Regulations, 28 December 1935, File 301, MDF-RB.

17. This description of TLE is gleaned from Stock Certificate Plan, 14 July 1941, Washington Office Circulars File, Subject Correspondence File, RB; By-Laws of the Tribal Land Enterprise, 1943, TLE Records, RST; Reservation Program Data, 1943, RB; Credit Agent to Commissioner, 4 August 1945, File 45014−1938−031, Rosebud, CCF; Annual Meeting of Holders of Interest in the Tribal Land Enterprise, 4 October 1945, Minutes of the Board of Directors File, TLE Records, RST; Chairman to Holders of Interest, 4 October 1945, Minutes of the Board of Directors File, TLE Records, RST; Auditor to Board, 21 September 1945, Minutes of the Board of Directors File, TLE Records, RST; Minutes, Board of Directors, 12 December 1945, Minutes of the Board of Directors File, TLE Records, RST.

18. Stock Certificate Plan, 14 July 1941, Washington Office Circulars File, Subject Correspondence File, RB.

19. Superintendent to Critchfield, 10 April 1944, Minutes of the Board of Directors File, TLE Records, RST. Shareholders who did not receive land assignments from TLE received dividends approximating the rental incomes they had previously received for their land. Seventy-five individual shareholders received dividends ranging from less than one dollar to $33.50 in 1945.

20. Economic and Social Data on the Rosebud Indian Reservation, File 19712−1936−259, pt. 1, Rosebud, CCF; Annual Extension Report, 1941, File

486–1942–031, Pine Ridge, CCF; Annual Extension Report, 1943, File 13778–1944–031, Pine Ridge, CCF.

21. Indian Cattle Purchase Program, *Indians at Work* 2, no. 3 (15 September 1934): 10; Annual Extension Report, 1938, File 6687–1939–031, Pine Ridge, CCF; Reservation Program Data, 1940, RB; U.S. Congress, Senate, *Survey of Conditions*, 21823, 21917.

22. Extension Report, 1941, File 2658–1942–031, Rosebud, CCF; Jennings and Field Agent to Commissioner, File 64695–1938–031, Rosebud, CCF; Audit Report, 28 February 1946, File 35929–1946–259, Rosebud, CCF.

23. File 215, Reimbursable Funds, MDF-PR; Narrative Report of Revolving Loan Program of the Oglala Sioux Tribe, 30 June 1945, File 28440–1944–031, Pine Ridge, CCF; Our Tribal Loans, *Voice of the Sioux People*, 1945, File 2682–43–054, pt. 1, Pine Ridge, box 328, Accession 56A–588, Record Group 75, NA.

24. Adult Education Program, n.d., File 749, MDF-PR.

25. Annual Extension Report, 1935, File 13401–1936–031, Rosebud, CCF; Reservation Program Data, 1944, File 720, MDF-PR.

26. Annual Extension Report, 1935, File 13396–1936–031, Pine Ridge, CCF; Annual Extension Report, 1935, File 13401–1936–031, Rosebud, CCF; Community Work at Grass Creek, Pine Ridge, South Dakota, *Indians at Work* 4, no. 2 (1 September 1936): 46–47; The News from Medicine Bow Day School and Potato Creek Community, *Indians at Work* 6, no. 2 (October 1938): 46; Annual Extension Report, 1938, File 6687–1939–031, Pine Ridge, CCF; Superintendent to Commissioner, 9 January 1939, File 9712–E–1936–054, Rosebud, GRCIO; Reservation Program Data, 1940, RB; File 749, MDF-PR; Rehabilitation (Exhibit B), 1941, File 6989–1936–056, pt. 1, Rosebud, CCF; Reservation Program Rosebud-Yankton, pt. 5, box 44, Rehabilitation Project Records, Record Group 75, NA.

27. Rosebud Community Gardens, *Indians at Work* 3, no. 2 (1 September 1935): 46; Irrigation Helps Gardens at Kyle, South Dakota, *Indians at Work* 5, no. 6 (February 1938): 21; Annual Extension Report, 1939, File 5277–40–031, Pine Ridge, box 1287, Accession 53A–367, Record Group 75, NA; U.S. Congress, Senate, *Survey of Conditions*, 21923; Extension 1941–46, Rehabilitation Garden Project File, Pine Ridge Records, RA; Reservation Program, Rosebud-Yankton, pt. 5, box 44, Rehabilitation Project Records, Record Group 75, NA.

28. Livestock Activities of Pine Ridge Indians, *Indians at Work* 3, no. 11 (15 January 1936): 37–40; Annual Extension Report, 1940, File 13–1941–031, Rosebud, CCF; Annual Extension Report, 1941, File 2658–1942–031, Rosebud, CCF; Annual Extension Report, 1941, File 486–1942–031, Pine Ridge, CCF; Annual Extension Report, 1942, File 712–1943–031, Pine Ridge,

CCF; Annual Extension Report, 1943, File 13778–1944–031, Pine Ridge, CCF; Annual Extension Report, 1944, File 5521–1945–031, Pine Ridge, CCF; Annual Extension Report, 1945, File 8706–1946–031, Pine Ridge, CCF.

29. This description of rehabilitation colonies on Rosebud is based on: Grass Mountain Colony, *Indians at Work* 6, no. 10 (June 1939): 28–29; Superintendent to Commissioner, 4 May 1940, Extension and Credit File, Rosebud Records, RA; Housing Development Records, RB; U.S. Congress, Senate, *Survey of Conditions*, 21922–3; Reservation Program, Rosebud-Yankton, pt. 5, box 44, Rehabilitation Project Records, RG 75, NA.

30. Red Shirt Table—A Community Working Toward Self-Support, *Indians at Work* 4, no. 20 (1 June 1937): 36. On the Red Shirt Table project, see also Red Shirt Table Development, *Indians at Work* 6, no. 8 (April 1939): 16–20; File 532, Red Shirt 1937, MDF-PR; Annual Extension Report, 1939, File 5277–40–031, Pine Ridge, box 1287, Accession 53A–367, Record Group 75, NA; U.S. Congress, Senate, *Survey of Conditions*, 21821; 1941–49 Land Management File, Pine Ridge Records, RA; Superintendent to Commissioner, 8 May 1942, File 9684–C–1936–057, pt. 2, Pine Ridge, GRCIO; DeMallie 1978: 280–83.

31. Superintendent to Commissioner, 8 May 1942, File 9684–C–1936–057, pt. 2, Pine Ridge, GRCIO.


Chapter 6

1. Collier 1945:275, 1963:346. On the influence of the philosophy of indirect rule on the Indian New Deal, see Hauptman 1986.

2. Superintendent to Commissioner, 21 April 1936, File 9684–C–1936–057, pt. 1, Pine Ridge, GRCIO.

3. President to Commissioner, 14 August 1936, File 9684–C–1936–057, pt. 1, Pine Ridge, GRCIO.

4. Jennings to Commissioner, 20 June 1938, Unlabeled File, Correspondence with Officials, Records of the Indian Organization Division, Record Group 75, NA.

5. Statements Concerning Indian Service Policies, 1939, File 011, MDF-RB.

6. Superintendent to Commissioner, 11 January 1936, File 9684–C–1936–057, pt. 1, Pine Ridge, GRCIO; Minutes of the Rosebud Sioux Tribal Council, 4–5 January 1939, File 9712–E–1936–054, pt. 2, Rosebud, GRCIO; Semi-Monthly Report of Organization Field Personnel, 23 July 1941, File 51571–1931–054, pt. 2, Pine Ridge, CCF; Superintendent to Commissioner, 5 August 1941, File 51571–1931–054, pt. 2, Pine Ridge, CCF; McCaskill to Field Agent, 23 October 1941, File 6989–1936–056, pt. 1, Rosebud, CCF.

7. Law and Order Code of the Rosebud Sioux Tribe, 1937, Tribal Records, RST; Minutes of the Rosebud Sioux Tribal Council, 8 April 1937, File 9712–E–1936–054, pt. 1, Rosebud, CCF; Law and Order Code of the Oglala Sioux Tribe, 1937, U.S. Congress, Senate, *Survey of the Conditions of the Indians of the United States* (1940), Hearings before a Subcommittee of the Committee on Indian Affairs, 76th Cong., pt. 37:21749–66.

8. Superintendent to Commissioner, 20 November 1937, File 11435–1936–172, Rosebud, CCF.

9. Superintendent to Commissioner, 11 December 1937, File 9712–1936–054, vol. 1, Rosebud, CCF.

10. Jennings to Commissioner, 14 December 1937, File 9712–1936–054, vol. 1, Rosebud, CCF.

11. Mekeel to Commissioner, 13 December 1937, File 9712–1936–054, vol. 1., Rosebud, CCF.

12. Westwood to Jennings, 13 December 1937, File 9712–1936–054, vol. 1, Rosebud, CCF; Cohen to Commissioner 17 December 1937, File 9712–1936–054, vol. 1, Rosebud, CCF.

13. Commissioner to Chairman, 13 January 1938, File 9712–1936–054, vol. 2, Rosebud, CCF.

14. Agency Physician to Agency Clerk, 30 December 1932, File 073, General Correspondence File, RB.

15. Judges to Superintendent, 26 February 1932, File 073, General Correspondence File, RB.

16. The Question of the Indian Dance, Rosebud Reservation, 22 August 1932, File 073, Correspondence File, RB.

17. Correspondent to Superintendent, 20 February 1933, File 073, Correspondence File, RB.

18. Meiklejohn to Harper, 18 December 1936, File 9712–1936–054, vol. 1, Rosebud, CCF.

19. The supervisory function was not always used to disempower the tribal government, but, on occasion, to protect it. In 1938, for example, the secretary's office rescinded a tax ordinance enacted by the Oglala Sioux Tribal Council because it delegated some discretionary administrative power to the superintendent. The secretary's office insisted that the tribal constitution did not authorize delegation of tribal powers to the superintendent, but only to tribal authorities. Acting Secretary of the Interior to Tribal President, 19 May 1938, File 9684–C–1936–057, Pine Ridge, GRCIO.

20. Minutes of the Rosebud Sioux Tribal Council, 12–14 January 1938, File 9712–E–1936–054, pt. 1, Rosebud, CCF. On *yuwipi* see W. Powers 1982.

21. Zimmerman to Superintendent, 29 October 1937, Correspondence File, Tribal Records, RST.

22. Superintendent to Chairman, 23 January 1938, Correspondence File, Tribal Records, RST; Superintendent to Chairman, 26 January 1938, File 9712–1936–054, vol. 2, Rosebud, CCF. The distinction between practicing medicine and practicing religion would not have been recognized by Lakota practitioners.

23. Resolution of the Rosebud Sioux Tribal Council, 3 May 1937, File 9712–1936–054, vol. 1, Rosebud, CCF; Superintendent to Rosebud Sioux Tribal Council, 1 June 1937, File 9712–1936–054, vol. 1, Rosebud, CCF.

24. Secretary to Commissioner, 1 June 1937, File 9712–1936–054, vol. 1., Rosebud, CCF.

25. Ibid.

26. Zimmerman to Tribal Chairman, 30 September 1937, File 9712–1936–054, vol. 1., Rosebud, CCF.

27. Native American Church to Commissioner, 1 September 1941, File 623–1940–054, Pine Ridge, box 1287, Accession 53A–367, Record Group 75, NA; Commissioner to Correspondent, 17 March 1942, File 9684–C–1936–057, pt. 2, Pine Ridge, GRCIO; Superintendent to Secretary, 25 April 1942, File 51571–1931–054, pt. 2, Pine Ridge, CCF.

28. Superintendent to Commissioner, 22 July 1943, File 2682–43–054, pt. 1, Pine Ridge, box 238, Accession 56A–588, Record Group 75, NA.

29. Jennings to Zimmerman, 23 August 1943, File 2682–43–054, pt. 1, Pine Ridge, box 238, Accession 56A–588, Record Group 75, NA; Zimmerman to Assistant Secretary of the Interior, 23 September 1943, File 2682–43–054, pt. 1, Pine Ridge, box 238, Accession 56A–588, Record Group 75, NA.

30. Chapman to Tribal President, 14 October 1943, File 2682–43–054, pt. 1, Pine Ridge, box 238, Accession 56A–588, Record Group 75, NA; Chapman to Chairman, 4 May 1944, File 2682–43–054, pt. 1, Pine Ridge, box 238, Accession 56A–588, Record Group 75, NA; Stewart 1972; United States Department of the Interior, *Opinions of the Solicitor of the Department of the Interior Relating to Indian Affairs, 1917–1974* (1979), vol. 1, 846; Robert Stahl, personal communication, 1989.

31. Daiker to Superintendent, 26 September 1936, File 11435–1936–172, Rosebud, CCF; Correspondent to Commissioner, 14 January 1937, File 9712–1936–054, vol. 1, Rosebud, CCF; Superintendent to Commissioner, 12 February 1945, File 9684–1936–066, Pine Ridge, GRCIO; McCaskill to Superintendent, 10 July 1945, File 9684–1936–066, Pine Ridge, GRCIO; Superintendent to McCaskill, 16 July 1945, File 9684–1936–066, Pine Ridge, GRCIO.

32. Hearing Before Commissioner, 11 May 1939, File 6989–1936–056, pt. 1, Rosebud, CCF; Narrative Report, Revolving Credit Operations, 1942, File 45014–1938–031, Rosebud, CCF; Unofficial Code of Laws, 1942, Ordinances and Resolutions Adopted by the Rosebud Sioux Tribal Council and Other Tribal Groups, RB.

33. Hearing Before Commissioner, 11 May 1939, File 6989–1936–056, pt. 1, Rosebud, CCF; Statements Concerning Indian Service Policies, 1939, File 011, MDF-RB; Delegates to Commissioner, 3 May 1940, File 066, MDF-RB.

34. Resolutions of the Rosebud Sioux Tribal Council, 5–6 January 1943, File 2699–1947–054, Rosebud, Accession 56A–588, box 263, Record Group 75, NA; Program of Delegation, 7 January 1943, File 6989–1936–056, pt. 1, Rosebud, CCF; Zimmerman to Delegates, 2 February 1943, File 6989–1936–056, pt. 1, Rosebud, CCF.

35. Resolution of The Rosebud Sioux Tribal Council, 12–15 January 1938, File 9712–1936–054, vol. 2, Rosebud, CCF; Minutes of the Rosebud Sioux Tribal Council, 24 April 1939, File 9712–E–1936–054, pt. 2, Rosebud, GRCIO; Proceedings of Special Committee to Re-Draft the CCC-ID Program for the Fiscal Year 1941–42, 15 April 1941, File 9712–1936–054, vol. 4, Rosebud, CCF.

36. Resolution of The Rosebud Sioux Tribal Council, 12–15 January 1938, File 9712–1936–054, vol. 2, Rosebud, CCF; Zimmerman to Case, 16 March 1939, Rosebud Indian Agency File, Francis Case Papers, Layne Library, Dakota Wesleyan University, Mitchell, S.D.; Minutes of the Rosebud Sioux Tribal Council, 2–4 October 1939, File 9712–E–1936–054, pt. 2, Rosebud, GRCIO; Minutes of the Rosebud Sioux Tribal Council, 1 August 1940, File 9712–E–1936–054, pt. 2, Rosebud, GRCIO; Proceedings of Special Committee to Re-Draft the CCC-ID Program for the Fiscal Year 1941–42, 15 April 1941, File 9712–1936–054, vol. 4, Rosebud, CCF; Memo from Superintendent, 18 April 1941, File 9712–1936–054, vol. 4, Rosebud, CCF.

37. Memo from Tribal Employment Committee, 19 July 1940, Memorandum File, Tribal Records, RST; Superintendent to Tribal Chairman, 22 July 1940, File 9712–1936–054, vol. 4, Rosebud, CCF.

38. Resolution of the Rosebud Sioux Tribal Council, 1 August 1940, File 9712–1936–054, vol. 4, Rosebud, CCF; Tribal Secretary to Secretary of the Interior, 8 August 1940, File 9712–1936–054, vol. 4, Rosebud, CCF.

39. Superintendent to Commissioner, 22 July 1943, File 2682–43–054, pt. 1, Pine Ridge, box 238, Accession 55A–588, Record Group 75, NA.

40. Superintendent to Chairman, 31 January 1938, File 9712–1936–054, vol. 2, Rosebud, CCF.

41. Minutes of the Oglala Sioux Tribal Council, 15–16 April 1936, File 9684–E–1936–054, pt. 1, Pine Ridge, CCF.

42. Executive Committee to Commissioner, 28 April 1936, File 9684–C–1936–057, pt. 1, Pine Ridge, GRCIO; Commissioner to President, 21 May 1936, File 9684–C–1936–057, pt. 1, Pine Ridge, GRCIO.

43. Westwood Memo, 30 June 1936, File 9684–C–1936–057, pt. 1, Pine Ridge, GRCIO.

44. Minutes of the Oglala Sioux Tribal Council, 10–13 April 1945, File 9684–1936–054, pt. 3, Pine Ridge, CCF.

45. Superintendent to Commissioner, 12 February 1945, File 9684–1936–066, Pine Ridge, GRCIO; Assistant Tribal Secretary to Secretary of the Interior, 26 March 1945, File 2682–43–054, pt. 1, box 238, Accession 56A–588, Record Group 75, NA.

46. Superintendent to Commissioner, 11 May 1945, File 9684–1936–066, Pine Ridge, GRCIO.

47. Commissioner to Mueller, 8 November 1945, File 9684–1936–066, Pine Ridge, GRCIO; Report of Efficiency Rating, 1 April 1946, U.S. Office of Personnel Management, St. Louis [deaccessioned by repository; now in possession of author].

48. Indian Organization, 29–30 January 1937, File 076, MDF-PR; Superintendent to McCaskill, 30 July 1945, File 9684–1936–066, Pine Ridge, GRCIO; McNickle to Commissioner, File 9684–1936–066, Pine Ridge, GRCIO; Report of Efficiency Rating.

49. Transfer and Promotion, Effective 1 September 1946, U.S. Office of Personnel Management.

50. Cohen 1960b.

51. Shepard to Commissioner, 19 June 1942, File 067, MDF-RB; Superintendent to Commissioner, 28 July 1942, Correspondence with Officials, Records of the Indian Organization Division, Record Group 75, NA.

52. Mekeel 1944:211.

Chapter 7

1. Local Treaty Council, n.d., Black Hills Claim File, Francis Case Papers, Layne Library, Dakota Wesleyan University, Mitchell, S.D.; Minutes of the Ring Thunder Local Council, n.d., File 9711–1936–066, Rosebud, CCF; Treaty Council, n.d., File 9684–C–1936–057, Pine Ridge, GRCIO; Correspondent to Collier, 12 May 1937, File 9684–C–1936–057, Pine Ridge, GRCIO; Correspondent to Case, 23 January 1938, Black Hills Council File, Francis Case Papers; Superintendent to Commissioner, 4 March 1938, File 31330–

1937−054, General Service, CCF; Great Plains Sioux Congress, 1−2 July 1938, File 17822−1938−066, General Service, CCF; Proceedings and Debates of the Eight Reservation Indians, 22−24 June 1939, Black Hills Council File, Francis Case Papers; Resolution of the Great Sioux Nation Black Hills Claim Treaties Council, 11 December 1943, Folder 1, box 3, Ralph Case Papers, RA.

2. Chairman to Commissioner, 28 September 1936, File 9712−C−1936−057, Rosebud, CCF; Correspondent to Commissioner, 1 June 1937, File 9712−1936−054, vol. 1, Rosebud, CCF.

3. U.S. Congress, Senate, *Survey of Conditions of the Indians of the United States* (1940), Hearings before a Subcommittee of the Committee on Indian Affairs, 76th Cong., pt. 37:21826.

4. Superintendent to Commissioner, 4 March 1938, File 31330−1937−054, General Service, CCF; Superintendent to Commissioner, 8 April 1940, File 076, MDF-PR.

5. 1934 Census, Rosebud, Roll 444, ICR; 1937 Census, Pine Ridge, Roll 383, ICR; personal communications, U.S. Department of the Interior, Bureau of Indian Affairs, Pine Ridge Agency and Rosebud Agency, Pine Ridge and Rosebud, S.D. Data are not available for two of the Rosebud old dealers.

6. Reports of Industrial Surveys, Pine Ridge, Record Group 75, NA; Competency Commission Reports, Pine Ridge, Roll 12, Major James McLaughlin Papers, Microfilm copy, Assumption Abbey Archives, Richardton, N.D.

7. None of the most prominent old dealers ran for office in the 1938 election on Pine Ridge, the only election for which records have survived. Election Report, 11 February 1938, File 9684−C−1936−057, Pine Ridge, GRCIO; Correspondent to Commissioner, 14 February 1938, File 9684−C−1936−057, Pine Ridge, GRCIO.

8. WPA Anthropological Schedules, RA; Minutes of Meeting of Special Delegates, 20 November 1943, Roll 104, Karl E. Mundt Papers, Microfilm copy, Karl E. Mundt Historical and Educational Foundation, Dakota State College, Madison, S.D.

9. Economic Survey and Related Records, 1940−41, PR; Audit Report, 28 February 1946, File 35929−1946−259, Rosebud, box 55, Accession 68A−4937, Record Group 75, NA.

10. Acting Secretary to Chair et al., 27 April 1936, File 9711−1936−066, Rosebud, CCF; Minutes of the Ring Thunder Local Council, n.d., File 9711−1936−066, Rosebud, CCF; Zimmerman to Chairman, 8 May 1937, File 9684−C−1936−057, Pine Ridge, GRCIO; Minutes of the Treaty Council, 18−20 September 1937, File 9684−C−1936−057, Pine Ridge, GRCIO.

11. Minutes of the Rosebud Sioux Tribal Council, 15−16 April 1936, File 9684−E−1936−054, pt. 1, CCF; Letter to Commissioner, 12 June 1937, File 9684−C−1936−057, pt. 1, Pine Ridge, GRCIO; Superintendent to Education

Division, 15 February 1938, File 9684–c–1936–057, pt. 1, Pine Ridge, GRCIO; Superintendent to Commissioner, 14 April 1939, File 9684–c–1936–057, pt. 2, Pine Ridge, GRCIO; Head Community Worker to Commissioner, 29 January 1940, File 6844–1940–013, Pine Ridge, box 1287, Accession 53A–367, Record Group 75, NA; Work of the Oglala Sioux Tribal Council, 11 November 1944, File 9684–1936–066, Pine Ridge, GRCIO.

12. Proceedings of the Treaty Council, 8 May 1937, File 9684–c–1936–057, Pine Ridge, GRCIO; Resolution of the Rosebud Sioux Treaty Council, n.d. [1939], Rosebud Indian Agency File, Francis Case Papers; The Black Hills Treaty and Claim Council, 11 May 1943, Roll 104, Mundt Papers.

13. Correspondent to Mundt, 9 April 1943, Roll 104, Mundt Papers.

14. Jennings to Daiker, 21 November 1938, File 9684–a–1936–068, Pine Ridge, GRCIO; Superintendent to Commissioner, 26 April 1939, File 9684–c–1936–057, pt. 2, Pine Ridge, GRCIO; Daiker to Tribal President, 17 February 1939, File 9684–c–1936–057, pt. 1, Pine Ridge, GRCIO; Superintendent to Commissioner, 26 April 1939, File 9684–c–1936–057, pt. 2, Pine Ridge, GRCIO; U.S. Congress, Senate, *Survey of Conditions*, 21597–21604.

15. Commissioner to Petitioner, 14 November 1938, File 9784–a–1936–068, Pine Ridge, GRCIO; Commissioner to Superintendent, 14 November 1938, File 9784–a–1936–068, Pine Ridge, GRCIO; Zimmerman to Superintendent, 17 March 1939, File 064, MDF-PR; Superintendent to Commissioner, 14 April 1939, File 9684–c–1936–057, pt. 2, GRCIO; Memorandum on the Pine Ridge Constitution, 14 April 1939, File 9684–c–1936–057, pt. 2, GRCIO; Minutes of the Oglala Sioux Tribal Council, 14–18 July 1941, File 9684–e–1936–054, pt. 2, Pine Ridge, CCF; Complaint, 18 April 1941, File 51571–1931–054, pt. 2, Pine Ridge, CCF.

16. Chief Special Officer to Commissioner, 3 October 1939, General Correspondence of the Chief Special Officer, Records of the Law and Order Section, Record Group 75, NA.

17. Superintendent to Commissioner, 4 March 1938, File 31330–1937–054, General Service, CCF.

18. U.S. Congress, Senate, *Survey of Conditions*, 21481.

19. Ibid., 21471.

20. Ibid., 21829.

21. Commissioner to Pine Ridge Superintendent, 2 March 1938, File 31330–1937–054, General Service, CCF.

22. The conviction was appealed to the Oglala superior court where federally-appointed superior judges heard the case and reversed the lower court decision. Superintendent to Commissioner, 4 March 1938, File 31330–1937–054, General Service, CCF.

23. U.S. Congress, Senate, *Survey of Conditions*, 21615.

24. Superintendent to Commissioner, 26 April 1939, File 9684–C–1936–057, pt. 2, Pine Ridge, GRCIO.

25. U.S. Senate, *Survey of Conditions*, 21829.

26. Petition, December 1939, File 6844–1940–013, Pine Ridge, box 1287, Accession 53A–367, Record Group 75, NA; McCaskill Memo, 13 May 1940, File 6989–1936–056, pt. 1, Rosebud, CCF.

27. Chairman to Case, 12 May 1936, Rosebud Reservation File, box 128, SSC; U.S. Congress, House, *Conditions on Sioux Reservations* (1937), Hearings Before the Committee on Indian Affairs on HR 5753, 75th Cong., 1st sess., 11 (emphasis in original); Memorandum of Meeting of the Old Treaty Council, n.d., File 062, MDF-PR; Abstract of Treaty Council Committee's Request, 16 October 1945, File 9684–1936–066, Pine Ridge, GRCIO.

28. Memorandum of Meeting of the Old Treaty Council, n.d., File 06, MDF-PR.

29. U.S. Congress, Senate, *Survey of Conditions*, 21610–11, 21861. These old dealers had more in mind than the tribal councils in these criticisms. They probably referred to most aspects of the New Deal, including unit leasing and cooperative organization.

30. Correspondent to Thomas and Bulow, 15 April 1938, File 23780–1938–155, Rosebud, CCF; Abstract of Treaty Council Committee's Request, 16 October 1945, File 9684–1936–066, Pine Ridge, GRCIO.

31. 1934 Census, Rosebud, Roll 444, ICR; Forestry and Grazing Report, 1937, Pine Ridge, File 47762–1937–031, Pine Ridge, CCF; 1937 Census, Pine Ridge, Roll 383, ICR; Forestry and Grazing Report, 1938, File 6687–1939–031, Pine Ridge, CCF; Superintendent to Commissioner, 1 June 1939, File 6989–1936–056, Rosebud, CCF; Forestry and Grazing Report, 1939, Pine Ridge, File 54274–1939–031, Pine Ridge, CCF; Land Use Report and Proposed Indian Range Unit Records, RB; U.S. Congress, Senate, *Survey of Conditions*, 21858, 21890–1.

32. Report of Loans, 1944, File 28440–44–031, Pine Ridge, box 238, Accession 56A–588, Record Group 75, NA; Audit Report, 28 February 1946, File 36929–1946–259, Rosebud, box 55, Accession 68A–4937, Record Group 75, NA; Macgregor 1946:25; Useem 1947:23.

33. U.S. Congress, Senate, *Survey of Conditions*, 21459 (emphasis added). This, of course, was a partisan representation of the past. It involved, among other things, pointed propositions about the *voluntary* nature of fee patenting—*forced* fee patenting was erased in this historical representation—and about fee patenting being equivalent to tribal disenrollment. Some of my contemporary consultants on Rosebud believe that there were no forced fee patents. They insist that mixedbloods voluntarily sought removal of trust status

in the early twentieth century and were thereby "terminated"; they voluntarily "disenrolled" themselves, "relinquished rights as being part of that tribe"; they "became *waśicun*" (white).

There were other, similarly delegitimating, historical representations of mixedbloods during the New Deal period. U.S. Congress, House, *Conditions on Sioux Reservations*, 17; U.S. Congress, Senate, *Survey of Conditions*, 21863; Correspondent to Sharpe, 23 March 1944, Folder 1, box 3, Ralph Case Papers.

34. Correspondent to Thomas and Bulow, 15 April 1938, File 23780–1938–155, Rosebud, CCF.

35. Treaty Council of the Sioux Tribe, 11−12 March 1937, File 062, MDF-PR; Abstract of Treaty Council Committee's Request, 16 October 1945, File 19834–1936–066, Pine Ridge, GRCIO.

36. Schneider, Schneider, and Hansen 1972:331.

37. U.S. Congress, Senate, *Survey of Conditions*, 21540.

38. Correspondent to Mundt, 29 July 1944, Roll 104, Mundt Papers.

39. *Oun t'anni* was a Lakota neologism. Black Hills Treaty Council, 23 April 1938, Pine Ridge and Rosebud Sioux Delegates File, SSC.

40. Useem 1947:156.

41. Resolutions of the Black Hills Treaty Council, 4−6 April 1938, Pine Ridge and Rosebud Sioux Delegates File, box 128, SSC. See also Resolutions of the Eight Reservations Treaty and Claims Council, 4−6 April 1940, Repeal Wheeler-Howard Act File, box 36, SSC; Resolutions of the Black Hills Claim and Treaty Council, 14−15 May 1940, File 6844–1940–013, Pine Ridge, box 1287, Accession 53A–367, NA; Black Hills Treaty and Claim Council, 11 May 1943, Roll 104, Mundt Papers.

42. Correspondent to Thomas, 29 September 1944, box 128, SSC; Correspondent to Thomas, 6 February 1945, box 128, SSC.

43. U.S. Congress, Senate, Committee on Indian Affairs, *Analysis of the Statement of the Commissioner of Indian Affairs in Justification of Appropriations for 1944, and the Liquidation of the Indian Bureau* (1943), 78th Cong., 1st sess., Senate Partial Rept. 310; U.S. Congress, House, *Investigate Indian Affairs* (1945), Hearings on House Resolution 166, 78th Cong., 2d sess., pt. 3:188−89, 209, 212, 214, 220.

44. Conference Report, 26−28 July 1943, File 9684−E−1936−054, pt. 2, Pine Ridge, CCF; Minutes of the Black Hills Sioux Nation Council, 13, 16−17 September 1943, Black Hills Treaty Council File, box 126, SSC; Minutes of the Oglala Sioux Tribal Council, 10−15 January 1944, File 9684−E−1936−054, pt. 2, Pine Ridge, CCF.

45. The disempowerment of IRA tribal councils and its role in conditioning reservation politics has been recognized by other scholars: Thomas 1966a, 1966b; Gearing 1970:104; Jorgensen 1972:223–24; Schusky 1975: 193, 225; Bee 1981:96. Compare this with the situation among the Wind River Arapaho where council members have been effective intermediaries, securing per capita payments and other material benefits from the federal government. Tribal government there does not face the crisis of authority common on other reservations (Fowler 1978, 1982).

46. Minutes of the Rosebud Sioux Tribal Council, 29 April–1 May 1936, File 9712–E–1936–054, pt. 1, Rosebud, CCF; Assistant Range Examiner to Commissioner, 20 February 1941, File 9712–1936–054, vol. 4, Rosebud, CCF; Memo from Superintendent, 18 April 1941, Memorandum File, Tribal Records, RST; Superintendent to Commissioner 16 August 1941, Memorandum File, Tribal Records, RST; Minutes of the Oglala Sioux Tribal Council. 10–15 January 1944, File 9684–E–1936–054, pt. 2, Pine Ridge, CCF.

47. It is true that the OIA's use of the law and order apparatus may have seemed less arbitrary to the Lakota than did the activities of the IRA tribal courts. After all, the OIA did not use the courts to pry money from individuals for the enrichment of judges and policemen, as tribal junior judges and tribal policemen were reputed to do under the court fee system. Two points should be noted, however. First, the number of cases involving abuse of the fee system apparently constituted a minority of the cases heard in the tribal courts. Second, even if abuse was rampant in the court system, why would the Lakota want abolition of the entire system of IRA tribal government rather than reform of the court system?

48. *Statutes at Large of the United States,* vol. 40:586; ibid., vol. 41:26, 429, 434, 1248; ibid., vol. 42:576, 1174; ibid., vol. 43:411, 1161; ibid., vol. 44:474, 954; ibid., vol. 45:223, 1584; ibid., vol. 46:301, 1138; U.S. Department of the Interior, Office of Indian Affairs, *Minutes of the Plains Congress* (1934), Haskell Institute, Lawrence, Kan., 34.

49. Proceedings of the Medicine Post [sic] District Meeting, 31 December 1937, Pine Ridge and Rosebud Sioux Delegates File, box 128, SSC.

50. Petition, 31 January 1942, Rosebud Indian Reservation File, Francis Case Papers; Woehlke to Case, 28 May 1942, Rosebud Indian Reservation File, Francis Case Papers.

51. Superintendent to Commissioner, 17 January 1939, File 9712–066, Rosebud, GRCIO. Jorgensen (1972:233–34) has noted that, among the Ute and Shoshone, acts of tribal councils are confused with acts of the federal government, and that tribal councils are held accountable for things beyond their control.

52. Chairman to Case, 27 July 1939, Rosebud Indian Agency File, Francis Case Papers (emphasis added).

53. Resolutions of the Black Hills Treaty and Claim Council, 29 January 1940, S2103 File (76th Cong.,), Record Group 46, NA; U.S. Congress, Senate, *Survey of Conditions*, 21537.

54. Selznick 1966:261. See also Lacy 1982.

55. Felix Cohen, How Long Will Indian Constitutions Last? *Indians at Work* 6, no. 10 (June 1939): 40, 42, 41.

## Conclusion

1. *The New York Times*, 12 March 1973; *The Washington Post*, 12 March 1973; *Akwesasne Notes* 1974; Burnette and Koster 1974; Ortiz 1977; Dewing 1985.

2. Dewing 1985.

3. *Oyate*, the people, is often translated as nation.

4. U.S. Congress, Senate, *Occupation of Wounded Knee* (1974), Hearings before the Subcommittee on Indian Affairs of the Committee on Interior and Insular Affairs, 93d Cong., 1st sess., 233.

5. U.S. Congress, Senate, *Wounded Knee*, 184; Dewing 1985. Clearly the issue of sovereignty and the issue of the Oglala Sioux Tribal Council were related. As Tom Holm (1985:138) puts it: "It followed that if the Sioux Nation was sovereign, the people had the right to establish the type of government they wanted." My point is one of emphasis. I see mainly resistance to the tribal government and not a demand for independence from the United States in the activities of Oglala activists and their sympathizers during the Wounded Knee incident. Holm and Raymond DeMallie (1978:304–10) also emphasize this issue for Lakota people. Compare this interpretation with that of Vine Deloria, Jr. (1985), Steve Talbot (1981), and Laurence Hauptman (1984), who emphasize the Indian insistence on a *national* status, independent from the United States, behind the Wounded Knee incident. The latter writers, of course, do not argue that the occupiers were not attempting to dissolve the Oglala Sioux Tribal Council and/or oust its president. Rather, they see the fight for sovereignty as the ultimate agenda behind abolition of the tribal council.

6. For similar interpretations of the Indian New Deal, see Jorgensen 1972:138–39, 1978:17; Taylor 1980:ch. 6; Talbot 1981:70–75; Hauptman 1984, 1986; and Clow 1987.

7. Cornell 1988:95.

# References

## Archival and Unpublished Sources

Chicago, Illinois. The Newberry Library.
> Ayer Collection. *The Word Carrier.*
> Ayer Indian Linguistic Collection. Dakota on Wiwicaygapi kte cin. Dakota item 47.

Kansas City, Missouri. National Archives. Record Group 75 (Bureau of Indian Affairs).
> Pine Ridge Agency Records:
>> Account of a Council of Pine Ridge and Rosebud Indians, 29–24 February 1892.
>> Economic Survey, 1940–41.
>> Main Decimal File, 1900–1965.
> Rosebud Agency Records:
>> Economic and Social Survey, 1934.
>> Family Income Reports, 1940.
>> General Correspondence File, 1878–1933.
>> Housing Development Records, 1936–44.
>> Land Use Report and Proposed Indian Range Unit Records.
>> Main Decimal File, 1930–1950.
>> Minutes of Tribal Group Meetings other than the Tribal Council, 1937–65.
>> Ordinances and Resolutions Adopted by the Rosebud Sioux Tribal Council and Other Tribal Groups, 1934–1965.
>> Reservation Program Data, 1940, 1943.
>> Subject Correspondence File, 1908–45.

Madison, South Dakota. Karl E. Mundt Historical and Education Foundation, Dakota State College. Karl E. Mundt Papers, Microfilm copy.

Milwaukee, Wisconsin. Archives, Marquette University Library. Bureau of Catholic Indian Mission Records. St. Francis Mission Records.

Mitchell, South Dakota. Layne Library, Dakota Wesleyan University. Francis Case Papers.

New Haven, Connecticut. Manuscripts and Archives, Yale University Library. John Collier Papers. Microfilm copy.

Pierre, South Dakota. South Dakota State Historical Society. Chiefs' Certificates.

Pine Ridge, South Dakota.
    Pine Ridge Agency, Bureau of Indian Affairs, U.S. Department of the Interior:
        U.S. Department of Agriculture, Soil Conservation Service, Range Management of the Pine Ridge Indian Reservation, 1940 [copy in possession of author].
    Red Cloud Indian School:
    Tiyospaye, 1974.

Richardton, North Dakota. Assumption Abbey Archives. Major James McLaughlin Papers. Microfilm copy.

Rosebud, South Dakota.
    Lakota Archives and Historical Research Center, Sinte Gleska University. Tribal Records.
    Realty Office, Rosebud Agency, Bureau of Indian Affairs, U.S. Department of the Interior. Allotment Folders.
    Rosebud Sioux Tribe:
    Law and Order Code, 1937.
    Tribal Land Enterprise Records.
    Tribal Records.

St. Louis, Missouri. U.S. Office of Personnel Management. Personnel Records.

Sioux Falls, South Dakota. Center for Western Studies, Augustana College. Archives of the Episcopal Diocese of South Dakota:
Wilbert D. Swain Papers, 1921–1950.
*South Dakota Churchman.*

Vermillion, South Dakota. University of South Dakota.
    Dorris Duke Oral History Project. American Indian Research Project.
    Institute of Indian Studies. A Report on the Bureau of Indian Affairs Fee Patenting and Canceling Policies, 1900–1942.
    Richardson Archives, I. D. Weeks Library:
    Ralph Case Papers.

Peter Norbeck Papers.
Rosebud Records, Indian Tribal Series.
Pine Ridge Records, Indian Tribal Series.
William Williamson Papers.
WPA Anthropological Schedules.

Washington, D.C. National Archives.
Record Group 46 (U. S. Senate):
Records of the Investigating Subcommittee of the Senate Committee on Indian Affairs.
S2103 (76th Congress) File.
Record Group 48 (Secretary of the Interior):
Correspondence of the Office of the Solicitor.
Record Group 75 (Bureau of Indian Affairs):
Annual Reports and Work Programs, 1934–43, Records of the Division of Extension and Industry.
Central Classified Files, 1907–1939, Pine Ridge, Rosebud, and General Service.
Correspondence with Officials, 1934–46, Records of the Indian Organization Division.
General Correspondence of the Chief Special Officer, 1933–47, Records of the Law and Order Section.
General Records Concerning Indian Organization, 1934–1956, Pine Ridge and Rosebud.
Indian Census Rolls, 1885–1940. Microfilm Publication M595.
New Accessions.
Procedural Issuances: Orders and Circulars, 1854–1955. Microfilm Publication M1121.
Records Concerning the Wheeler-Howard Act, 1933–1937.
Reports of Industrial Surveys, 1922–29, Records of the Industries Section.
Reports of Inspection of the Field Jurisdictions of the Office of Indian Affairs, 1873–1900. Microfilm Publication M1070.
Records of the Rehabilitation Division.
Special Cases File 147, Rosebud.
Superintendents' Annual Narrative and Statistical Reports from Field Jurisdictions of the Bureau of Indian Affairs, 1907–1938. Microfilm Publication M1011.

## Government Documents

South Dakota. South Dakota State Planning Board (Brookings). *Indians of South Dakota.* 1937.

U.S. Bureau of the Census. *Agriculture*, vol. 1, pt. 2. Sixteenth Census of the United States (1940). 1942.

U.S. Congress. House. *Right of Way to Dakota Central Railway Through Sioux Reservation, Dakota.* 48th Cong., 1st sess., 11 December 1883. Exec. Doc. 11.

————. *To Divide a Portion of the Reservation of the Sioux Nation of Indians in Dakota in Separate Reservations.* 48th Cong., 1st sess., 31 May 1884. Rept. 1724.

————. *Agreements with Rosebud and Lower Brule Indians for Cession of Lands in South Dakota.* 55th Cong., 2d sess., 3 May 1898. Doc. 447.

————. *Conditions of the Indians of the United States.* Hearings before the Committee on Indian Affairs on HR 8360. 74th Cong., 2d sess., 1936.

————. *Conditions on Sioux Reservations.* Hearings before the Committee on Indian Affairs on HR 5753. 75th Cong., 1st sess., 1937.

————. *Investigate Indian Affairs.* Hearings before a Subcommittee of the Committee on Indian Affairs, pt. 3. 78th Cong., 2d sess., 1945.

U.S. Congress. Senate. *Message from the President of the United States.* 48th Cong., 1st sess., 19 December 1883. Exec. Doc. 20.

————. *Letter from the Secretary of the Interior.* 48th Cong., 1st sess., 23 January 1884. Exec. Doc. 70.

————. *In the Senate of the United States.* 48th Cong., 1st sess., 7 March 1884. Rept. 283.

————. *Message from the President of the United States, Transmitting Reports Relative to the Proposed Division of the Great Sioux Reservation, and Recommending Certain Legislation.* 51st Cong., 1st sess., 10 February 1890. Exec. Doc. 51.

————. *Agreement with Indians of Rosebud Agency, S. Dak.* 57th Cong., 1st sess., 9 December 1901. Exec. Doc. 31.

————. *Rosebud Indians of South Dakota.* 58th Cong., 2d sess., 15 February 1904. Doc. 158.

————. *Survey of Conditions of the Indians of the United States.* Hearings before a Subcommittee of the Committee on Indian Affairs, pt. 7. 71st Cong., 2d sess., 1930.

————. *To Grant Indians Living under Federal Tutelage the Freedom to Organize for Purposes of Local Self-Government and Economic Enterprise.* Hearings before the Committee on Indian Affairs on S. 2755. 73d Cong., 2d sess., 27 February 1934.

————. *Repeal of the So-Called Wheeler-Howard Act.* 76th Cong., 1st sess., 2 August 1939. Rept. 1047.

———. *Survey of Conditions of the Indians of the United States.* Hearings before a Subcommittee of the Committee on Indian Affairs, pt. 37. 76th Cong., 1940.

———. *Analysis of the Statement of the Commissioner of Indian Affairs in Justification of Appropriations for 1944, and the Liquidation of the Indian Bureau.* 78th Cong., 1st sess., 1943. Senate Partial Rept. 310.

———. *Occupation of Wounded Knee.* Hearings before the Subcommittee on Indian Affairs of the Committee on Interior and Insular Affairs. 93d Cong., 1st sess., 1974.

U.S. Department of the Interior. *Opinions of the Solicitor of the Department of the Interior Relating to Indian Affairs, 1917–1974.* 2 vols. 1979.

U.S. Department of the Interior. Office of Indian Affairs. *Reports of the Commissioner of Indian Affairs.* 1846–1906.

———. *Regulations of the Indian Office.* 1904.

———. *Indians at Work.* 1933–45.

———. *Minutes of the Plains Congress.* Haskell Institute, Lawrence, Kansas. 1934.


## Newspapers

*Mellette County Pioneer,* White River, South Dakota.

*The Missouri Republican,* St. Louis, Missouri.

*The New York Times,* New York.

*Sioux Falls Argus Leader,* Sioux Falls, South Dakota.

*The Washington Post,* Washington, D.C.


## Books, Articles, and Dissertations

Akwesasne Notes
    1974    *Voices from Wounded Knee, 1973: In the Words of the Participants.* Rooseveltown, N.Y.: Akwesasne Notes.

Bee, Robert L.
    1981    *Crosscurrents along the Colorado: The Impact of Government Policy on the Quechan Indians.* Tucson: University of Arizona Press.

Bromert, Roger
    1978    The Sioux and the Indian CCC. *South Dakota History* 8: 340–56.

1980        The Sioux and the Indian New Deal, 1933–1944. Ph.D. diss.,
            University of Toledo.

Buechel, Eugene S., S.J.
    1970    *A Dictionary of the Teton Dakota Sioux Language: Lakota–En-
            glish, English–Lakota.* Edited by Paul Manhart, S.J. Pine Ridge:
            Red Cloud Indian School.

Buecker, Thomas R.
    1984    Fort Niobrara, 1880–1906: Guardian of the Rosebud Sioux. *Ne-
            braska History* 80:300–25.
    1987    The 1887 Expansion of Fort Robinson. *Nebraska History* 68:
            83–93.

Burnette, Robert, and John Koster
    1973    *The Road to Wounded Knee.* New York: Bantam Books.

Castile, George P.
    1974    Federal Indian Policy and the Sustained Enclave: An Anthropo-
            logical Perspective. *Human Organization* 33 (3): 219–228.

Clow, Richmond Lee
    1987    The Indian Reorganization Act and the Loss of Tribal Sover-
            eignty: Constitutions on the Rosebud and Pine Ridge Reserva-
            tions. *Great Plains Quarterly* 7:125–34.

Cohen, Felix S.
    1960a   Colonialism: A Realistic Approach [1945]. In *The Legal Con-
            science: Selected Papers of Felix S. Cohen,* edited by Lucy Co-
            hen, 364–83. New Haven: Yale University Press.
    1960b   Indian Self-Government [1949]. In *The Legal Conscience: Se-
            lected Papers of Felix S. Cohen,* edited by Lucy Cohen, 305–14.
            New Haven: Yale University Press.

Collier, John
    1922    The Red Atlantis. *The Survey* 49 (October):15–66.
    1945    United States Indian Administration as a Laboratory of Ethnic
            Relations. *Social Research* 12:265–303.
    1963    *From Every Zenith: A Memoir and Some Essays on Life and
            Thought.* Denver: Sage Books.

Comaroff, Jean, and John Comaroff
    1991    *Of Revelation and Revolution.* Vol. 1, *Christianity, Colonial-
            ism, and Consciousness in South Africa.* Chicago: University of
            Chicago Press.

Cornell, Stephen
    1988    *The Return of the Native: American Indian Political Resur-
            gence.* New York: Oxford University Press.

Daniels, Robert E.
    1970    Cultural Identities among the Oglala Sioux. In *The Modern Sioux: Social Systems and Reservation Culture*, edited by Ethel Nurge, 198–245. Lincoln: University of Nebraska Press.

Deloria, Ella C.
    1983    *Speaking of Indians*. Vermillion, S.D.: State Publishing Company. Orig. pub. 1944.

Deloria, Vine, Jr.
    1985    *Behind the Trail of Broken Treaties: An Indian Declaration of Independence*. Austin: University of Texas Press. Orig. pub. 1974.

Deloria, Vine, Jr., and Clifford Lytle
    1984    *The Nations Within: The Past and Future of American Indian Sovereignty*. New York: Pantheon Books.

DeMallie, Raymond J.
    1976    Sioux Ethnohistory: A Methodological Critique. *Journal of Ethnic Studies* 4(3):77–83.

    1978    Pine Ridge Economy: Cultural and Historical Perspectives. In *American Indian Economic Development*, edited by Sam Stanley, 237–312. The Hague: Mouton.

    1982a   Preface. In *Lakota Society*, by James R. Walker, edited by Raymond J. DeMallie, ix–xiv. Lincoln: University of Nebraska Press.

    1982b   Introduction to Part I. In *Lakota Society*, by James R. Walker, edited by Raymond J. DeMallie, 3–13. Lincoln: University of Nebraska Press.

    1988    Introduction to the Reprint Edition. In *Among the Sioux of Dakota: Eighteen Months Experience as an Indian Agent, 1869–70*, by D. C. Poole, xi–liii. St. Paul: Minnesota Historical Society. Orig. pub. 1881.

Dewing, Roland
    1985    *Wounded Knee: The Meaning and Significance of the Second Incident*. New York: Irvington Publishers.

Dragenett, Charles E.
    1907    The Work of the Indian Employment Bureau. *Proceedings* (25th Annual Meeting): 24–27. Lake Mohonk, N.Y.: Lake Mohonk Conference of Friends of the Indian and Other Dependent Peoples.

Eicher, Carl K.
    1961–2  An Approach to Income Improvement on the Rosebud Sioux Indian Reservation. *Human Organization* 20:191–96.

Erikson, Erik H.
   1963      *Childhood and Society.* 2d ed. New York: W. W. Norton and
            Company. Orig. pub. 1950.

Feraca, Stephen E.
   1964      The History and Development of Oglala Sioux Tribal Govern-
            ment. Washington, D.C.: Office of Tribal Operations, Bureau of
            Indian Affairs.
   1966      The Political Status of the Early Bands and Modern Communi-
            ties of the Oglala Dakota. *Museum News* 27 : 1–19.

Foucault, Michel
   1979      *Discipline and Punish: The Birth of the Prison.* Translated by
            Alan Sheridan. New York: Vintage Books.
   1980      *The History of Sexuality, Volume I: An Introduction.* Trans-
            lated by Robert Hurley. New York: Vintage Books.

Fowler, Lorretta
   1978      Wind River Reservation Political Process: An Analysis of the
            Symbols of Consensus. *American Ethnologist* 5 (4): 748–69.
   1982      *Arapahoe Politics, 1851–1978: Symbols in Crises of Authority.*
            Lincoln: University of Nebraska Press.

Frank, Andre Gunder
   1969      *Capitalism and Underdevelopment in Latin America: Histori-
            cal Studies of Chile and Brazil.* New York: Monthly Review
            Press.

Frideres, J. S.
   1974      *Canada's Indians: Contemporary Conflicts.* Scarborough, On-
            tario: Prentice Hall of Canada, Ltd.

Garbarino, Merwyn S.
   1980      Independence and Dependence among the Seminole of Florida.
            In *Political Organization of Native North Americans,* edited by
            Ernest L. Schusky, 141–62. Washington, D.C.: University Press
            of America.

Gearing, Frederick O.
   1970      *The Face of the Fox.* Chicago: Aldine.

Giddens, Anthony
   1987      *The Nation-State and Violence.* Berkeley: University of Califor-
            nia Press.

Gramsci, Antonio
   1971      *Selections from the Prison Notebooks.* New York: International
            Publishers.

Haas, Theodore
1947    *Ten Years of Tribal Government under the Indian Reorganization Act.* Washington, D.C.: Department of the Interior.

Hagan, William T.
1966    *Indian Police and Judges: Experiments in Acculturation and Control.* New Haven: Yale University Press.

Hagen, Everett E.
1962    *On the Theory of Social Change: How Economic Growth Begins.* Homewood, Ill.: Dorsey Press.

Hassrick, Royal B.
1964    *The Sioux: Life and Customs of a Warrior Society.* Norman: University of Oklahoma Press.

Hauptman, Laurence M.
1984    The Indian Reorganization Act. In *The Aggressions of Civilization,* edited by Sandra L. Cadwalader and Vine Deloria, Jr., 132–48. Philadelphia: Temple University Press.
1986    Africa View: John Collier, The British Colonial Service and American Indian Policy, 1933–45. *The Historian* 48 (3): 359–74.

Holm, Tom
1985    The Crisis in Tribal Government. In *American Indian Policy in the Twentieth Century,* edited by Vine Deloria, Jr., 135–54. Norman: University of Oklahoma Press.

Hoover, Herbert T.
1980    Yankton Sioux Experience in the "Great Indian Depression." In *The American West: Essays in Honor of W. Eugene Hollon,* edited by Ronald Lora, 53–71. Toledo: University of Toledo.

Howard, James H.
1951    Notes on the Dakota Grass Dance. *Southwestern Journal of Anthropology* 7:83–85
1966    The Teton or Western Dakota. *Museum News* 27 (9–10): 1–26.

Hoxie, Frederick
1979    From Prison to Homeland: The Cheyenne River Indian Reservation before World War I. *South Dakota History* 10 (1): 1–24.
1984    *A Final Promise: The Campaign to Assimilate the Indians, 1880–1920.* Lincoln: University of Nebraska Press.

Hyde, George
1956    *A Sioux Chronicle.* Norman: University of Oklahoma Press.
1974    *Spotted Tail's Folk: A History of the Brule Sioux.* Norman: University of Oklahoma Press. Orig. pub. 1961.

1975        *Red Cloud's Folk: A History of the Oglala Sioux Indians.* Nor-
            man: University of Oklahoma Press. Orig. pub. 1937.

Jorgensen, Joseph G.
    1972        *The Sundance Religion: Power for the Powerless.* Chicago: Uni-
                versity of Chicago Press.
    1978        A Century of Political Economic Effects on American Indian So-
                ciety. *Journal of Ethnic Studies* 6 (3): 1–82.

Lacy, Michael G.
    1982        A Model of Cooptation Applied to the Political Relations of the
                United States and American Indians. *The Social Science Journal*
                19 (3): 23–36.

Leacock, Eleanor, and Nancy Ostreich Lurie, eds.
    1988        *North American Indians in Historical Perspective.* Prospect
                Heights, Ill.: Waveland Press. Orig. pub. 1971.

Lears, T. S. Jackson
    1985        The Concept of Cultural Hegemony: Problems and Possibilities.
                *American Historical Review* 90: 567–93.

McDonnell, Janet A.
    1980        Competency Commissions and Indian Land Policy. *South Da-
                kota History* 11 (1): 21–34.
    1991        *The Dispossession of the American Indian, 1887–1934.* Bloom-
                ington: Indiana University Press.

McGillycuddy, Julia B.
    1941        *McGillycuddy, Agent: A Biography of Dr. Valentine T. Mc-
                Gillycuddy.* Stanford: Stanford University Press.

Macgregor, Gordon
    1946        *Warriors without Weapons: A Study of the Society and Person-
                ality Development of the Pine Ridge Sioux.* Chicago: University
                of Chicago Press.

Mekeel, Haviland Scudder
    1932a       A Discussion of Culture Change as Illustrated by Material from
                a Teton-Dakota Community. *American Anthropologist* 34:
                274–85.
    1932b       A Modern American Indian Community in the Light of its Past:
                A Study in Culture Change. Ph.D. diss., Yale University.
    1936        The Economy of a Modern Teton Dakota Community. *Yale
                University Publications in Anthropology* 6: 1–14. New Haven:
                Yale University Press.
    1943        A Short History of the Teton-Dakota. *North Dakota Historical
                Quarterly* 10: 136–205.

1944     An Appraisal of the Indian Reorganization Act. *American Anthropologist* 46:209–18.

Meriam, Lewis, et al.

1928     *The Problem of Indian Administration.* Baltimore: Johns Hopkins University Press.

Mirsky, Jeanette

1966     The Dakota. In *Cooperation and Competition among Primitive Peoples,* edited by Margaret Mead, 382–427. Boston: Beacon Press. Orig. pub. 1937.

Mooney, James

1965     *The Ghost Dance Religion and the Sioux Outbreak of 1890.* Edited by Anthony F. C. Wallace. Chicago: University of Chicago Press. Orig. pub. 1896.

Moore, Sally Falk

1986     *Social Facts and Fabrications: "Customary" Law on Kilimanjaro, 1880–1980.* New York: Cambridge University Press.

1988     Legitimation as a Process: The Expansion of Government and Party in Tanzania. In *State Formation and Political Legitimacy,* edited by Ronald Cohen and Judith D. Toland, 155–72. New Brunswick, N.J.: Transaction Books.

Olson, James C.

1975     *Red Cloud and the Sioux Problem.* Lincoln: University of Nebraska Press. Orig. pub. 1965.

Ortiz, Roxanne Dunbar

1977     *The Great Sioux Nation: Sitting in Judgment on America.* Cincinnati: General Board of Global Ministries, The United Methodist Church.

Parkman, Francis

1946     *The Oregon Trail.* Garden City, N.Y.: Doubleday. Orig. pub. 1849.

Parman, Donald

1971     The Indian and the Civilian Conservation Corps. *Pacific Historical Review* 40:39–56.

Philp, Kenneth R.

1977     *John Collier's Crusade for Indian Reform, 1920–1954.* Tucson: University of Arizona Press.

Poole, D. C.

1988     *Among the Sioux of Dakota: Eighteen Months Experience as an Indian Agent, 1869–70.* St. Paul: Minnesota Historical Society. Orig. pub. 1881.

Powers, Marla N.
    1986    *Oglala Women: Myth, Ritual, and Reality.* Chicago: University of Chicago Press.

Powers, William K.
    1975    *Oglala Religion.* Lincoln: University of Nebraska Press.
    1982    *Yuwipi: Vision and Experience in Oglala Ritual.* Lincoln: University of Nebraska Press.

Prucha, Francis Paul
    1984    *The Great Father: The United States Government and the American Indians.* Abridged ed. Lincoln: University of Nebraska Press.
    1988    The Indians in American Society: *From the Revolutionary War to the Present.* Berkeley: University of California Press.

Schell, Herbert S.
    1975    *History of South Dakota.* 3d ed. Lincoln: University of Nebraska Press. Orig. pub. 1961.

Schneider, Peter, Jane Schneider, and Edward Hansen
    1972    Modernization and Development: The Role of Regional Elites and Non-Corporate Groups in the European Mediterranean. *Comparative Studies in Society and History* 14:328–50.

Schusky, Ernest L.
    1970    Political and Religious Systems in Dakota Culture. In *The Modern Sioux: Social Systems and Reservation Culture,* edited by Ethel Nurg, 140–47. Lincoln: University of Nebraska Press.
    1975    *The Forgotten Sioux: An Ethnohistory of the Lower Brule Reservation.* Chicago: Nelson Hall.

Scott, James C.
    1985    *Weapons of the Weak: Everyday Forms of Peasant Resistance.* New Haven: Yale University Press.

Selznick, Philip
    1966    *TVA and the Grass Roots: A Study in the Sociology of Formal Organization.* New York: Harper Torchbooks. Orig. pub. 1949.

Standing Bear, Luther
    1978    *Land of the Spotted Eagle.* Lincoln: University of Nebraska Press. Orig. pub. 1933.

Stewart, Omer C.
    1972    The Native American Church and the Law [1961]. In *The Emergent Native Americans: A Reader in Culture Contact,* edited by Deward E. Walker, Jr., 382–97. Boston: Little, Brown and Company.

Talbot, Steve
  1981      *Roots of Oppression: The American Indian Question.* New
            York: International Publishers.

Taylor, Graham D.
  1980      *The New Deal and American Indian Tribalism: The Adminis-
            tration of the Indian Reorganization Act, 1934–1945.* Lincoln:
            University of Nebraska Press.

Thomas, Robert K.
  1966a     Colonialism: Classic and Internal. *New University Thought* 4:
            37–43.
  1966b     Powerless Politics. *New University Thought* 4:44–53.

Tyler, S. Lyman
  1964      *Indian Affairs: A Study of the Changes in Policy of the United
            States Toward the Indians.* Provo: Institute of American Indian
            Studies, Brigham Young University.

Useem, John, Gordon Macgregor, and Ruth Useem
  1943      Wartime Employment and Cultural Adjustments of the Rosebud
            Sioux. *Applied Anthropology* 2:1–9.

Useem, Ruth Hill
  1947      The Aftermath of Defeat: A Study of Acculturation among
            the Rosebud Sioux of South Dakota. Ph.D. diss., University of
            Wisconsin.

Walker, James R.
  1980      *Lakota Belief and Ritual.* Edited by Raymond J. DeMallie and
            Elaine A. Jahner. Lincoln: University of Nebraska Press.
  1982      *Lakota Society.* Edited by Raymond J. DeMallie. Lincoln: Uni-
            versity of Nebraska Press.

Wax, Murray L.
  1971      *Indian Americans: Unity in Diversity.* Englewood Cliffs, N.J.:
            Prentice Hall.

Wax, Murray, Rosalie H. Wax, and Robert V. Dumont
  1964      *Formal Education in an American Indian Community.* Supple-
            ment to *Social Problems* 11:4.

Williams, Raymond
  1977      *Marxism and Literature.* New York: Oxford University Press.

Wissler, Clark
  1912      Societies and Ceremonial Associations in the Oglala Division of
            the Teton-Dakota. *Anthropological Papers* 11 (1): 1–99. New
            York: American Museum of Natural History.

1916      General Discussion of Shamanistic and Dancing Societies. *Anthropological Papers* 11 (12): 853–76. New York: American Museum of Natural History.

1971      *Red Man Reservations.* New York: Collier Books. Orig. pub. 1938.

Wolf, Eric R.

1990      Distinguished Lecture: Facing Power—Old Insights, New Questions. *American Anthropologist* 92 (3): 586–96.

# INDEX

Adult education, 121–22
Agent. *See* Superintendent
Agreements, 5, 17, 39–41
Agricultural Adjustment Administration, 209n. 8
Agriculture, Indian, 3, 23–24, 110–12. *See also* Grass Mt. Colony; Livestock operations; Red Shirt Table Development Association
*Akicita* (soldier), 35–36, 45, 49–50, 57
Allen, S. D., 96, 97
Allotments: ended, 62; proposed, 40–41; protected in Howard Bill, 68–69, 70, 75–76; supervised sales of, 14, 111, 123n. 25. *See also* Fee Patenting; Land: heirship infractionation of; leasing of; Range units; Tribal Land Enterprise; Trust restrictions
American Indian Movement, 182
Annuities, 5, 6, 37–39
Anthropology, 104, 105, 107
Applied Anthropology Unit, 131
Artificial economies: agency employment in, 25–27; and credit, 28; and dependence, 28–29; reinforced during New Deal, 115–16, 185; and per capita payments, 28; and per diem labor, 27–28; and poverty, 29; and resignation, 29; role of, in subsistence, 23–24. *See also* Rations

Bands, 35, 43, 105
Bear Creek Project, 124
Bennett County, 6
Berry, Tom, 74, 75
Black Hills Agreement, 5, 17, 40
Black Hills claim, 40, 47
Black Hills Council, 53, 54, 151
Blood quanta. *See* Degree of blood
Boarding schools, 64, 65, 201n. 9
Boss farmer. *See* Farmer
Brave Bear, 5
Brophy, William, 146, 147
Burke Act, 14

Case, Ralph, 54, 77
Castile, George Pierre, 31
Cattle business. *See* Livestock operations
Charter of incorporation, 120

## About the Author

THOMAS BIOLSI received his Ph.D. in anthropology from Columbia University. He is an associate professor of anthropology at Portland State University in Oregon. He has a long-standing interest in the history of Indian-white relations and is co-editor (with Larry J. Zimmerman) of *Indians and Anthropologists: Vine Deloria, Jr., and the Critique of Anthropology* (University of Arizona Press, 1997). He is presently completing a book on legal conflict between the Rosebud Sioux Tribe and the state of South Dakota.